THE WELL-SPOKEN WOMAN SPEAKS OUT

ALSO BY CHRISTINE K. JAHNKE

The Well-Spoken Woman:
Your Guide to Looking and Sounding Your Best

THE WELL-SPOKEN WOMAN SPEAKS OUT

HOW TO USE YOUR VOICE TO DRIVE CHANGE

CHRISTINE K. JAHNKE

Prometheus Books

59 John Glenn Drive
Amherst, New York 14228

Published 2018 by Prometheus Books

Interior illustrations by Kersti Frigell © Christine K. Jahnke
Cover illustration by Kersti Frigell © Christine K. Jahnke
Cover design by Jacqueline Nasso Cooke
Cover design © Prometheus Books

Inquiries should be addressed to
Prometheus Books
59 John Glenn Drive
Amherst, New York 14228
VOICE: 716–691–0133 • FAX: 716–691–0137
WWW.PROMETHEUSBOOKS.COM

22 21 20 19 18   5 4 3 2 1

Library of Congress Cataloging-in-Publication Data

Names: Jahnke, Christine K., 1963- author.
Title: The well-spoken woman speaks out : how to use your voice to drive change / Christine K. Jahnke.
Description: Amherst : Prometheus Books, 2018. | Includes index.
Identifiers: LCCN 2018021613 (print) | LCCN 2018037529 (ebook) | ISBN 9781633885011 (ebook) | ISBN 9781633885004 (paperback)
Subjects: LCSH: Public speaking for women. | BISAC: LANGUAGE ARTS & DISCIPLINES / Public Speaking.
Classification: LCC PN4192.W65 (ebook) | LCC PN4192.W65 J35 2018 (print) | DDC 808.5/1082—dc23
LC record available at https://lccn.loc.gov/2018021613

Printed in the United States of America

For everyone who's ready to change the conversation

CONTENTS

Introduction   9

PART I—ONCE UPON A TIME . . .

Chapter 1: The Future Is Female   17
Chapter 2: The Self-Awareness Quotient   35

PART II—A GIRL SET OUT TO DRIVE CHANGE . . .

Chapter 3: Reading the Room   65
Chapter 4: Resisting Boors and Bullies   91

PART III—THE NEW FACE OF LEADERSHIP . . .

Chapter 5: Power Words—Intentional Storytelling   113
Chapter 6: Power Words—Persuasive Media Messages   139
Chapter 7: The New Look and Sound of Leadership   163

PART IV—SHE SPOKE IN ARENAS FAR AND WIDE . . .

Chapter 8: Preparation Is Queen   199
Chapter 9: Media Interviews and Debates   223
Chapter 10: Keynotes, Panels, Introductions, and Awards   249

PART V—NOW YOUR STORY IS THE ONE TO TELL

Epilogue   279

Acknowledgments   293

Appendix: Well-Spoken Women Great Moments   295

Notes   303

Index   327

INTRODUCTION

Respect Existence or Expect Resistance
                    —Sign at the Women's March, 2017

The woman in the first row would not be ignored.

The room was packed but she stood out. Persistently and insistently she waved her hand until I called her to join me up front. It was a cold Saturday morning in February, and nearly everyone in the room was attending their first political-candidate training.

College students, small-business owners, corporate lawyers, nurses, moms, daughters, and grandmothers. What they had in common is they had never before considered themselves candidate material.

The woman in the front was running for Congress in 2018 because as a daughter of an immigrant and mother to a gay daughter she could not sit on the sidelines. That's why Pennsylvania's Chrissy Houlahan was so eager to practice her speaking skills that winter morning.

Women are taking their anger—about the lack of representation, rampant sexual harassment, violence against black lives, immigration bans, mass shootings, pay inequity, cuts to healthcare, the dangers of being transgender, and more—and using it to drive change. In the streets. At town halls. In boardrooms and Hollywood studios. In state capitals and Capitol Hill. Through podcasts and TV studios.

This book is a celebration of women who are raising their voices. And it is a guide for every woman who wants to join in. For every woman who wants to be a better speaker.

A sea change is under way. It used to be that when a man spoke, people listened; and when a woman spoke, her credentials were questioned, appearance found lacking, and message dismissed.

Not. Any. More.

The Well-Spoken Woman Speaks Out picks up where my first book, *The Well-Spoken Woman*, left off. Women of all races, ethnicities, ages, and gender identities face double standards and bias. This book categorizes the challenges and presents strategies to overcome the barriers. A note about the use of the word *woman* and the binary pronouns *she/her/hers*, since they are not all-encompassing. Language is important, especially as it relates to how you self-identify. This book is meant to help a diverse readership, including people who use nonbinary pronouns such as *they/them/theirs*. It is intended for all leaders, activists, and candidates who are committed to making progressive change.

I feel fortunate to have learned from amazing elected officials, organizers, campaign managers, pollsters, and funders who toil in the political arena. Women who have had their "faces marred by dust, sweat, and blood."[1] Badass women who follow the advice of Eleanor Roosevelt: "You must do the thing you think you cannot do."[2]

There's no rougher business than electing a woman to office, especially to an executive post such as president, governor, or mayor. The 2016 US presidential election made more people aware of just how tough it is. For twenty years, the Barbara Lee Family Foundation has been studying the obstacles and opportunities female candidates face. With the research and the political muscle of groups like Emily's List and Emerge America, progress is being made. For example, we've elected more women governors in the last two decades than in the previous century. However, only thirty-nine women have ever served as governor, and a Democratic woman of color has not yet held that office.

I have a long track record of working with other coaches, speechwriters, and consultants, and I have shared my methods and techniques with them. As a veteran of five Democratic National Conventions, I've been backstage for the drama and the glory. My approach is always focused on giving practical, tactical direction you can use and benefit from. There is plenty of cookie-cutter advice out there: suggestions like "Punch it up" and "Just be yourself." Women don't have time to be patronized or given vague pointers.

The course of my life was changed in 1991 by a woman who courageously came forward with a message many people didn't want to hear. Too few believed Professor Anita Hill when she delivered meticulous factual testimony with incredible poise about how Clarence Thomas sexually harassed her. Professor Hill had reluctantly traveled from her home in Oklahoma to appear before an all-male, all-white Senate judiciary committee that grilled her as if she had committed a crime. Watching the hearings on TV and seeing how she was treated made my blood boil. I couldn't do anything to help her, but I *could* do something to help other woman who wanted a voice.

I had recently moved to Washington, DC, after a year spent on the road working as a press secretary and organizer for a presidential campaign. My background was in journalism, and, having grown up watching *The Mary Tyler Moore Show*, I thought I wanted to make it in TV news like Mary Richards of WJM-TV. But, rather than covering the news, I wanted to be with the people who were making the news.

In Washington there were national groups committed to recruiting and electing women to office. After watching the few women in Congress courageously fight for Professor Hill's right to be heard, I joined the effort to increase their ranks. As former Senator Barbara Mikulski used to say, we need to kick doors open for other women.

At the Women's Campaign Fund, I coached pro-choice Democratic and Republican women candidates. That may sound odd now, in our current political climate, but not that long ago you could work with progressive women on both sides of the aisle. It was a different time, when elected officials would work together and seek compromise. But I'm a pro-choice voter who believes women must have control over their bodies. No legislative body should be able to dictate or limit our reproductive healthcare decisions.

That's why I'm committed to helping the courageous, determined leaders at Planned Parenthood and I admire the doctors with Physicians for Reproductive Health who sometimes have to risk everything to care for their patients. I thank them for the care they provide and for telling their stories.

With advocacy work, you learn to take the long view—progress is too slow. It often seems for every battle won another is already waging. Nowhere is this truer than with the health of the planet and its people. In the past two decades I've worked with thought leaders at the Bill & Melinda Gates Foundation who are elevating the welfare of women here and around the world. The scientists at the Union of Concerned Scientists who were early reasoned voices for taking action on climate change. And advocates at the Sierra Club who took on big coal so America could be energy smart.

Now a new generation is insisting on change. The #MeToo movement has blown the lid off sexual harassment. Leaders at Black Lives Matter are raising the collective consciousness about police brutality. Student activists around the country are holding the NRA accountable, even without enough political support. Transgender activists stand against hate-based legislation. As Oprah Winfrey proclaimed in her mighty speech at the 2018 Golden Globes, the end of sexual harassment and gender inequity is possible. Change can come.

The Well-Spoken Woman Speaks Out will help you be a part of the change. This book will take you on a journey to discover how you can best use your voice. Each section provides specific advice and best practices to build the skills necessary to run for office, push an issue, and mobilize people.

PART I—ONCE UPON A TIME . . .

In complicated times such as when a tornado hits, it's important to have a path forward. Thought-provoking questions will help you understand what kind of speaker you are and what kind you want to be. I provide encouragement from iconic role models who open a world of possibilities. Like Glinda the Good Witch who advises Dorothy and her dog, Toto, to follow the Yellow Brick Road to the Emerald City, these role models will help guide you along your own path.

PART II—A GIRL SETS OUT TO DRIVE CHANGE . . .

Just as Anita Hill met resistance, so too will you. But you can prepare yourself for the friendlies and the not-so-friendlies. On the way to meet the Wizard of Oz, Dorothy is befriended by companions who join her quest. They have unexpected encounters with sweet-faced Munchkins and face grave danger with the Wicked Witch. Likewise, in any speaking environment, there can be pleasant surprises as well as difficult obstacles. In this section, you will learn how to deal with toxic people and their flying monkeys.

PART III—THE NEW FACE OF LEADERSHIP . . .

Well-spoken advocates use power words, sounds, and moves. With the right tools, you can turn back opponents and drive change. Arriving in Emerald City, Dorothy is not the naive girl who left Kansas, and her friends have found their courage, heart, and brains. Emboldened, Dorothy confronts Oz, the Great and Terrible. Pulling back the curtain, she sees that there is no leader. The Oz is just an ordinary man who has puffed himself up with smoke and mirrors. A man who is a fake and can do nothing to help her.

PART IV—SHE SPOKE IN MANY ARENAS
FAR AND WIDE . . .

Throughout the adventure, Dorothy learned she could do anything she set her mind to: a splash of water on the Wicked Witch was all it took to free the Munchkins. The farther Dorothy traveled, the more she came to know herself and to believe in herself. In a similar fashion, the closing chapters will provide you with everything you need to master new and different arenas.

PART V—NOW YOUR STORY IS THE ONE TO TELL

Books must end, but the journey never does. Through exploration and challenge we become stronger. Dorothy learned she had the power all along. To go back home, all she needed to do was click her ruby-red slippers. With inspiration and instruction, you can accomplish your goals.

The march to progress is under way. This book offers the resources every well-spoken woman needs to join the parade.

Let's celebrate our victories along the way. Three cheers for the band of sisters who inspired millions to join the Women's March. Cheers to the women who broke the silence on sexual harassment. Cheers to women young and old who are taking on gun violence. Cheers to all the women like Chrissy Houlahan who are stepping forward and running for office.

The passion is evident.

Our sleeves are rolled up.

The sisterhood is rising.

The Well-Spoken Woman Speaks Out is an invitation to explore how you can speak up for yourself, your cause, and your country.

PART I

ONCE UPON A TIME . . .

CHAPTER 1

THE FUTURE IS FEMALE

"It would have been more comfortable to remain silent."
—Anita Hill, opening statement to
Senate Judiciary Committee, 1991

There once was a time when a woman would speak and few would bother to listen.

A new story is now being told.

#TimesUp #MeToo #SheShouldRun #BlackLivesMatter #NeverAgain #PowerToThePolls #ShePersisted

It is our time.

For too long, what we had to say was dismissed. For too long, our words were discounted. For too long, we were disbelieved.

That is why we're speaking out. The barriers and biases we are overcoming take many forms:

- We are shut down
- Our accusations are ignored
- Our qualifications are questioned
- Our ideas are coopted
- Sexist, racist language is minimized as a "joke" or "harmless"
- We are interrupted
- We are called names (like "bitch" or "c—t")
- We are met with eye rolling
- We are subject to comments on our hemlines or hairstyles

- Our personal life is judged
- Our voice is demeaned as shrill
- We are told to smile

These toxic tactics have been used to intimidate women and keep us in our place on the margins. Who's going to speak up if an idea will be slammed—or left unacknowledged? The deafening sound of crickets can be humiliating.

Why does this matter? Shouldn't we put on our big-girl pants and get over it? If we expect to be taken seriously, why don't we toughen up? Isn't it up to us to "step up" or "lean in" as we have been advised?

The limitations and intimidations do matter. The consequences of not listening to diverse points of view are more severe than hurt feelings or a bruised ego. When every person doesn't feel free to contribute or if her attempts to do so are stifled, everyone loses. Groupthink dictates. Up until now, groupthink was dominated by the views, voices, and life experiences of the people who hold the power. When outside perspectives and different insights are not aired, it means they do not become part of the decision-making process. The result is bad policy, bad practices, and bad products.

We see examples all around us. If women are not seated at the table when healthcare is discussed, the result is legislation that leaves out maternity care. Alt-right protestors spew misogynistic, racist propaganda while claiming their First Amendment rights are under attack. All male, all white television panels discuss abortion rights. Transgender people are viciously attacked online and in the streets. Tech bros design apps that can't answer questions about sexual assault or menstruation cycles. It goes on and on.

What is different now is more of us will no longer sit back, hold our tongues, or wait to be called upon. Nor are we going to lean in to systems that don't accept us for who we are. No more will we live by the wrong set of rules. Women, young and old, are changing the rules.

*"For all of the people who felt like their voice wasn't
heard. I said I'll run and I'll be your voice."[1]*
—First-time candidate Ashley Bennett describing her
"from the gut" decision to run for public office

"Fight for your lives before it is someone else's job."[2]
—Mass-shooting survivor Emma González
speaking at the March for Our Lives

Emma González and Ashley Bennett are two remarkable women who are leading the call to resist, insist, and persist. They are two women who are doing it on their own terms. They are not changing themselves to fit into a system. They are changing the system. And thousands of women are hearing their call and following their lead.

Women of color are ruling social media. Transgender people are claiming the public square. White women are finally angry enough to get off the sidelines. Together we are channeling our passions to change business as usual.

One speech.

One TV interview.

One staff meeting.

One rally.

One march at a time.

If you are reading this book, you are already standing up or are eager to join in.

Hoorah!

The Well-Spoken Woman Speaks Out will help you formulate strategies to work around the deck that has been stacked against us for too long. The best practices and tools that follow will help you speak out with force and thoughtfulness. Techniques will ensure you are ready for any speaking venue. This is about maximizing your unique voice so we can work together to bring progressive change.

Based on decades of experience, coaching women for countless speeches and thousands of media interviews, this book shares the secret sauce of effective speaking—*you*.

It is about taking all aspects of your life and integrating them into a message you share with the world. The following pages will show you how to shine a light on your specialness, whatever it is. It's about telling what it means to be a woman, a woman of color, or LGBTQ. Let them know you are a dedicated teacher, scientific expert, brilliant lawyer, courageous first responder, ardent activist, creative entrepreneur, or caring public servant. You have something to add to the public dialogue, and your voice needs to be heard.

It all starts with a belief in yourself. Emma and Ashley said to themselves—*I can do this. I will do this.* When your mind is set, the next step is to fortify yourself. Wonder Woman didn't leave home without her golden bracelets and Lasso of Truth. This book shows you how to fortify yourself with the Vitamin Cs of public speaking—Certainty, Conviction, Credibility, Confidence, and Collective Action.

THE WELL-SPOKEN WOMAN'S PRINCIPLES TO DRIVE CHANGE

- Embody Certainty
- Show Your Conviction
- Own Your Credibility
- Claim Confidence
- Power the Collective Voice

These are the principles that enable you to stand against bias, exploitation, and hatred. Core principles sustain you when the speaking terrain is rough. They enable you to hold your head high should anyone attempt to disrespect you. They prepare you to manage the criticism of opponents and the doubts of the skeptics.

These are the qualities that enable you to set the record straight, share facts, take a stand, and motivate people to think and to take action.

PRINCIPLE 1: EMBODY CERTAINTY

The first step is, as the Swedish women's national soccer team showed on their game-day uniforms, "Believe in your damn self."[3] The team members switched the player's names that typically appeared on the backs of jerseys with motivational phrases. Hoping to inspire the next generation of athletes, one player said, "Together we can show everything is possible."[4]

Understanding what makes you tick and gaining the ability to express it clearly is central to presenting your authentic self. Your life experiences set you apart and will make your presentation stand out. In the past, you may have been made to feel that sharing what you have gone through wasn't worth talking about. Perhaps others have tried to marginalize your voice because of who you love or where your people come from. Don't allow others to do that to you. Let it go. That's what Ashley Bennett did.

Ashley Bennett followed her gut all the way to winning her very first campaign for elected office. It started the day of the Women's March in 2017. Ashley's work as a psychiatric emergency screener at a 24-hour crisis center prevented her from marching. But the action she took that day after viewing a social-media post by a local elected official is what changed her life. Local politician John Carman posted a Facebook meme that included the line "Will the women's protest be over in time for them to cook dinner?"[5]

Furious that her representative would mock his constituents, Ashley wrote a letter to Carman asking him: "How did he have time for ridicule when there was so much that needed to be done?"[6] As she told the New Jersey *Inquirer Daily News*, "It is never wrong to ask your elected official to hold themselves to a higher standard."[7] When there was no reply, Ashley showed up at the next Atlantic County freeholder meeting along with other women who confronted Carman about the misogynistic post. Carman said it "was a joke" and added that the "strong and confident" women in his life weren't "offended."

The dismissal of their concerns was the last straw. Ashley decided to run against Carman. And she pledged not to make dinner until she had won. On the campaign trail, Ashley shared how she felt blessed to help community members with her work at the crisis center. She talked about graduating from the local high school and how her best memories are tied to the community. When Ashely was a little girl, her grandmother worked security at the local basketball games. Ashley recounted standing outside the locker room, waiting to get player autographs, because she thought it was the NBA.

Less than a year later, with help from her co-workers at the crisis center who covered her shifts, Ashley had won a seat on the commission that controls the county budget. The joke turned out to be on Carman, but Ashley had more than just the last laugh. Her candidacy is a reminder of how democracy is supposed to work. Citizens of any age, background, and experience can run and win. Now, young girls and boys will be asking for Ashley's autograph.

Women's March ✓
@womensmarch

(Follow) ∨

Ashley Bennett, who showed up at an Atlantic County Freeholder's meeting to protest comments made by Freeholder John Carman mocking the Women's March, and then decided to run for his seat, knocked Carman off the board on Tuesday. Congrats Ashley!

Ashley believed she could do a better job. The ability to believe in yourself is foundational. Trust yourself. Trust what you've learned from life. Trust that your ideas are sound and your opinion is worthy. When you do, you'll find that plenty of others believe in you, too.

Authentic speakers draw upon the richness of where they come from, the people they spend time with, and the places they go. When the "who you are" is the sustenance of your advocacy, it helps audiences understand why you care. And why they should, too. Women's March national co-chair Carmen Perez opened a panel at the Women's Convention by saying, "I'm a Mexican American, Chicana woman who grew up in Southern California in a poor community where there were gangs. I also grew up playing basketball. There are different things that I identify with, but intersectionality allows me to be my whole self."[8]

The power of intersectionality is that when individual and group identities come together, they create a whole that constitutes a unique and worthy point of view. This concept is important for the women's movement, which has in the past been dominated by white, middle-class women. Intersectionality ensures a more inclusive movement that allows the voices of women from all backgrounds to be heard and respected.

PRINCIPLE 2: SHOW YOUR CONVICTION

Make it evident to audiences just how much you care.

> *"I'm done being polite. I'm done being politically correct.*
> *I'm mad as hell. My people's lives are at stake. We are but*
> *one nation. We may be small, but we are huge in dignity*
> *and zealous for life. I ask the press to send a Mayday call*
> *around the world. We are dying here."* [9]
>
> —San Juan Mayor Carmen Yulín Cruz,
> after Hurricane Maria

As the mayor of the largest city in Puerto Rico, Carmen Yulín Cruz was not deterred by repeated attempts to discredit her leadership in the wake of the worst storm to hit the island in eighty years. When the winds subsided, the mayor personally led a rescue effort at an assisted-living center, wading through chest-high water with bullhorn in hand. Accused of showboating for cameras, she responded, "That is my job."

As she told *The New York Times*, "My job is to make life better for people, and you cannot make life better if you are in a helicopter. You can't make life better for them if you can't touch them." [10]

In the days following the storm, very little aid reached the island, leaving thousands without basic necessities of water, food, and electricity. The mayor took to the airwaves to generate urgency about the horror taking place on the streets and demand the federal government fix the logistical delays. Rather than collaborating with her to aid people, Donald Trump tweeted that she was a "nasty" woman who "lacked leadership skills."[11]

The backlash didn't end there. It was the mayor who called out a $300 million clean-up contract that had been awarded to a Montana company with ties to the Trump administration. The company's initial response was to threaten a work stoppage, which would endanger people without electricity and clean water. But the mayor held firm, demanding the "no-bid" contract be voided and the award process operate with transparency. Shining a light on the highly suspect trans action ultimately led to the cancelation of the contract.[12]

Throughout the ordeal, the mayor stood firm, showing real leadership on behalf of the people of Puerto Rico. Taking on big interests is always risky. Stating what you believe in opens you up to condemnation and pushback. Telling people what they don't want to hear can bring disparagement and physical threats. The blowback can be harsh, if not cruel, and overwhelming.

The bigger the step, the higher the risk. Putting yourself out there means making yourself vulnerable. Sociologist Brené Brown has spoken extensively about the power of vulnerability. Brown says vulnerability may be excruciating, but above all else it is necessary: "To allow ourselves to be seen, deeply seen, vulnerably seen . . . it means I'm alive . . . and I'm enough."[13] The act of sharing your vulnerability creates a powerful connectivity with the audience. There is risk involved and also reward. You show that you have the guts to put what you believe in on the line. And the satisfaction of knowing you are driving change.

PRINCIPLE 3: OWN YOUR CREDIBILITY

It's time to validate what you know and what you do.

In another time, Danica Roem would not have been elected to the

Virginia state legislature. But this is a different time, and the thirty-three-year-old transgender journalist defeated a man who described himself as the state's "chief homophobe."[14] State delegate Bob Marshall began holding office when Danica was in elementary school. He used his office to push "bathroom bills," ban marriage equality, require ultrasounds before abortions, and define life as beginning at conception.[15]

Danica's response was clear and direct: "Discrimination *should be a disqualifier*."[16]

On the campaign trail, she made it clear that her opponent was using his office as a platform for his extreme ideological agenda rather than serving the people. As a life-long resident of the northern Virginia community she now represents, Danica campaigned on an issue people care about. When she was in high school, because of traffic congestion, she sometimes had to wait two hours after school for her mom to pick her up. Tapping into the hell of rush hour that still exists on the infamous Route 28, she pledged to do something about it.

Media reporters described Danica's campaign as "boring, boring, boring."[17] Refusing to engage in the negative identity politics of her opponent, she talked unceasingly about infrastructure—installing stoplights and replacing outdated water pipes. This is the experience she pledged to bring to the state legislature.

Danica's victory is a life lesson for any woman who has doubted her own qualifications. As she said, "All Donald Trump's election showed me is that there is literally nothing in my background that disqualifies me."[18] Self-doubt is experienced by everyone regardless of gender or sexual orientation, but research shows that women are more likely to be held back by it.[19] This is not surprising, given that our life experiences haven't been as valued as those of men.

It's no wonder that imposter syndrome plagues women more than men.[20] Imposter syndrome is the feeling that you don't belong, that the only reason you made it where you are is by dumb luck or accident. This is especially evident in how women make the decision to reach for the next rung on the ladder. The questions they pose include: "How do I build a résumé to run?" "How can I be taken seriously?" "How do I demonstrate qualifications?" Men don't ask those questions enough. And, when they do, we see evidence all around us that they don't allow subpar answers to hold back their ambition.

PRINCIPLE 4: CLAIM CONFIDENCE

> *"I'm done. This is conversation is over. I'm yanking mics.*
> *Good-bye. See ya. That was entirely inappropriate."*[21]
> —CNN anchor Brooke Baldwin
> shutting down offensive behavior

BROOKE BALDWIN   LIVE CNN

"First Amendment and boobs," was the comment from a guest that caused CNN anchor Brooke Baldwin to abruptly end a segment on her daytime program. At first, Brooke couldn't believe what she had just heard spew from the mouth of Fox Sports commentator Clay Travis. When she gave Travis a chance to clarify, he reiterated the sexist comment without hesitation. What happened next is what was new and what we need to see more of. Travis apparently thought the line was a good one, as he had used it previously on the radio.[22] But this time it wasn't ignored as another "boys will be boys" moment. Brooke cut off his mic.

It's exciting to watch women who've seen a lot and are not taking it anymore.

Confidence need not be elusive or mysterious. It can be acquired through preparation and gained over time from experience. This is especially true for public speaking. If you lack confidence now, you can change that. Where you are today doesn't have to be where you are tomorrow, next week, and next year.

We have all worked with people like Travis—men who may feel emboldened by the coarseness of some public leaders who openly sanction sexist and racist comments. Brooke showed that such ugliness in the public dialogue won't be tolerated. Cutting the mic took power away from a white dude who was abusing his opportunity to speak. Claiming your confidence puts you in control.

> *"I'm reclaiming my time."*[23]
> —Congresswoman Maxine Waters controls the clock

Who knows what Treasury Secretary Steve Mnuchin was thinking when he attempted to give nonanswers to Congresswoman Maxine Waters during a House Financial Services Committee hearing. Maybe he didn't understand whom he was dealing with. Mnuchin appeared before the committee to testify on the state of the international finance system. When the congresswoman asked why he had not responded to

a letter about the Trump administration's financial ties to Russia, he tried to run out the clock by dodging her answers with platitudes.

With each of his slippery evasions, Congresswoman Waters, who was the ranking member on the committee, invoked a House procedure to "reclaim" her speaking time. She unabashedly interrupted each and every one of his nonanswers, displaying a command of procedural rules that ensured her point was made. It is clear that she won't be pushed around by Mnuchin or anyone else.

Maxine's mantra, "Reclaiming my time," is an apt metaphor for all who feel there is no time to waste.

PRINCIPLE 5: POWER THE COLLECTIVE VOICE

Nothing can make you feel more vulnerable than standing alone.

> I have been silenced for twenty years. I have been slut-shamed. I have been harassed. I have been maligned. And you know what? I'm just like you. Because what happened to me behind the scenes is what happens to all of us in this society. And that cannot stand. It will not stand.[24]

Rose McGowan finally wasn't alone when she took the stage at the 2017 Women's Convention to share her story of sexual abuse that had haunted her adult life. She was one of dozens of women who came forward with allegations of rape and sexual harassment by Harvey Weinstein, dating back decades.[25] Onstage, the actress joined hands with Tarana Burke, the advocate who initiated the #MeToo movement ten years ago to help people who've been sexually harassed or abused. Tarana has dedicated her life to helping people who were afraid to tell or who did tell but were not believed. It has taken decades and decades, but finally the issue of sexual harassment is being taken seriously.

The stories of Rose and Tarana resonated loud and clear from that stage, reverberating across the country and enabling thousands of women to speak up and be heard. Throughout history, women have been denied access to formal networks of power, and what we have learned is that nothing will change unless we take things into our own hands.

As Maya Angelou said, "Each time a woman stands up for herself, without knowing it possibly, without claiming it, she stands up for all women."[26] We are standing together and speaking out for one another now.

Emma González exemplifies the power of the collective voice.

This teenager is representative of young people across the country who are fighting to save their own lives against the threat of gun violence. Along with her classmates who survived the mass shooting at Marjory Stoneman Douglas High School, and with activists in cities

like Chicago, where guns have long posed a daily threat, students like Emma are stepping in where adults have failed.

Days after a gunman with an AR-15 semi-automatic rifle slaughtered her classmates, Emma emerged as a leader among leaders. At an anti-gun rally, fighting to control tears, she publicly mourned the loss while making it clear the reaction to the shooting at her school would be different: "We are going to be the students you read about in textbooks. Not because we are going to be another statistic about mass shootings in America. But, because . . . we are going to be the last mass shooting."[27]

Young people are not settling for knee-jerk condolences like "our thoughts and prayers are with you" but are putting themselves forward to be the change they want to see. They are calling on politicians to pass sensible gun laws and calling for voters to reject lawmakers who side with the NRA rather than keeping kids safe. They have witnessed the pointlessness of waiting for others to act and are taking their grief and channeling it into action.

With a coherent, reasonable message and the savvy use of social and traditional media, the students showed they mean business with the organization of the 2018 March for Our Lives, which was accompanied by over eight hundred events across the country.[28] In Washington, DC, Emma spoke volumes when she took a moment of silence before a crowd of over 800,000 people. Dubbed the "6 Minute and 20 Second Speech" because Emma stood silent, eyes closed, tears streaming, until a timer beeped to mark the amount of time it took the school shooter to gun down seventeen people and injure seventeen more.

Emma's poise is all the more commendable given the ugly attacks she has weathered, most often from adult, white, male conservatives. A state legislative candidate in Maine called her a "skinhead lesbian."[29] Iowa Congressman Steve King's campaign posted on Facebook, "This is how you look when you claim Cuban heritage but don't speak Spanish . . ."[30] While the politicians who disagree with her resort to offensive tactics, support for Emma grows. In one month, she attracted more followers on Twitter than the NRA, which joined the website in 2009. The message of school safety is resonating beyond students, parents, and educators to everyone who cares about preventing senseless death and protecting lives.

Let the leadership displayed by these women inspire you. Ashley Bennett believed in herself. Mayor Cruz stood up to a bully. Danica Roem owns her qualifications. Brooke Baldwin controlled the mic. "Auntie Maxine" made it clear who was running the show. Rose McGowan and all of the silence breakers have moved sexual assault and harassment out of the shadows. Perpetrators are paying for their crimes. Emma González and the students organized against gun violence are mobilizing a multitude.

These are the qualities leaders use to drive change.

WELL-SPOKEN WOMEN RESIST, INSIST, PERSIST

Women are rewriting the rules.
Yes, we can, begins with yes, I can.
Your story matters.
Together we can bring change.

CHAPTER 2

THE SELF-AWARENESS QUOTIENT

"I am not lucky. You know what I am? I am smart, I am talented, I take advantage of the opportunities that come my way and I work really, really had. Don't call me lucky. Call me a badass."

—Shonda Rhimes, *Year of Yes*

"I never watch myself on video."

Unfortunately, this is an all-too-common refrain I hear when rehearsing a speech with a new client. It is usually accompanied by a shudder. It's spoken not so much as a confession but rather as an assertion—*Why would I put myself through that?*

Without fail, the top three pushbacks to reviewing practice on tape are: "Augh—my hair;" "I sound just like my mother;" and "Why did I say that?" Author Nora Ephron pretty much summed up the collective distorted view with the line she used as a title for one of her books: "I feel bad about my neck."

As a point of comparison, the reaction of male clients watching themselves is generally favorable. There may be a bit of grousing about "Jeez, my belly . . ." But they are quick to point out positives: "See how I reigned in my hand gestures?" "I really like the joke I told."

In my experience, both women and men often have a distorted view of how they come across to an audience. Women tend to be too hard on themselves. Men tend to be too easy on themselves. Watching a video of yourself is one way to get a more accurate read on your speaking ability. It provides some distance from what you experienced while you were giving the talk. Being able to step back helps you develop a more accurate sense of what you were projecting, which is essential to accelerating improvement.

Heightened self-awareness is a trait shared by well-spoken women. Do you know how you come across to others? Do you emanate credibility? Does your warmth come through? Do you telegraph your anxiety? Are you responsive to the audience? Once you know more about what you are projecting, then you can work on what you would like to improve. This chapter provides best practices to jump-start the process.

The first is a personal assessment tool called the Self-Awareness Quotient (SAQ). It is designed to help you more accurately diagnose what works and what doesn't work so well. The SAQ will help you avoid fixating on petty concerns or minor flaws, which can erode confidence. It will ensure you don't keep making the same mistakes, by providing a clearer understanding of why you do what you do.

Ultimately, the SAQ will help you develop your signature style so you can present the best you. The SAQ is not about changing who you are to fit a norm. The well-spoken woman doesn't fit into a single prototype. The well-spoken woman is many women.

SELF-AWARENESS QUOTIENT

How Do You See Yourself?
What Are Your Core Strengths and Weaknesses?
What Changes Are Needed to Be the Best You?
What Kind of Speaker Do You Want to Be?

Self-Awareness Quotient Factors

Four factors comprise the SAQ—personality type, impetus, experience, and anxiety. Examining these factors will help you shed false views about your speaking style and abilities. You will be able to replace those notions with more accurate insights. View the SAQ factors as a compass to help you orientate yourself to how you truly come across. The questions below are intended to help you get your bearings. Your responses will begin to shed light on:

- Personality type and how it affects your delivery style;
- The role of impetus;
- How experience impacts performance; and
- What triggers anxiety.

Self-Awareness Factors

Personality Type

1. Does talking to people boost your energy or sap it?
2. Do you thrive on consensus or on debate?
3. Do you seek out people to share new ideas or stick to what you know in familiar venues?
4. Do you worry to excess or roll with the punches?
5. Are you meticulous about details or do you tend to be lax?

Impetus

1. How motivated are you to give the talk?
2. Do you really care or could you not care less?
3. Do you feel compelled to speak or to seek excuses to avoid talking?

Experience

1. How many years have you been talking at meetings, giving presentations, or making speeches?
2. How many times per month do you speak publicly? 0–1, 2–7, or 8 or more?
3. Is your topic the same or do you address a number of different topics?
4. Are you speaking to the same people or to different groups?

Anxiety

1. Does nervous energy cause panic or feel exhilarating?
2. Does preparation reduce your stress level?
3. Do you have effective coping techniques?

The next section takes a closer look at each of the four SAQ factors. Each of the factors will help you think more deeply about what you are good at and what's holding you back. Once you have your bearings you can chart a course to becoming the speaker you want to be.

SAQ—Personality Type

There are dozens of traits that make up an individual's overall personality. Psychologists have identified what they call the "Big Five" that underlie the foundation of each person's character: extraversion, openness, neuroticism, agreeableness, and conscientiousness.[1] Each trait affects your speaking style. With a better understanding of what drives your personality, you can better play to your speaking strengths and correct your weaknesses.

One way to view the role of personality is to view the five traits as either driven by the brain or by the heart. Broadly speaking, a brain-driven approach to public speaking focuses on reaching people with intellect and data. The brain-driven presenter prefers to communicate information—analyze numbers, explain research, review policy, describe strategy, and so on. Technologists, scientists, engineers, lawyers, and professors tend to be more brain-driven. Their attention to detail can leave lay audiences confused, and their depth of knowledge can overwhelm people who are not as well versed in the subject matter.

Presenters with a heart-driven approach put the focus on winning people over with passion and physical energy. The heart-driven presenter is demonstrative because she wants the audience to feel what she is saying. Marketers, salespeople, coaches, religious leaders, and politicians are often good storytellers who freely share personal experiences. However, too much focus on emotion can result in an audience that gets wrapped up in the moment and is entertained but later is unclear about what the speaker was getting at.

Personality—Brain or Heart?

1. Extraversion

Extroverts get their energy from social settings and relish making heart-to-heart connections with audience members. They love to talk and often come across as approachable because of their outgoing nature. While these qualities do lend themselves to the stage, some extroverts expect to get by on the strength of personality alone. Thus, they may spend less time preparing and often the audience will see through the polished veneer. They may rest on their laurels versus pushing themselves to get better. As extroverts advance in their careers and speak before more influential audiences, their gregarious personality does not automatically guarantee success.

Introverts tend to get their energy from themselves and can feel drained simply by spending time with others. The act of public speaking can leave them physically and emotionally exhausted. They are in their heads and prefer listening rather than speaking. It takes more of a physical effort for them to perform. However, a strength among introverts is that they know the talk should be more about the audience and less about themselves. They will strive to compensate for a less-outgoing personality by working to make a substantive connection with the audience.

2. Openness

Just as you would expect, openness refers to being open to new experiences. The heart is open to meeting people and exploring ideas. Open people are often imaginative and have a wide range of interests, but they may lack practicality and spend time on impulses that threaten deadlines. Open people value the exchange of new ideas and are well suited for panel discussions and talk shows. They are comfortable accommodating last-minute changes to program agendas such as speaking slots, new speakers, and questions. However, too many good ideas can spread you thin. Stay focused on a few key points to avoid diluting your impact by talking about everything.

People who are low in openness prefer to stick to their habits and don't seek out adventure. They are comfortable with the tried-and-true versus the unknown. Less-open people can do well when speaking about topics in which they feel well-versed. If you are on the low side of openness, it may take a greater effort for you to speak before new people in unfamiliar surroundings. If you are asked to give a speech addressing a subject beyond your area of expertise, be sure to schedule extra time to prepare.

3. Neuroticism

Neuroticism is a measure of emotional stability. Neurotics tend to be emotionally volatile and feel higher levels of stress. Public speaking can feel like an insurmountable challenge because the mere thought of getting up in front of people causes immediate feelings of dread. This may be linked to an earlier bad experience of facing ridicule or criticism in front of others. Neurotics tend to focus on the negative and obsess about what will go wrong, which leaves them feeling insecure and inadequate. It is difficult for them to roll with the punches, so it's essential to channel the nervous energy into constructive preparation. Having a set routine for writing and rehearsal can help alleviate stress.

People with a low level of neuroticism take a more rational approach to public speaking. They are more calm, hardy, and in control of their emotions. They are much less easily upset and less reactive. However, a too-calm, too-steady speaking style can come across as flat if the presenter appears to be disinterested in what she is talking about. Emphasis should be placed on using delivery techniques to add energy, such as a slightly quicker speaking pace or the use of hand gestures. Physical movement is one way to show you are invested in the subject matter. The use of dynamic visuals is another way to prevent a presentation from coming across as dull or dry.

4. Agreeableness

Agreeable people are heart-centered and strive to ensure everyone gets along. They are less comfortable challenging social norms or rules. Friendly interactions and consensus are preferred over scoring points or conflict. Point-counterpoint discussions and interviews may push agreeable speakers beyond their comfort zone. Those formats require the ability to assert viewpoints and push back against opposing ideas. The use of facts, data, and third-party validators are ways that agreeable speakers can more comfortably support their point of view.

People with low levels of agreeableness are quick to assert themselves and confidently state opinions. They challenge norms and think outside the box. They do not necessarily care what others think of them and have a thick skin to tolerate criticism. These speakers have the potential to be highly persuasive in debate forums if they can avoid alienating people with their self-interested and sometimes brusque manner. They must recognize that what they view as an independent point of view can be seen as rude, mean-spirited, or manipulative. Developing patience is key so that they can listen to other views and not dismiss them with snap judgements.

5. Conscientiousness

The unconscientious presenter is heart-centered. They will react in the spur of the moment and may come across as unreliable or careless. These speakers are more impulsive than diligent and, their spontaneity can bring moments of vitality such as when they wow the audience with something unexpected. But the lack of planning can result in misfires or, worse, a hot mess. These speakers can be difficult to work with because they sometimes surprise themselves and their support staff with what comes out of their mouth.

The conscientious presenter is mindful to never be late, is well-organized, and is self-disciplined. However, conscientious people can also be the ultimate planners who overthink the details. They tend to put things into lists, which, when recited to an audience, sound tedious. The high expectations they set for themselves can result in seeking perfectionism. This is a formula for failure because a speech that looks neat and tidy on paper and meets all deadlines can come across as monotonous when delivered. Giving a perfect speech should never be the goal—it will feel too tightly scripted and will lack the freshness of being in the moment with the audience.

SAQ—Impetus

In the movie *Norma Rae*, Sally Field's character is about to be arrested for her efforts to organize a union in a Southern textile mill. In the pivotal scene, she shouts to be heard above the roaring factory looms, "I'll wait for the sheriff to come and take me home. And I ain't gonna budge till he gets here."[2] Grabbing a marker, she scrawls the word

"UNION" on a scrap of cardboard, jumps on a table, and displays the sign for all to see. Slowly, one by one, her co-workers turn off their noisy machines in a sign of solidarity.

It's a dramatic climax because Norma Rae and all the mill workers have been threatened and intimidated by the company bosses. They are risking their personal safety and their jobs. There's a lot on the line, but Norma Rae is compelled to speak out. She knows what she is doing is right and can no longer remain quiet about the intolerable working conditions and low pay.

Are you speaking because you are compelled to do so? Does your belief in something bigger than yourself drive you to take action you might not otherwise take? Are you motivated by the energy from the crowd?

Compelled

The impetus factor can be viewed on a sliding scale from 1 to 5, with 5 representing a high level indicating that you feel compelled to speak out, or you have a personality type that relishes public speaking. From Latin, the word *impetus* originally meant assault or force—the force or energy with which a body moves. Being driven by impetus goes beyond simply being motivated. If you are impelled to do something, sitting on the sidelines or keeping quiet is not an option. There is a strong desire to come forward and sometimes a feeling of being duty bound to speak up. If there is one SAQ factor that is more essential than the others to driving social change, it is impetus.

"I continue to be surprised by how little black lives matter."[3] That social-media post by Alicia Garza would become the latest rallying cry in the long, hard road traveled by advocates for black freedom in America. When a Florida jury acquitted George Zimmerman after he shot and killed seventeen-year-old Trayvon Martin, labor organizer Alicia was compelled to send a message for action on civil rights. The hashtag #BlackLivesMatter signaled a revitalized effort in the ongoing battle to end police violence and the oppression of black people.

High impetus may arise from the need to fight back against discrimination or marginalization. It may also spring from love and joy—the celebration of a momentous occasion. A victorious campaign. Introducing a personal hero. Pitching a brilliant idea. Eulogizing a beloved community leader. Accepting an award. Feeling compelled can also be the force that allows you to push aside the anxiety that might normally hold you back.

Obligated

There are a number of scenarios in which the level of impetus is lower on the sliding scale, closer to 1 than 5. Some speaking situations are routine—there isn't always something on the line. Other speaking engagements are obligations, simply a task that must be completed. Some speakers experience a high level of anxiety which overrides any compulsion they might otherwise feel. Other speakers, such as introverts, prefer to drive action by being a behind-the-scenes player. The low end of the scale includes routine speaking assignments, such as a biweekly project update to the team or when a friend wrangles you into facilitating a meeting or an annual report to a difficult board of directors.

Procrastination can be a downfall in scenarios when you feel obligated to speak. It's more likely that the necessary prep work will be delayed when there isn't much at stake or you don't feel anything will be accomplished. Recognize the routine, the obligation, or the task for what it is and consider how it might be turned into an opportunity to challenge yourself or to learn something new.

Every speaking situation can feel obligatory if you do not enjoy talking in front of others. The SAQ factor that addresses anxiety will help you pinpoint what is causing the apprehension or dread you experience. Additionally, chapter 8 provides detailed information about proactive steps to calm your nerves.

SAQ—Experience

The amount and level of experience you have matters and can be measured in four ways.

1. How long have you been speaking? Are you a novice who is just starting out with little experience under your belt? Or have you been presenting for years? If you're new, you are still learning much about yourself and how you best interact with others. It may take you more time to process new information at a level in which it can be effectively shared with others. Tackling new subjects can be more challenging because you are starting at ground zero with your understanding of the material.

   Experience gained over time helps good speakers become great speakers, if they are committed to improving. Michelle Obama was a good, if reluctant, campaigner on behalf of her husband when he first ran for the presidency. After eight years in the White House, she matured as a speaker and is widely respected and admired for the causes she championed. The First Lady turned what had initially been an obligation with low impetus into an opportunity to advocate for children and inspire millions.

2. How frequently do you speak? Fewer than one or two opportunities per month is a low frequency. More than eight is a high frequency. The more you speak publicly, the more opportunity you have to hone skills through experimentation with new techniques, gain insights from interacting with audiences, and make adjustments based on feedback.

3. What are you speaking about? Are you speaking about the same topic, or do you need to be ready to address different subjects? Speaking more frequently helps you improve, but if you need to address different topics, that may be challenging. For example, political candidates give what's called a "stump speech" nearly

every day on the campaign trail. They repeat the same material almost verbatim, which allows them to more quickly refine the content and improve their delivery technique.

4. Where are you speaking? Not all speakers are proficient in all forums. Some people do well with a large crowd, while others are less comfortable in front of a camera. Don't expect that you should be able to perform at the same level in all types of venues.

What it takes to excel with a PowerPoint presentation in an auditorium is different from what it takes to connect with community members in a rec center. Some people are in the zone using a slide deck but feel lost sitting at a roundtable discussion. Each forum requires particular skills and techniques. The physical layout of the room, equipment setup, audience size, and visual aids can all present different challenges. Only by trying out a variety of forums will you begin to identify the places where you feel most comfortable.

Types of Public Speaking Forums:

- Staff or board meetings
- Informal briefings to small groups
- Live, in-studio interviews
- Presentations at large conferences
- Keynote addresses to thousands
- Panel discussions
- Training workshops
- Edited TV interviews
- Radio talk shows or podcasts

SAQ—Anxiety

How high is your anxiety level? Everyone experiences nervousness but to widely varying degrees. Are you scared or relatively calm? Do the nerves feel like a shot of adrenaline that provides a spark? Or are you overwhelmed by feelings of dread?

It's important to identify by what, where, and when anxiety is triggered. There are a host of variables that can cause you to feel a high level of stress. The following situations may help you identify what causes your anxiety level to spike.

- Audience size
- Familiarity with audience members
- Judgment of peers or higher-ups
- Level of impetus
- First time addressing a topic
- A controversial subject
- Lack of familiarity with a topic
- Inadequate preparation time
- Question-and-answer period
- Use of visual aids
- Livestream or recording

How you are able to handle anxiety is linked to the other SAQ factors. For most people, adequate preparation time is key to alleviating nervousness. Each of the five personality types approach preparation differently. Introverts and neurotics generally need more preparation time than the others to reduce the stress they experience. Extroverts and low-level conscientious presenters may mistakenly believe they don't need to schedule time for preparation, and, as result, they don't improve. People with low levels of openness will feel less stress if they give themselves more prep time when discussing new topics.

Presenters who are driven by a strong impetus may be anxious, but the discomfort will not keep them from speaking out. In their case, maintaining the status quo is more stressful than the idea of speaking out is. A low-level of impetus can result in procrastination, which can result in a lackluster performance. For everyone, the amount of speaking experience and the type of speaking situation will directly impact the level of anxiety.

Use the SAQ Factors to better understand all of the variables that impact your ability to perform. Once you know more about yourself and your speaking strengths and weaknesses, you can explore where you might take your abilities. Another best practice is having a role model. Role models provide important life lessons while they inspire and motivate us. They come in all ages and from all backgrounds. At the March for Our Lives, the granddaughter of the Reverend Dr. Martin Luther King Jr. and Coretta Scott King led the crowd in a chant that would have made her grandparents proud. Nine-year-old Yolanda Renee King asked the crowd to share her dream that "Enough is enough. And that this should be a gun-free world, period."[4]

WELL-SPOKEN ROLE MODELS

Whom do you admire as a public speaker? Have you considered adopting a public-speaking role model?

It might surprise you to learn that practicing in front of a role model can improve your skills. Researchers in Switzerland have found that just seeing an image of a strong, woman leader caused other women to speak more confidently. In the study, two groups of female students were recruited to give a persuasive speech before an audience of real people. Some of the students spoke in a room with a photograph of a leader like Angela Merkel or Hillary Clinton hanging on the back wall. In the other room there was no photo. The results were astonishing: the students who spoke in a room with a photo spoke longer—a sign of dominance.

Even more significantly, the presence of the photographs positively impacted how the student speakers rated their speaking skills. They viewed themselves as more confident and their talks more fluid. Outside observers also rated them higher. In the *Journal of Experimental Social Psychology*, the researchers concluded, "Female political role models can inspire women and help them cope with stressful situations that they encounter in their careers, such as public speaking."[5]

Clearly, a muse is a must. Even if it is just a photo! I shared this research with a group of women I was coaching, and one participant said she always practices her speaking technique while standing in front of a picture of Harriet Tubman.

Having a role model is a way to stretch the limits of your own persona by tapping into the charms of an accomplished presenter. Role models or, as actress Laverne Cox would say, "possibility models" help us find our way.[6] As a black transgender girl in Mobile, Alabama, who was raised by a single mother, Laverne says she learned that the sky is the limit when you apply yourself to achieving your dreams.

Initially you may gravitate to a role model style that is the closest match to your self-awareness factors. As your experience deepens, anxiety lessens, and confidence grows, you may want to integrate attributes from other styles. Each of the role models below has distinct, endearing charms. The charms are positive attributes you may want emulate. Just as it is possible to learn by adopting the strength of an admired person, it is also possible to learn from her weaknesses. Just like the rest of us, role models have areas in need of improvement or Achilles' heels that may undermine their speaking strengths, too. We all have things to work on! Explore the possibility models below to push your potential to new heights.

BE WHAT YOU SEE

Activist

Malala Yousafzai, Nobel Prize Laureate, Pakistani Advocate for Girls' Education, and Co-Founder of the Malala Fund

Charms: Single-issue focus. Long-term commitment. Challenges followers to take on big problems that directly impact many lives.

Achilles' Heel: Intense. Solemn. Gravity could be leavened with more personal anecdotes.

Soul Sisters: Cecile Richards, former president of Planned Parenthood and reproductive healthcare expert.

Ai-jen Poo, director of National Domestic Workers Alliance advocating for the working people who are often most invisible.

Conversationalist

Laverne Cox, Actress and Transgender Advocate

Charms: Professional who speaks from the heart. Makes you laugh, cry, and think.

Achilles' Heel: So good she often makes it look as if it is easy.

Soul Sisters: Meryl Streep, actress and philanthropist.

Tina Fey, comedian and film and theater producer.

Viola Davis, actress and producer.

Debater

Ana Navarro, Political Strategist and TV Commentator

Charms: Well-reasoned. Succinct. Quick on her feet. Provides sharp contrast on issues while avoiding personal attacks.

Achilles' Heel: Fast talker. Emotive. Should be mindful to avoid ideological spats that the broader audience doesn't care about.

Soul Sisters: Symone Sanders, political strategist and TV commentator.

Jessica Valenti, author and blogger.

Ana Navarro CNN Political Commentator CNN

Leader

Hillary Clinton, Presidential Nominee and Former Secretary of State

Charms: Visionary. Depth of knowledge. Battle-tested. Willing to listen.

Achilles' Heel: Technical. Measured. Didactic. Storytelling would help the audience understand the big picture.

Soul Sisters: Melinda Gates, philanthropist and global advocate for women and girls.

Ruth Bader Ginsburg, Supreme Court justice, aka Notorious RGB.

Orator

Oprah Winfrey, Media Executive and Philanthropist

Charms: Inspiring. Strong call to action. Big personality.
Achilles' Heel: Self-focused. Long-winded. Showy.
Soul Sisters: Elizabeth Warren, US senator and bankruptcy expert.
Ann Richards, former governor of Texas.

Professor

Alicia Garza, Co-Founder of
Black Lives Matter and Civil Rights Leader

Charms: Powerful insights. Astute observations. Consciousness-riser.

Achilles' Heel: Overly earnest. Detailed. Moralizing. Personalization and humor would ensure arguments are relatable.

Soul Sisters: Gloria Steinem, journalist and social-justice activist. Rebecca Traister, author and editor.

Promoter

Sallie Krawcheck, CEO and Co-Founder of Ellevate Network

Charms: Storyteller. Convincing. Likeable. Sense of humor.
Achilles' Heel: Self-promoting. Salesperson. Controlling.
Soul Sisters: Sheryl Sandberg, technology executive and author.
Carla Harris, banker, motivational speaker, and gospel singer.

Protestor

Linda Sarsour, Co-Chair of the Women's March and American Muslim Advocate

Charms: Rousing. Strongly held views. Hellraiser. Willing to push the envelope.

Achilles' Heel: Hell-raiser. Risks alienating potential allies.

Soul Sisters: Ashley Judd, activist and Global Goodwill Ambassador for United Nations.

Angela Davis, academic and author.

Storyteller

Chimamanda Ngozi Adichie, Nigerian Writer and Recipient of MacArthur Foundation Genius Grant

Charms: Shares life lessons. Poignant imagery. Strong yet vulnerable.

Achilles' Heel: The combination of intellect and command of language can make her appear high and mighty.

Soul Sisters: J. K. Rowling, British author and queen of tweets.

Maya Angelou, author, poet, and civil rights activist.

Surrogate

Michelle Obama, Former First Lady, Lawyer, and Author

Charms: Team player. Dedicated. Unique perspective.

Achilles' Heel: Proxy. Overshadowed. Would love to see her headlining.

Soul Sisters: Samantha Bee, comedian, writer, and TV producer.

Jill Biden, former Second Lady, community college teacher, and co-founder of the Biden Foundation.

The possibility models are women who themselves remain open to new ways of growing and learning. They seek out best practices and ideas that will empower them to stretch beyond any limits—self-imposed or societal. By doing so they exceed audience expectations and are a joy to watch in action.

Today's movements for social justice are providing an environment in which young women and girls can be role models. Younger speakers are taking charge of their lives by telling their stories in their own way. Young women have witnessed how silence and powerlessness go hand in hand. As Rebecca Solnit wrote, "Being unable to tell your story can be a living death, sometimes a literal one."[7] Many women were raised to keep quiet, to not tattle, and to avoid talking about subjects because they are embarrassing or shameful. This is changing.

Young people are brazenly speaking out to save their own lives. The Dreamers who are advocating for immigration reform so they can remain in the country they were raised in. The Olympic gymnasts who confronted the doctor who claimed to be providing "special treatment" when he was sexually assaulting them. The gun-violence survivors who are standing up to the politicians who take NRA money. By exposing how they have been wronged and sharing the pain they have suffered, they are creating a culture shift.

Five amazing young women were among the voices raised at the 2018 March for Our Lives. They are focused, compassionate, principled possibility models.

*"We Need Change Now. Yes, I am a Parkland survivor
and an MSD student. But before this I was a regular
black girl and after this I am still black and I am still
regular. And I will fight for all of us."*[8]
—Aalayah Eastmond, sixteen-year-old

"I learned to duck bullets before I learned to read."[9]
—Edna Lizbeth Chavez, seventeen-year-old
south Los Angeles student and youth leader
with the nonprofit Community Coalition.
Edna lost her hero when her brother Ricardo
became a victim of gun violence.

*"Look to your left. Look to your right. Brothers and sisters
is what I see. Together we unite to make a whole."*[10]
—Tyra Hemans, Marjory Stoneman Douglas senior.
When she spoke to Florida legislators,
Tyra held a photo of her friend Joaquin,
so they could see the true cost of gun violence.

Emma González's moment of silence was a testament to her resolve
and humanity.

*"I am here today to acknowledge and represent the
African American girls whose stories don't make the
front page of every national newspaper. . . I represent the
African American women who are the victims of gun
violence who are simply statistics and instead of vibrant,
beautiful girls full of potential."*[11]
—Naomi Wadler, eleven-year-old who organized
a student walkout at her elementary school in
Virginia to honor the Parkland victims
and an African American teen
who was at risk of being forgotten.
Courtlin Arrington died after being shot
in her Alabama high school.

Good role models abound in public speaking. Seek out someone who makes it possible for you to envision a world in which women's voices are heard and opinions respected. Let a possibility model inspire you to push the boundaries so you can drive change.

WELL-SPOKEN WOMEN RESIST, INSIST, PERSIST

Where you are is a starting point.
Self-awareness is foundational.
Stepping outside of your comfort zone can reveal inner strengths.
Role models present possibilities.

PART II

A GIRL SET OUT TO DRIVE CHANGE . . .

CHAPTER 3

READING THE ROOM

"Fasten your seatbelts. It's going to be a bumpy night."
—Bette Davis, *All about Eve*

We've looked at you. Now what about them? The people in the audience.

Here's the good, the bad, and the ugly.

The good news about audiences is most people generally show up with open minds and ears. They are rooting for you to do well, are eager to hear your insights, and may even share a laugh.

The bad news is occasionally you will encounter a difficult audience or individual. This may not have anything to do with you or your subject matter. Any audience can have a bad day. The room can lack energy, or people can be distracted.

The ugly is the encounter with bias. Some people—women and men—can't get past a speaker's race, sexual orientation, or gender to listen. They are stuck in the, "Who does she think she is?" mind-set. And they can be quick to tell you what they think. This chapter will help you identify these people and the environments in which they lurk. With this knowledge in mind, you can prepare yourself to handle any curveballs that may come your way.

RECOGNIZING IT

The "IT" here is implicit or explicit bias that you may encounter. *Explicit bias* refers to beliefs and attitudes that are conscious. *Implicit bias* is deep-seated unconscious bias that steers an individual's thoughts and actions. Recognition of bias is critical to avoid blaming yourself for IT when IT occurs. Let's put an end to thinking to yourself, "It must have been something I said or did." It is unlikely you have brought this upon yourself.

Recognizing that you will likely face bias at some point can help take the shock and awe out of IT. Being caught off guard can leave you rattled. That's what happened to a congressional candidate when she walked into a local VFW during the 2016 election cycle.[1] A college instructor and an elected county council member in a Midwestern state, the candidate was accustomed to fielding questions from students and constituents. Nonetheless, she was blindsided by an old man who walked up to her and asked: "Are you the stripper?" The question left her speechless and then infuriated. Where had that come from? Did the old jerk really not know any better? Or was he deliberately trying to rattle her?

THE TOXIC, TAXING CLIMATE

The suggestion to expect bias isn't meant to create within you a sense of paranoia by presupposing it lurks around every corner. Nor is it meant to imply that you should look for it where it doesn't exist. Again, most speaking situations are not hostile, and most people in the room are not antagonistic. At a snail's pace and with the efforts of many speakers, the climate is improving. The change has been hard-fought. It didn't evolve organically; it has come about because of those who bravely ventured into venues where they were not invited or welcome. And where they stayed even when confronted with condemnation, criticism, or physical harm.

There are climate indicators that will help you to assess how and when you might be hit with implicit and/or explicit bias. The indicators provide a measure of the atmospheric conditions in different speaking environments—a sense of which way the wind is blowing. Is the sky clear, or are clouds forming on the horizon? Should you expect turbulence, if not outright stormy conditions?

Use the below indicators to gauge the degree to which you will experience negativism that could potentially undermine your credibility or shake your confidence. The unfavorable conditions under which bias exists can be linked to three primary sources—outdated cultural norms, an unbalanced media environment, and the presence of toxic individuals.

CLIMATE INDICATORS

- Atmospheric Bias—It's Still a Man's World
- Unbalanced Media—A Stalled Pattern
- Toxic People—They Create Disturbances

ATMOSPHERIC BIAS

The "manel" is a relatively new descriptor, but all-male and often all-white panel discussions are not new. Women have long been excluded from these and other public forums. From the dawn of Western civilization, women were denied entry into the places where the techniques for public speaking and rhetoric were developed. And women were forbidden to publicly and sometimes privately voice an opinion on issues that impacted their lives.

Exclusionary practices date way back. For example, across centuries, biblical passages have been interpreted as restrictive admonitions. In 1 Corinthians 14:34, the Apostle Paul says, "Let your women keep silent in the churches." In ancient Greece, philosophers and politicians established academies where privileged citizens were taught public-speaking skills so they would be prepared to participate in society. Participation in those centers of learning was limited to men of means who created and defined what constitutes excellence in oration. The female perspective has played no role in shaping the communication models and best practices.

THE QUEEN'S WORDS

Cleopatra was a rare woman who was permitted into an exclusive club. She had access to something most women would be denied for hundreds of years—an education. As the daughter of a king, she was permitted to learn and was tutored by the best minds of the day in subjects such as rhetoric. Cleopatra's speaking ability was so commanding that her contemporaries praised her skill: "She learned to marshal her thoughts precisely, express them artistically, deliver them gracefully."[2]

Although it was noted that Cleopatra was a good speaker, we don't know what she actually said. There is no surviving record of any speech or pronouncement from her twenty-two-year reign. No one bothered to write anything down, so her words are lost to history. Rather than a first-person account of her governing style, we have only what others chose to describe.

The principles that guided early orators have been handed down for generations and remain a cornerstone of what is taught in rhetoric classes today. Students are instructed in Aristotle's three pillars of persuasion—the ethos, pathos, and logos—which he developed 2,500 years ago. Together the pillars form three basic tools of rhetoric. Logos is argument by logic. Pathos is argument by emotion. And ethos is argument by character. An early definition of what constitutes effective public speaking came from Roman teacher and writer Quintilian (who lived from 35 CE until after 96 CE). Many would consider it fit today: "A good man speaking well."[3]

The political thought and practices of ancient Greece and Rome profoundly influenced America's founding fathers. They conceived a constitution that denied women and people of color the right to vote. And they gave only white men the practical right to exercise free speech in the public square. The slave-owning Thomas Jefferson stated that if women were allowed to engage in the public meetings of men, doing so would result in a "depravation of morals."[4]

HISTORY REDUX

Residual vestiges of these cultural norms are barriers that continue to limit the ability of women to fully participate as citizens in government. Women won the right to vote in 1920 and in recent decades have voted in higher numbers than men, but they lack equal representation in government.[5] According to the Center for American Women and Politics, in 2018 women made up roughly 20 percent of the US Congress and held just six gubernatorial seats. Additionally, women were only 25 percent of state legislators. Keep in mind that women represent more than half of the US population.[6]

The dearth of women extends to the decision-making tables in the public and private sector. The Old Executive Office building, which is a stone's throw from the White House, operates under the Billy Graham Rule.[7] Vice President Mike Pence adopted the practice advocated by the evangelical pastor that discourages married men from spending time alone with women who are not their wives.[8] By refusing to meet alone with women, the vice president is limiting women's access to the highest levels of government.

In professional forums and conferences, women's voices remain in the minority. The extent to which women are kept out of panel discussions was first revealed by scholar Tamara Cofman Wittes. As the director of Middle East policy at the Brookings Institution, she blew the lid off the imbalance with an insider's look at foreign-policy discussions. Tamara found that in 2014, six leading think tanks presented 150 events focused on the Middle East and did not include one single women speaker.[9]

The manel is a mainstay of academic, industry, and scientific conferences and meetings. At the 2018 J. P. Morgan Health Care Conference—the largest healthcare investment symposium in the country—there were more speakers named Michael (22) than there were women CEOs (20) giving presentations.[16] At MarTech (marketing and technology) conferences in 2017, two-thirds of the speakers were men even though 50 percent of all marketing and advertising professionals are women.[17]

A particularly egregious example of women speakers being excluded is the Consumer Electronics Show. When the organizers of the 2018 show announced the lineup for main-stage speakers, there were no white women or women of color represented. The tech trade show is a global event that draws close to 200,000 technologists annually and it is one of the largest and best-known industry shows. This tone deafness on diversity in the tech community has deep roots. The fifty-year-old conference is known for its mostly male attendees and the female "booth babes" who show off the latest technology but do not have a speaking role.

All white, all male speaker lineups are a form of explicit bias that send the erroneous signal that only those voices matter. That only those opinions are worthy of attention. It's imperative to widen the scope of who is held up as an expert by elevating more women and people of color. Forums that showcase diversity and inclusion draw strength from speakers with a range of experiences, backgrounds, and talent. Everyone learns and grows when diverse views are presented.

THE PROBLEM WITH MANELS

The most egregious manels are the ones in which the so-called male experts exchange ideas about subjects related to women:

- The 115th Congress is made of less than 20 percent women. Not surprisingly, the US Congress lacks a comprehensive anti–sexual harassment policy.[10]
- In 2017, the leadership in the US Senate created a thirteen-man working group to reform healthcare. Their proposal didn't require insurance coverage for maternity care.[11]
- At eleven of the largest healthcare conferences in 2013, the participation rate of women speakers ranged from 12 percent to 38 percent.[12] For decades, countless women have been misdiagnosed for heart disease because the medical community never realized their symptoms were different from those experienced by men.[13]
- In 2015, only 25 percent of speakers at the top tech conferences in the San Francisco Bay area were women.[14] In 2014, Apple released a health-tracking app that didn't track menstruation.[15]

Being seen but not heard is a chronic problem for women that goes far back in our history. For instance, in 1840, a delegation of women activists from the United States traveled to a world anti-slavery convention in London only to be turned away.[18] The exclusion was protested until a compromise was reached. A special women-only (meaning white women) section was curtained off so that women could listen to but not participate in the conference proceedings.

The women were separated from the male attendees because the mixing of the sexes in public forums went against British customs. The old "we've always done it this way" argument was used to deny them an active role. Further, the men considered the involvement of women in politics to be "promiscuous" and "un-Christian."[19]

Two of the women stuck behind the curtain became founding mothers of the suffragist and abolitionist movements—Elizabeth Cady Stanton and Lucretia Mott. They were so angry about the mistreatment that upon their return home they began organizing the first women's rights convention. At the Seneca Falls gathering, women and men attended and sat together. Yet even for these progressive thinkers it was considered unseemly for women to run public meetings, so Mott's husband was called upon to chair the event. For the decades that followed, the leaders of the women's movement would be hamstrung by societal norms and their own prejudices.

White suffragists were divided on whether to open their ranks to women of color. Many felt collaboration with women of color would hurt their cause and delay the effort to win the vote. A glaring example was the attempt to exclude women of color from the first women's march held in Washington, DC, in 1913.[20] Black women were instructed to march at the end of the parade. Several prominent African American women refused to be segregated. Ida Wells-Barnett, who was a leading voice against lynching, ignored the insult and joined the procession to march with supporters from her home state. This is a problem that continues today, and the answer to this bias is promoting intersectionality.

RISKY BUSINESS

As we can see from Mott to manels, getting in the room is the first hurdle. Once you are there, the reception might be anything but welcoming. For glass-ceiling breakers, the right to free speech has always come at a cost. Women speakers face the risk of degradation, humiliation, and, worse, threats to their personal safety. Even the most prestigious speaking events can be unsafe and threatening environments.

TED Talk events have featured numerous women and men speaking on the topics of feminism, gender equity, and sexual violence. But women speakers and attendees have come forward with stories of being harassed at the exclusive TED events, where people pay $10,000 to attend. In 2017, the *Washington Post* reported on a rise in the number of women who said the "atmosphere of predatory male behavior was getting worse."[21] TED organizers had earlier told the *Post* that they had added language to their code of conduct to prohibit harassment and had instituted a policy of banning "sexual harassment of any kind, including unwanted sexual attention and inappropriate physical contact."

Women have had to stare down intimidation and physical threats since the barrier-breaking suffragists took to the campaign trail. In the 1850s, the first and for many years the only woman in America to advocate full-time for women's rights was Lucy Stone. A trailblazer, Lucy was one of the first women to earn a college degree when she graduated from Oberlin College in 1847.[22] Although she was chosen by her classmates to deliver a commencement address, Lucy refused the speaking engagement because she would not be allowed to deliver her remarks onstage with her male classmates. The restrictions on female public speakers meant that her speech would have to have been read by a male professor.

Lucy earned the nickname "Locomotive Lucy" for the thousands of miles she traveled alone via train and stage coach. Disowned by her parents for behavior they deemed ungodly, the activist dedicated her life to the cause and campaigned whether or not people wanted to listen. She often faced down unruly crowds that threatened violence and tried to drive her off the stage. When hit with an egg mid-speech, she challenged the hecklers "to rid their minds of her spoken truth" as easily as she wiped away the sticky mess.[23]

Violence can also come from the people who are supposed to be providing the protection. The founders of #BlackLivesMatter, Patrisse Cullors, Alicia Garza, and Opal Tometi, attest to the real, live threat of police brutality. From the outset, the impassioned speeches of #Black-LivesMatter activists have been incorrectly interpreted by many as anti-white propaganda rather than as an affirmation that "black lives matter, too." This bias has resulted in tense stand-offs between peaceful activists and police officers in Ferguson, Chicago, Baltimore, and too many other cities where black lives have been lost.

> *"We gave tongue to something we all knew was happening. We were courageous enough to call it what it was. But more than that to offer an alternative. An aspirational message: Black lives matter."*[24]
>
> —Opal Tometi

This physical violence taking place in the streets can be stoked by alt-right groups and other trolls online who direct their hatred at people of color and the LGBTQ community. For example, the Human Rights Campaign documented an increase in the killings of transgender people in 2017.[25] Human-rights advocates say the physical violence can't be separated from the hate in social media and a wave of anti-transgender legislation like "bathroom bills." These bills attempt to prohibit transgender people's access to public restrooms. In *Rants and Retorts*, journalist Anita Samuels has documented how bigots monopolize the comment sections of online news sites. Her findings show how racism is thriving under the guise of free speech online.[26]

The threat of violence has kept young activists from being able to speak out against misogyny and racism on college campuses. Women who are working to make change in the video-game industry have received death threats. In 2014, a speech by a video blogger scheduled at Utah State University was canceled due to the threat of a mass shooting.[27] Anita Sarkeesian took on the rampant misogyny in mainstream video games with a series of videos that document the abuse. The FBI investigated dozens of death and rape threats made against Sarkeesian and other women gamers, but to date no one has been prosecuted. Anger about the lack of FBI intervention in online threats prompted the CEO of a game studio to take action. Brianna Wu decided to run for Congress in Massachusetts because she had tracked one hundred death threats made against herself in a nine-month period that were unsolved.[28]

SPEAKING WHILE OTHER

This abuse against women extends beyond video gaming into other arenas typically dominated by men. For some baseball fans, it felt like hell had frozen over. A woman was calling a Major League Baseball playoff game. Fans did not hold back on what they thought about broadcaster Jessica Mendoza. When the former Olympic softball champion joined the guys in the ESPN booth in 2015, the reaction was brutal:

"I just switched the channel to ESPN2 so I could stop listening to Jessica Mendoza. BTW I don't understand Spanish."[29]

"Why do I turn on baseball and hear a women's voice in the broadcast booth. I watch sports to get away from women."[30]

The abuse has continued, and in 2016 it came from a baseball player:

Mike Bell @mikebell929   1h

yes tell us Tits McGhee when you're up there hitting the softball you see a lot of 95 mile an hour cutters?

Boiled Sports
@BoiledSports

A woman made history tonight calling an MLB Playoff game for ESPN. This is what an Atlanta radio guy thought of it.

11:28 PM - Oct 6, 2015

♡ 77   💬 177 people are talking about this

Mike Bell
@mikebell929   ⚙   +⚹ Follow

I've been trending for all the wrong reasons tonight. I apologize for calling Jessica Mendoza Tits McGee.

When a woman breaks into an announcer's booth or any other formerly all-boys club, she can expect to have the way she talks belittled. And the woman who dares to express a strong opinion can expect to be scorned. For instance, ESPN sports commentator Jemele Hill was suspended by the cable channel for tweeting that Donald Trump is a white supremacist.[31] The White House had used its bully pulpit to call for the firing of someone at a private company who had been hired to express her opinion. Jemele was co-anchor of an atypical sports program that wasn't just game highlights and box scores but a mix of opinion and commentary on sports and popular culture.

Institutions like major league sports and sports channels are not the only places where some want the high-profile speaking roles to remain the province of men. Engaging in verbally dominant behaviors such as self-promotion, public disagreements, or defending turf is tricky and risky business for women in the workplace. For decades, white women and women of color have had to navigate a labyrinth of double standards around conference tables. The male style of asserting oneself, holding the floor, and interrupting tends to dominate and be accepted only if it is a man who is doing the talking. If a woman is talking, the audience perceives her differently and there is less tolerance of her adopting a more aggressive, "masculine" speaking style.

In the 1990s, linguistics professor Deborah Tannen wrote that the "world of words" children grow up in is worlds apart for boys and girls even though they may be raised in the same community or family.[32] Boys tend to play in larger groups with leaders who take center stage, give orders, argue, and compete for status. Girls are more likely to play in small groups or pairs where the focus is on cooperation and friendship. Girls traditionally give suggestions rather than orders, avoid boasting, and don't directly challenge one another. The lessons children learn at a young age stay with them and follow them into the workplace.

Leaders take charge, but a woman with a dominant speaking style is viewed as too abrasive or pushy. In particular, black women who assert themselves are told "they have an attitude."[33] On the other hand, women who develop a leadership style based on qualities people associate with women, such as being helpful and sympathetic, can be viewed as pushovers. The woman who achieves a position of authority can find herself in what is known as a double bind, that is, "a feeling of being trapped . . . that nagging sense that whatever you do, you can do no right."[34]

In 2015, *Lean In* author Sheryl Sandberg dubbed this the double bind the "speaking while female" problem.[35] If a woman speaks up at work, she's likely to be ignored or viewed as too aggressive, so women tend to keep quiet. That was the finding of a study conducted by Yale psychologist Victoria L. Brescoll, who found that women executives feared a backlash so they tended not to speak out as much as their male colleagues.[36] Her research revealed that male executives who voiced their opinions more frequently were rated 10 percent higher for competence. Women executives who spoke more than their peers were punished with a 14 percent lower competence rating.

UNBALANCED MEDIA

"You can't be what you can't see." This is the mantra of women advocates who are working to change who controls what and how news is reported. From global entertainment companies to locally owned newspapers, the people with their hands on the power levers remain white males. Across all media realms—television, radio, print, and online—there is a dramatic lack of diversity in the gatekeepers who control what gets covered and who writes the stories.

The Women's Media Center's 2017 report on the status of women in the media shows glaring, persistent disparities. The report found that at the nation's top twenty news outlets, male journalists produced two-thirds of all news reports. The gender gap was most pronounced in television network newscasts, with men reporting three times as much news as women. WMC co-founder Gloria Steinem says an inclusive press is an imperative to a well-functioning democracy: "When men or women turn to or on the media, yet fail to see women in our true diversity, there is a sense that all or some women literally don't count. It's crucial that the media report and reflect, not conceal and distort."[37]

The power imbalance in who is telling the stories directly impacts how stories are told. The person who tells the stories gets to interpret what and who is important. In 2017, a woman considering a run for the US Senate in Colorado was surprised when a newspaper doing a piece on her possible candidacy described her as single.[38] She didn't consider this relevant to her candidacy. Even more dismaying was the commentary about her marital status from online readers who felt that a single woman without children was not well-suited for the job.

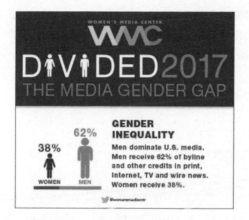

Used with permission from the Women's Media Center.

If you are invited to provide commentary on a cable news program, don't be surprised if you are the only woman on the studio set, even when the topic primarily affects women. The media watchdog group Media Matters looked at how abortion was covered on cable channels in 2017 and found that 60 percent of the people who commented on the issue of abortion were men. Fox had the greatest imbalance, with 68 percent male commentators; and at CNN, 58 percent were men. Stunningly, Media Matters found that across all cable shows, 64 percent of the comments about abortion were inaccurate.[39] One wonders whether if more women had been at the news desk, the information presented to the general public would have been more accurate, since women are most directly affected by the abortion debate.

Likewise, the #MeToo movement has raised questions about the practices of highly influential men who covered the 2016 presidential campaign and who have since faced accusations of sexual harassment. Former MSNBC commentator Mark Halperin, who was accused of harassment by several women co-workers, had dismissed reports that Donald Trump groped women.[40] For twenty-one years, Matt Lauer hosted the *Today* show until numerous allegations were made public against him.[41] Similar to how Halperin's biases showed at MSNBC, Lauer's interviews were colored by his own issues. For instance, his interviews with Hillary

Clinton and Donald Trump were widely panned for the kid gloves he wore with Trump and the hammering he gave Clinton.[42] We see here that those at the mic bring their own biases against women into their reporting of the news, which is just one way in which it is harmful to have a lack of diversity among those who report the news.

STICKY STEREOTYPES

In 2007, the most frequently purchased stock photo for the search term "woman" was of an anonymous woman lying naked in bed, partially covered by a sheet. Ten years later, the *New York Times* reported the most popular photo was a woman dressed in trail gear hiking alone in the mountains.[43] The sea change in image selection from sex object to independent person didn't happen by accident. It was the result of Getty Images' *Lean In Collection*, which created a library of images of real women doing real things.

The realistic photo collection remains an aberration. Most of the images of women on screens large and small are dominated by clichés and stereotypes. This may be due to the lack of women in decision-making roles in the television and film industry. In 2016, women made up 7 percent of the directors of the 250 highest-grossing movies, according to San Diego State University's Center for the Study of Women in Television and Film.[44] Women make up only a third of all the speaking roles in top films. The same study found that fewer than 30 percent of the 100 top films had women playing lead roles, and the majority of those roles went to white actresses. For women of color, 13 percent of characters were black; 4 percent, Latina; and 3 percent, Asian.

This might be changing, slowly. *Wonder Woman* and *Black Panther* were breakthrough films with women and people of color in prominent roles in front of and behind the cameras. But, with few women calling the shots, the entertainment media remain littered with stereotypical images. Depictions of the fiery Latina, the Asian tiger mom, the big-hearted mammy, and the Spanish maid with an accent are more commonplace than female superheroes. In 2016's top films, women were much more likely to be seen in "sexy attire," and "teenage females were just as likely [as adult women] to be depicted in sexually revealing clothing and with some nudity."[46] Ava DuVernay, the director of *A Wrinkle in Time* and *Selma*, says that the Academy of Motion Picture Arts and Sciences has a problem with inclusion: "There's a belonging problem in Hollywood. Who dictates who belongs? The very body who dictates looks all one way."[47]

SUPREMELY BIASED

If there's one place where you would think women would be given the deference they deserve, it would be the stately chambers of the Supreme Court of the United States. Court proceedings are dictated by traditions that date back to 1790. The justices are seated according to seniority, and during oral arguments, the proper address is "Your Honor" or "Justice." It is a serious breach of decorum for anyone to talk while a justice is speaking. Lawyers presenting to the court are instructed to stop talking immediately when a justice begins to speak.

In that setting with those rules, who would have the nerve to interrupt Justice Ruth Bader Ginsburg, a justice whose image has been emblazoned on t-shirts with the moniker "Notorious RBG," in recognition of her ability to pack a legal punch? Well, plenty of attorneys don't hesitate to cut her off. Justice Ginsburg and her sisters on the court are three times more likely to be interrupted than their male colleagues are.[45] And—wait for it—most of the interrupting is done by men.

With the additions of Sonia Sotomayor and Elena Kagan in 2010, the court reached a milestone with a record number of women serving. However, this also increased the number of interruptions. The real clincher is that the justice who is most likely to be cut off is the only woman of color to serve. Male lawyers talking over Justice Sotomayor is the most common type of interruption.

TOXIC PEOPLE

Toxic people can be known troublemakers or unknown individuals who surprise you with sudden outbursts. The antics of these people can cause your stress levels to rise and take a toll on your self-confidence. They can cause you to question your sense of reality—*Did that person really just say that?*

This bad behavior is exhibited at the highest levels of power, starting at the White House. Donald Trump did not temper his crude commentary when the presidential campaign ended but instead brought it with him to the Oval Office. Trump refused to denounce the white supremacists responsible for the death of a woman at a protest in Charlottesville, Virginia. Rather, he said there was an "egregious display of hatred, bigotry, and violence on many sides."[48] In this way, he attempted to place blame at the feet of those who were violent and those who were protesting the violence. In another display of outright bias, during a White House meeting, he described immigrants from Haiti, El Salvador, and African countries as coming from "shithole countries."[49]

Trump has the biggest megaphone, but he is one of many who engage in uncivil, mean-spirited commentary. Here is a small sample of other conservative, white men who feel free to communicate their biases in public forums.

Old, White Men Say the Darndest Things!

> "...not having the estate tax recognizes the people that are investing, as opposed to those that are just spending every darn penny that they have, whether it's on booze or women or movies." —Sen. Charles Grassley to a *Des Moines Register* reporter, 2017

> "I think it [America] was great at the time when families were united, even though we had slavery. They cared for one another.... Our families were strong. Our country had a

direction." —Former judge and Senate candidate Roy Moore, campaign event, 2017

"Planned Parenthood isn't purely a 'healthcare provider' any more than a heroin dealer is a community pharmacist." —Former governor Mike Huckabee (father of Sarah Huckabee Sanders), Breitbart interview, 2015

"The incidence of rape resulting in pregnancy is very low." —Rep. Trent Franks, House Judiciary hearing, 2013

"I think that most people in the Middle East, at least 50 percent, believe in being Sharia-compliant." —Former Trump advisor and alt-right promoter Steve Bannon, 2015

Democrats "made up the concept of sexual harassment." —Tucker Carlson, MSNBC, December 14, 2006

"This whole 'white people' business, though, does get a little tired. . . . I'd ask you to go back through history and figure out where are these contributions that have been made by these other categories of people you are talking about. Where did any other subgroup of people contribute more to civilization . . . other than Western civilization, itself." —Rep. Steve King, MSNBC, 2016

This small sample gives you a sense of how comfortable conservative, white men with big microphones feel communicating their bias and hatred. A common excuse for this type of talk is that these people are telling it like it is—just as "grab them by the pussy" was excused away by some as "locker-room talk." But the problem with accepting this talk is that it normalizes language that is racist and misogynistic. These sentiments should have no place in the public dialogue.

EQUAL RIGHTS AMENDMENT

"Equality of rights under the law shall not be denied or abridged by the United States or by any state on account of sex."

Some of the most vocal opponents of the Equal Rights Amendment have been conservative women. Leading the opposition in the 1970s was a Harvard-educated lawyer, Phyllis Schlafly, who regularly demonized feminist leaders as "man haters" and "women-libbers." Her opposition was based on the argument that, "The family gives a woman the physical, financial, and emotional security of the home—for all her life."[50] When she ran for Congress in 1952, Schlafly described herself as an "average housewife" who had asked her husband for permission to campaign. Unfortunately, Schlafly's hypocrisy is alive and well in today's conservative women commentators, who have said the following:

"My position is women should not have the right to vote." —Ann Coulter, *Free Speech*, June 15, 2015.

"Twenty-first-century feminism: an embarrassment to my gender." —Kayleigh McEnany, *The Blaze*, March 22, 2013.

"I think a very compelling case could be made that [the women's movement] has set women back. The most powerful thing a woman can do is give birth." —Laura Ingraham, *The Laura Ingraham Show*, November 11, 2015.

"This whole sisterhood, this whole 'let's go march for women's rights' and just constantly talking about what women look like or what they wear or making fun of their choices or presuming they are not as powerful as the men around [them]. This presumptive negativity about women in power, I think, is very unfortunate." —Kellyanne Conway, Conservative Political Action Conference, February 23, 2017.

Toxic People with Toxic Tactics

Toxic people don't just operate at the White House and on cable television. Here's a glossary of the most common types found in workplaces and offices everywhere. Familiarizing yourself with their tactics and behaviors is the first step to ensuring these individuals are unable to disrupt, intimidate, or take over when you are talking.

Body Shamer

A body shamer is someone who draws attention to body type or appearance. The focus on appearance, whether positive, negative, or neutral, elevates the body at the expense of everything else, drawing attention away from the content of the speech and the reputation or qualifications of the speaker. One egregious example of this was when fashion designer Karl Lagerfeld described Grammy-winning singer-songwriter Adele as "a little too fat."[51] Body shamers are deflecting attention away from the quality of what you have to say and the value of the contribution you make.

Body shaming can take place when you are being introduced. For example, "She may be a small person, but she has big ideas," was how a senior scholar on security studies was introduced at a professional conference.[52] Or, "She is the best-looking attorney general in the country," as President Barack Obama said when introducing US Senate candidate Kamala Harris at a campaign event.[53]

Broviator

"Bros" or dudes make pompous pronouncements they mistakenly believe others are interested in. They are masters of talking at length and saying nothing. Broviators, that is, bros who bloviate, operate in all public-speaking settings.

A favorite tactic is bropropriating. This is when a dude appropriates, or takes, a woman's idea and claims it as his own in an attempt to steal the credit. Expect this in meetings and roundtable discussions.

Humblebragging

Humblebragging is a technique favored by bros to get away with self-promotion by couching an accomplishment in feigned humility. One example of this is when former White House press secretary Ari Fleischer infamously tweeted, "They just announced my flight at LaGuardia is number 15 for takeoff. I miss Air Force One!!"[54]

Male Chauvinist

This is an old-timey term for the dude who sees all women as inferior and will actively try to undermine what you say and do simply because you are a woman and he is a man. The behavior encompasses a wide range, from paternalistic put-downs to dangerously demeaning beliefs. For example, a male chauvinist would be the male boss who expects a female employee of the same rank as male employees to fetch coffee. Or the former Google engineer whose manifesto claimed women are less effective programmers because of biological differences.[55]

Manelist

Be wary of the panel discussions that engage in window-dressing in an attempt to hide the fact that they are really manels. "Pinkwashing" is a term used to describe the effort to hide the high levels of testosterone in a panel by selecting a woman to be the moderator while all the other speakers are manelists. This also happens when the panel attempts to hide its whiteness by including one woman of color.

Mansplainer

A mansplainer is a man who explains to a woman something about which he knows little, and that she didn't ask about. In these situations, it is not uncommon for the woman to be more knowledgeable on the subject than the explainer. Author Rebecca Solnit first described this behavior in her essay "Men Explain Things to Me."[56] She hilariously recounts an egregious example of a man attempting to explain a book he described as very important but clearly hadn't read. Rebecca knew the mansplainer hadn't read the book in question because she had written it.

Most mansplainers explain things that are obvious. Unfortunately, they are many in number, and you encounter them at the watercooler, at cocktail receptions, in meetings, or just about any place people gather to talk.

Manterrupter

A manterrupter is a man who makes pointless interruptions while a woman is speaking. A notorious example was when Kanye West jumped onstage at the 2009 MTV Video Music Awards and ripped the microphone out of the hands of Taylor Swift as she was about to accept an award. Kanye went on to deliver a diatribe, leaving Taylor speechless. As we have seen with the women justices on the Supreme Court, no woman is immune to the manterrupter.

Mean Girl

The mean girls who rule the lunchroom with their vicious gossip and exclusionary tactics eventually grow up and go to work. Not all of them evolve into better versions of themselves, such as the meanies portrayed in Tina Fey's classic movie, *Mean Girls*. Adult queen bees are still in competition with other women whom they attempt to undercut with covert or indirect aggression.

Common mean-girl tactics are to leave you out of meetings or subtly undercut you in front of the boss or colleagues.

Name-Caller

Name-calling is using personal attacks to mock, insult, or bully. Former and current Fox personalities such as Bill O'Reilly, Tucker

Carlson, and Sean Hannity are famous for having made a regular practice of insulting women, minorities, and LGBTQ people. In addition to hosting or appearing on Fox cable shows, name-callers often lurk in the back rows of auditoriums, where they can heckle and spread bile.

Plastic Feminist

These self-proclaimed feminists are women who often resemble real-life Barbie dolls, with curated outfits and shiny hair. Models of physical perfection, they claim to support their sisters when in reality they are pursuing their own agenda that actively undermines other women. Ivanka Trump, for instance, claims to be a champion of women but uses her high-profile position to sell shoes and purses while remaining silent on the anti-women policies of the Trump administration.

Plastic feminists are often seen on television talk shows spouting anti-feminist ideologies and vocalizing their opposition to the Equal Rights Amendment. Their queen bee was the late Phyllis Schlafly, who preached that women's work was housework while she traveled the country, raising money for conservative causes.

Shouter

For our purposes here, a shouter is someone who uses the voice as a weapon to drown out other speakers. Male shouters do not suffer penalties for this behavior; it is considered acceptable for them to bloviate at high decibels. For example, journalist Gail Collins noticed this in Senator Bernie Sanders's speaking style; she observed that while he was running for president, he acted as someone who "yells his mind and is admired for being grumpy."[57] There isn't a woman or person of color who can get away with that behavior without suffering major blowback for being perceived as screechy, shrill, or out of control.

Straightsplainer

Like the above-mentioned mansplainer, the straightsplainer is not well-versed on the issues faced by those within the LGBTQ community yet minimizes their experiences nonetheless. Straightsplaining often begins with the premise that gay people have laws to protect them, so now everything is all right for them (regardless of whether or not those laws are effective or widespread). In this way, straightsplaining is a variation of mansplaining, except that it is when straight people tell gay people how gay people think, feel, and act. The straightsplainer often begin sentences with, "I'm not a homophobe, but here's what I believe homosexuals should do . . ." or something to that effect.

Straightsplaining is the province of evangelicals and conservative politicians who rant from the pulpit and rave on conservative podcasts and talk shows. You might encounter them anywhere, though, to varying degrees of intensity.

Whitesplainer

Whitesplainers are white people who deliver paternalistic lectures to people of color about what should and should not be considered racist, while obliviously exhibiting their own racism. Most white people have done this, perhaps without realizing how belittling and painful it is.

Whitesplaining can occur in any situation when whites are talking to people of color, and it is noticeable particularly during media interviews when program hosts explain to minority guests how they should feel or what they should say.

WELL-SPOKEN WOMEN RESIST, INSIST, PERSIST

Expect interference when something is at stake.

The practice of "no girls allowed" has deep roots.

When racist, sexist, and homophobic comments fall on deaf ears, the perpetrator is enabled.

Internalizing toxicity erodes confidence.

CHAPTER 4

RESISTING BOORS AND BULLIES

"You can disagree without being disagreeable."
—Ruth Bader Ginsburg

A "young lady" who "doesn't know a damn thing what she's talking about"—that is how a white, eighty-four-year old, male member of Congress referred to a colleague while speaking on the House floor. Alaskan Don Young has a history of ugly outbursts in public venues, including using the racial slur "wetbacks" to refer to temporary immigrant workers.[1] The woman he was talking about was a fifty-one-year-old congresswoman and a longtime civil-rights activist with an MBA.

Rep. Pramila Jayapal of Washington immediately objected to the offensive comment and demanded that it be stricken from the official record. Seizing the moment, she then tweeted a word of encouragement to others who have been similarly disrespected.

 Rep. Pramila Jayapal ✓
@RepJayapal

A message to women of color out there:stand strong. Refuse to be patronized or minimized. Let the small guys out there be intimated by you.

8:24 PM - Sep 7, 2017

♡ 7,125 ♡ 2,404 people are talking about this

The reaction on Twitter from her sisters in the House was swift and supportive:

> Rep. Judy Chu: "I'm proud to work with [her] and I can tell you she knows quite a bit."
> Sen. Elizabeth Warren: "Keep fighting."
> Rep. Barbara Lee: "She handled an egregious display of sexism on the House floor with dignity and grace. I'm proud to call her my friend."

It's clear the congresswoman will not accept being treated as "less than." And her action was a best-practice example of how to push back. An immigrant who came to this country from India by herself at age sixteen to attend college, Representative Jayapal is the first Indian American to serve in the House. Young's insult wasn't the first; another Republican member told her "to learn how to read."[2] Before being elected, she said she heard the insult "Go back to your own country!" so many times that she lost count.[3]

REP. PRAMILA JAYAPAL

Her quick action to have the sexist comment stricken from the congressional record was an appropriate, professional response. It also ensured media coverage of the incident. As did the social-media post, which provided a channel for her colleagues to voice both support for her and disdain for way she was treated. The high level of attention may have contributed to Young's decision to apologize, which the congresswoman accepted. Doing so further demonstrated that she could rise above the pettiness that was directed at her.

The way Jayapal handled the situation is a case study on what to do should this type of boorish behavior be directed at you. It is an example of how flipping the script can help you and help others. The congresswoman took charge and took control of a dialogue that was being driven by someone else.

FLIP THE SCRIPT

- Keep calm.
- Call out bad behavior.
- Create a teachable moment.
- Welcome support.
- Accept an apology, if one is forthcoming.

The five-step process of flipping the script allows you to take a moment of bias and turn it into an opportunity to drive change. Rather than ignoring the incident or responding in anger, Jayapal showed how dignity can carry the day.

Accepting an apology is about more than taking the high road. Flipping the script creates a chance for the person who has said something sexist or racist to learn and do better. Or, minimally, to prevent further episodes. Resist the impulse to shame the ignorant, which can make the situation worse. Only the shamer feels good when that happens. It takes real conversations to end this type of offensive behavior.

Comedian Sarah Silverman's response to a Twitter troll was a master class on how a helping hand can do more than an angry fist. When a stranger using the Twitter handle @jeremy_jamyrose called her a c—t, she responded to his tweet with compassion and discovered the source of his anger was abuse he suffered as a child. When he went on to explain that he was using pot and pills to self-medicate, Sarah rallied her followers to find him medical help.

Jeremy jamrozy @jeremy_jamrozy28 Dec
Replying to @SarahKSilverman
Cunt

Sarah Silverman ✔
@SarahKSilverman

I believe in you. I read ur timeline & I see what ur doing & your rage is thinly veiled pain. But u know that. I know this feeling. Ps My back Fucking sux too. see what happens when u choose love. I see it in you.

9:36 PM - Dec 28, 2017

♡ 2,543   ⬭ 446 people are talking about this   ℹ

We need a continuous roll of flipping-the-script moments to move forward like an ongoing wave in the stands at sporting events. This chapter shows you how to apply the flip-the-script tactic to a variety of speaking environments. The approach is one that we all should have been taught when we were young, but instead many of us we were instructed to be "good girls." Rather than being encouraged to speak out, we were praised for biting our tongues, turning the other cheek, and not making a fuss. Don't be discouraged if the suggestions that follow feel uncomfortable at first. That is to be expected because they are new. It may be necessary to step outside of your comfort zone.

Every situation is different, and trusting your gut can help you decide whether and how to respond. In some situations, you may not be able to deal with the offending person or persons on your own. Backup support may be required to quell the toxicity. Sometimes the position and the title of the toxic individual must be taken into account. The guidelines for handling your boss are different from those when you encounter a toxic stranger.

KEEP CALM AND CARRY ON

If you take a wide-lens view of common offensive statements directed at people of color, working people, LGBTQ people, and women, you will notice the animosity fits a pattern. The powerful attack the less powerful often with taunts reminiscent of schoolyard bullies. Recognizing this reality can remove the element of surprise. An unexpected nasty comment can shock you in the moment, leaving you stunned, speechless, or breathless. Knowing that this bullying behavior fits a larger pattern may help you avoid personalizing and internalizing it.

Instead of personalizing the comments, view yourself as a proxy for a larger group of people who are under attack. The attacks are often vicious because progressives threaten the power the high and mighty use to keep other people down. Rep. Jayapal demonstrated how to carry out sage advice provided by First Lady Michelle Obama. In her emotional speech in support of Hillary Clinton at the 2016 Democratic National Convention, Obama advised not stooping to the level of bullies, "When they go low, we go high." Jayapal's actions were a showcase on how to take the high road and not end up feeling like roadkill.

Here is a cheat sheet of common low-road tactics, and suggestions on what to say in response. As you read through the suggested responses, ask yourself this question: "What would Michelle do—WWMD?" In other words, imagine that Michelle Obama was being disrespected, and envision how she would handle the boor. Then channel her style.

What Would Michelle Do?

Low Road—What They Say	High Road—What You Say
Name-calling	"You sound like a bully."
Body shaming	"That is so unkind and childish; I look great."
Ridicule your idea	"People without facts resort to personal attacks."
Belittle your credentials	"Why would you say that? I don't deserve it."
Disparage your opinion	"Hey, that sounded condescending; mind dropping the attitude?"
Criticize you personally	"Let's stick to our differences on policy."
Charge "fake news"	"Lay out the facts by citing an independent source."
Use coarse language	"Your mouth needs to be washed out with soap."
Tell you to shut up	"Let me speak my turn."

The high-road comments head off angry, knee-jerk responses you may later regret. With a preplanned retort, you can control your emotions and stay above the fray. Knowing in advance how you will respond to juvenile behavior keeps your focus on your agenda to drive change.

It is possible to flip the script in a variety of settings. Outlined below are specific techniques and tips for handling toxic people and offensive behavior in meetings, presentations, and audience question-and-answer sessions.

A WORD OF KINDNESS GOES A LONG WAY

A moment of graciousness occurred on a radio talk show the day after the November 2017 elections. Danica Roem, the transgender candidate who unseated a self-described homophobic state legislator in Virginia, was asked what she thought about how her opponent had campaigned against her. The incumbent, Bob Marshall, had repeatedly questioned her gender identity, referred to her with the wrong pronouns, refused to debate, and accused her of promoting transgender education in the public schools for children as young as five years old. His campaign produced a television ad accusing her of "lewd" and "shocking" behavior.[4] The day after her victory, when NPR's Kojo Nnamdi asked Danica about her opponent, she took the high road:

> Look, next year, Delegate Marshall is going to be my constituent. I'm not trying to make him feel bad. I'm sure [he] and his family are probably grieving. This is probably a pretty massive loss for him. I have no intention of trying to be disrespectful. I'm going to work on fulfilling my campaign promises.[5]

THE MEETING

1. Interruptions

Sometimes you need to know how to hold the floor when you're talking. And sometimes you need to take action in order to get the floor. Manterrupters are often repeat offenders, so you can anticipate that they will try to cut you off more than once.

If the interrupter is your boss or is higher up the food chain, cede the floor. This ensures that you don't appear disrespectful to people with more authority and responsibility than you. If the interruption is an ongoing problem with a supervisor, you have a couple of options. If you feel that you can approach this person directly, then do so privately at a time when you are not upset and he does not feel threatened or particularly stressed. Approaching the issue when you are both in a healthy and stable state is more likely to ensure a successful outcome. Calmly explain what has happened and be as specific as possible. If this isn't something you feel that you can do, then approach a supporter or mentor for his or her advice.

If the interrupter is a colleague, you don't need to defer to that person. The best way to hold the floor is to keep talking. The secret is how you modulate your voice. When interrupted, most people instinctively react by talking faster and louder. This can cause the speaker's vocal pitch to rise, sounding "shrill." It is more effective to ignore the annoying interruption and keep talking, but slow the pace and lower the pitch slightly.

Going slow and low keeps you in the driver's seat because you sound controlled and the interrupter comes off as rude. If you're feeling game, turn to the person who's trying to interrupt, give him or her a wide smile, and keep talking. This will prevent the encounter from feeling like a contest of wills. You want to project firm but pleasant control.

Hold the Floor:

- Keep talking.
- Slow your pace.
- Lower your tone.
- Smile at the person who's trying to cut you off.

There may be times when you need to interrupt to get a word in edgewise. Those situations require the "Amazing Interrupting Technique" outlined below. Every talker needs to come up for air, and that's the second you have to jump in. When the speaker takes a pause to breathe, look at that person, say his name, and use a transition. For instance, you can say, "Dave has a point, but he may be overlooking something I found in the research . . ." and keep talking. As you continue, look at Dave and smile. The facial expression is a secret weapon because you look benign while you cut someone off.

Amazing Interrupting Technique:

- Wait for the speaker to take a breath.
- Use his name to catch him off guard.
- Segue with a preplanned transition line.
- Turn away from the speaker and deliver your points.
- Smile at the interrupter as you continue holding the floor.

2. Broviators

These individuals attempt to control the room by pointedly disagreeing, often using the interruption, "Yes, but . . ." Broviators are know-it-alls who love to challenge others and put on a display of verbal tug-of-war by engaging in public debate when it's unnecessary. If you anticipate broviators being in the group, head them off at the pass. Set the stage by explaining that new information will be introduced and ask everyone to listen with an open mind, holding comments until the end.

If the broviator persists, mask any frustration or resentment with a neutral facial expression. Hear out the challenger by allowing him to share his perceived wisdom or grievance. Don't engage in a public power struggle. As you listen, maintain steady eye contact, and once he has finished, say, "It looks like we have a different opinion on this. Why don't we table it for now and plan to discuss it at another time? Now, let's move on to the other items on the agenda." It is usually easier to deal with challenging types one-on-one, when they are not putting on a show for others.

3. Silent Minority

Maybe the problem isn't about being interrupted but about getting up the nerve to speak in the first place. Turn the meeting into an opportunity to shine. You did the homework. You're prepared. It's time for others to know how conscientious you are. Leaning in here will help you gain confidence to do it in larger forums. Take yourself seriously by embracing something a wise woman once told me: "If you are in the room, recognize that you belong there. You don't have to take a test every day. If you are there, you belong there."

You don't have to prove that you belong in the room or at the table. But, if you typically hold back, set a reasonable goal for yourself to speak up. For example, make a pledge that you will talk at least once. And perhaps at one decibel higher, if need be. Ask to be included in the formal agenda, or raise your hand when your area of expertise is being discussed. A sincere and serious effort to contribute should be valued and respected by others in the room.

Then observe the reaction you get. As discussed in chapter 2, you may have a heads-up that a contribution might be dismissed or ignored if you are the only woman in the room or if the room is dominated by a broviator or two. Rather than stewing about a slight after the meeting is over, be ready with a plan of action.

That's what the women in the Obama White House had to do with a room full of Type A alpha males. They employed a strategy famously known as "amplification." It works this way: If you raise a point and it is ignored, you have an ally ready to repeat what you said, giving you credit for the idea. As reported in the *Washington Post*, the strategy forced the men in the room (it was mostly men in President Barack Obama's first term) to recognize the contribution and from whom it had come.[6] This prevents a bro from claiming the idea as his own, that is, in engaging in the previously mentioned bropropriation.

Apparently President Obama began to notice what was going on, and he altered his behavior by calling on women and junior aides more frequently. When word of their success got out, "amplification" went viral. If you don't have a team of women allies, then you can seek out anyone who will be sympathetic to your plight, regardless of gender. There are likely others who could use and benefit from your reciprocal support.

4. Poker Faces

Unresponsive people can be worse than aggressive troublemakers because you don't know where you stand. Rooms dominated by older, white men (and some women) are more likely to give you the poker face. From the front of the room it can be difficult to discern what's going on, and their blank expressions and crossed arms may not provide clues about what they are thinking—are they tolerating what you are telling them? Or perhaps you are telling them something they haven't heard before. Their body language is disconcerting because it is unclear how or if they are processing the information you are presenting. Are they quietly absorbing it or silently disagreeing? They may actually be preoccupied with something else going on in their lives. Or some may even be shy and unassertive, and they may be trying to avoid being called upon.

Since the behavior of the poker faces doesn't have much impact on others in the room, it is usually best to ignore them. If you are comfortable, try the technique of calling on them in an easygoing manner or asking an open-ended question to draw them out. If the silent types are VIPs, you can try to engage them one-on-one during a break or once the meeting has concluded. Don't expend too much energy worrying about what these people are thinking while you are delivering your speech; it's better to focus on the other audience members at that point in your presentation.

If everyone in the room is nonresponsive, don't take it personally. Sometimes the audience is having a bad day, and sometimes people are tired of being in meetings. Signal that you understand something is off by saying, "I'll keep my remarks brief so we have time for questions." If there aren't any questions, that's another signal that it's time to call it a day.

SPEECHES, TALKS, PRESENTATIONS

1. Getting the Crowd to Quiet Down

Some people don't know when to stop talking; they seem to lack the filter that gauges how much talking is too much. The talkers typically sit off to the side or in the back of the room and share running commentary. One proven technique borrowed from third-grade teachers is to move so that you can stand closer to the offenders. Without looking at them, simply walk toward them when they are chatting. Your physical presence will often make them more aware of their behavior because now everyone is looking in their direction. If they persist, make eye contact and say, "As I was saying . . ." Or, "Joe, did you have something to add?"

If it is not possible to move closer to them, try this: Stop talking and allow them to be embarrassed when their noise fills the silence. Again, you can consider directly calling out their behavior by posing a question, "Do you have something to share with the group?" If these people are high-energy individuals, you might encourage them to keep quiet by keeping them busy with a task. Ask them to take notes or list questions, if possible.

At some functions such as evening fundraisers or award ceremonies that kick off with a cocktail reception, it can be impossible to get the crowd to quiet down. In this situation, give up on the people who came to network. Focus your attention on the few at the front of the room who are listening. Avoid raising the volume of your voice in an attempt to speak over the din. Keep your voice at a normal level. Shouting won't help. If people want to listen, they will move closer to you.

2. Hecklers

Heckling by an audience member raises the stakes. It is an abusive or degrading interruption sometimes lobbed by an unseen assailant. How to react in the moment can be an agonizing decision. Should you ignore it or call it out?

When dealing with an unknown assailant, abusive colleague, or aggressive questioner, the first rule of thumb is to avoid showing an emotional reaction. Such a reaction may be the outcome the trouble-maker was hoping to achieve by heckling you. Lashing back in anger may cause you to say something in the moment that you'll later regret. Plus, it can throw you off your agenda. That's not to say the abuser should get a free pass. Rather, how you call out bad behavior will impact whether or not you achieve your goals.

Be cognizant that the way you react to a provocation matters because all eyes are fixed on you. It is, in many respects, a test. The other people are watching to see if you can keep your professional wits about you. Maintaining composure ensures that you are not the one who comes off looking petty, hotheaded, or insensitive. It might be tempting to let loose in a moment of infuriation, but losing your cool won't solve anything and likely will make the situation more unpleasant for everyone.

Bear in mind that the audience is there to hear you and not listen to some idiot in the audience. Allow yourself a second or two to manage your emotional state. Most people will feel angry and will want to lash back at the heckler. Recognize that your stress level is raised and you need to get it under control so it doesn't overwhelm you. The risk is that if you allow yourself to react defensively, it will be more difficult to recover and could ruin the remainder of the presentation. Pause, take a deep breath or two. Put a smile on your face to signal to the audience that you are OK. When you're ready, carry on.

Most comedians hate heckling and choose to ignore it because of the risks associated with dealing with it directly. Amy Schumer has the stage experience to shut down the worst abusers. When a guy at a show dared to yell, "Show us your tits," he was out the door before he knew what happened. She retorted, "If you yell again, you'll be yelling 'show your tits' to people in the parking lot."[7] The quick response that seems off the cuff was in reality a tried-and-true technique she had worked out during countless live performances.

Room size matters. If you are in a large room with more than two hundred people, the best response is usually no response. If the heckler doesn't have a microphone, it's likely most people in the room didn't hear what he said. If you are accompanied by a colleague, this person could photograph the heckler, and the picture could be posted online—after you've had a chance to think about what you want to say. Rather than coming off as mean-spirited, you may want to use the incident to make a bigger point, like Congresswoman Jayapal did.

If you suspect that there may be toxic people in the room, you can employ tactics that have been developed to combat online and street harassment. There are a number of steps recommended by Hollaback!, an organization whose goal is to combat harassment. First, plan to have a colleague who can directly intervene, if you anticipate trouble. That person can interject by saying, "That's inappropriate and disrespectful. It's not OK to say that." The colleague can also record what is happening so you have an accurate account of the exchange. On the Hollaback! website, the organization is collecting stories to document incidences of hate. Posting your story also helps other people understand that they are not alone in what they have experienced.

Deflecting or neutralizing the heckling is not about caving in. It is about staying calm so you can remain in control, keep the audience on your side, and finish the talk. Don't underestimate the power of the crowd. Social pressure can have an enormous impact on a heckler. The audience may also be offended and will frequently rise to the speaker's defense. Group dynamics take over, and the other audience members will tell the heckler to knock it off. Once the offender realizes he is outnumbered, he will usually pipe down.

College-campus auditoriums and other large venues require extra precautions. If you expect trouble, then it is necessary to inquire about security arrangements. Then hecklers can be managed by trained security personnel.

3. Rallies and Town Halls

Sometimes heckling involves a group of people who have planned to disrupt the event. For example, people will secretly bring banners into an auditorium to unfurl with a message for the media cameras. Here again, when you're at the lectern, the best response is to ignore what is happening in one area because most people will remain unaware. If you draw attention to it from the front of the stage, then everyone will be distracted.

For large events, get there early to meet and greet people as they are arriving. Engage them in conversation to introduce yourself and hear what's on their minds. Keep the length of your talk on the shorter side. If you plan a question-and-answer session, have an organized way to handle questions. One approach is to utilize a moderator to facilitate the program and call on questioners. It can be helpful to solicit questions at the beginning of the program so people have a chance to vent if they need to. When dealing with a contentious issue, giving the audience members a chance to blow off steam at the beginning can calm the room down. People often need to feel that they've been heard. Giving them a chance to speak helps them understand that you care about their concerns.

The most successful town hall events are not one-sided affairs with the speaker standing on a raised stage talking down to the citizenry. A community event should be a dialogue between the speaker and the audience, and it should look and feel like a dialogue. The event will be more successful if everyone has a fair chance to have their say and opposing points of view are listened to. It's important to communicate that the event is a two-way street when making decisions about logistics and the program agenda.

Be as accessible as you can. The optics on this matter. Select a venue where you can be standing level with the audience to avoid appearing as if you are lecturing the crowd. Former Rep. Jason Chaffetz of Utah practically invited the booing and angry chants at his town halls about repealing the Affordable Care Act. He stood on a large stage while literally looking down at his constituents who felt he was dismissing their concerns about maintaining access to healthcare.

If the topic under discussion is controversial, be prepared to stay until the very last question has been asked and answered. Don't attempt to duck out. If security is a concern, it must be planned in advance and carried out in conjunction with local law enforcement and event organizers.

HANDLING Q&A SESSIONS

The question-and-answer session following a presentation is an opportunity for direct interaction with the audience. It provides a chance to hear what's on the minds of others and to reinforce key message points. If you unintentionally left something out of the talk, you can work it into an answer or raise it for discussion at this point. The Q&A offers another chance to clarify any misconceptions or misunderstandings.

The protocol for the Q&A should be established by the event moderator if there is one or by you at the beginning of the program. Advise the audience when you prefer to take questions. You may elect to respond to queries during your talk or ask them to hold off until you have finished your prepared remarks.

Inform the audience how you will field the questions. Tell them if there are microphones available and where are they located. If questions are to be written down, it's helpful to supply small note cards and pencils. Let them know if you are taking questions electronically from online viewers. You may want to break the ice and start off the questioning yourself by saying, "A question often asked is . . ." Or have a colleague prepared to lead off with a planned question.

Important Technique: Get Their Names First

Always request that each questioner provide her or his name and affiliation before asking a question, especially if the topic is politically sensitive. With some information about the person who's doing the asking, you may be able to add more meaning or relevance to your answer. Also, when individuals have to state their name aloud, it slows down the questioner, and they may think more carefully about how their question is phrased. This can ward off overly aggressive questions.

When speaking on a noncontroversial topic, set a time limit for the Q&A period. Ten to fifteen minutes is plenty. After about eight questions or so, the quality of questions and answers can suffer as people raise redundant or off-topic subjects. If there aren't a lot of questions, it's best to end the session early versus dragging on or begging for questions.

Avoid judging individual questions with commentary, unless the question is exceptional. Remember that when you say, "That is an excellent question," it implies the others weren't so great.

Bring the Q&A session to a close by giving the audience a heads-up that it is about to end: "I have time for one or two more questions." End with the next question you answer well. It can be a downer after a strong presentation to close on a weak question. Wrap the entire session up with a brief summary of the talk's main points. The summary shouldn't run longer than 90 seconds or so. It is an opportunity to remind the audience of a main point before everyone heads off.

Q&A Protocol

1. State the ground rules prior to taking any questions.
2. Ask questioners to identify themselves before asking questions.
3. Be sure to understand the question before giving a response.
4. Address each individual with courtesy and respect.
5. Keep your answers short and to the point.

The Angry Questioner

Angry questioners are often releasing pent up frustration over a perceived slight or wrongdoing. Failure to listen to an emotional outburst can make you appear insensitive or downright cold. In the heat of the moment, be careful not to judge too quickly, as it may not be possible to understand the motivation or intention behind the question. The questioner may be a political plant from an opposing camp who is trying to discredit you, or he or she may be making an awkward or inappropriate plea for help.

Despite your best efforts, it is still possible to have an angry audience member. Here are the steps to ensure the encounter doesn't escalate. Patience is key to ensuring the person has a chance to be heard.

Managing the Angry Questioner

1. Allow the questioner to speak unfettered—this may take a minute or so. It will likely feel longer than it is. Face him while he is talking, maintain steady eye contact with him to demonstrate to him and the audience that you are listening and respectful.
2. Once the questioner has finished, tell him you heard what he said. At this point, the angry questioner may interrupt you. Again, let him speak his mind.
3. When he's finished, respond by looking directly at him. After about 10 seconds of eye contact, you can physically turn away or, when possible, walk away from the questioner. Look at other people in the room to bring group dynamics into play.
4. If the questioner pops up again, let him proceed one more time. When you respond, follow the same technique of initial eye contact and then break away, looking at other people.
5. When you finish your response, call on someone else.
6. If the angry questioner interrupts again, now the behavior is

very likely annoying other audience members. Group dynamics often take over, and other people might jump in to hush him.

7. If the group doesn't provide assistance, calmly explain to the questioner that it is time to hear from others and that you will be available after the talk or will follow up at a later time.

8. Once you've provided a fair opportunity for the individual to be heard, everyone will be ready to move on.

Being an advocate often isn't for the faint of heart. When you put yourself and your ideas out there, people will push back, sometimes with ugly comments or worse. But that doesn't mean you have to ignore a putdown or swallow your pride. Anticipating implicit and explicit bias lessens the likelihood that you will be stunned speechless or blurt out a knee-jerk response. Dealing with boors, bullies, and their BS is an essential survival skill. By standing up for yourself, you send the signal that you have the strength to stand up for the cause.

WELL-SPOKEN WOMEN RESIST, INSIST, PERSIST

Toxicity—call it for what it is.
Constructive pushback is fair play.
Strong women deescalate with dignity.

CREDENTIAL THYSELF

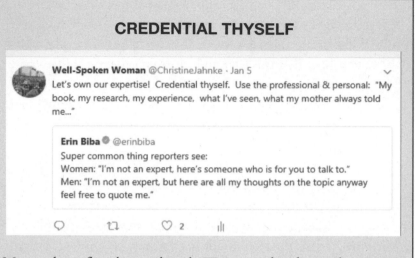

Well-Spoken Woman @ChristineJahnke · Jan 5
Let's own our expertise! Credential thyself. Use the professional & personal: "My book, my research, my experience, what I've seen, what my mother always told me..."

Erin Biba @erinbiba
Super common thing reporters see:
Women: "I'm not an expert, here's someone who is for you to talk to."
Men: "I'm not an expert, but here are all my thoughts on the topic anyway feel free to quote me."

Men tend to inflate their credentials. Women tend to dismiss their own. In fact, science writer Erin Biba tweeted about the difficulty she sometimes has in getting women to comment for her stories. Let's put an end to this and own our expertise. Credential yourself with the professional and the personal.

- Asked to be addressed by a title such as doctor or professor.
- Mention your years of experience.
- Refer to research you've authored: "My study found . . ."
- Tell a story that conveys firsthand knowledge: "When I toured the site . . .," "When I spoke to the president . . .," "When I ran the numbers . . ."
- Personalize your story, like Elizabeth Warren did when she campaigned for the US Senate: "I'm the daughter of a maintenance man who grew up to be a professor at a fancy law school . . ."
- Reference your publications: "My book is still being used at MIT . . ."
- Share what you have learned from life: "My mother always taught me . . ."
- On her Twitter profile, Ava DuVernay had written, "I'm a girl from Compton who got to make a 100-million-dollar Disney movie."
- Ask your introducer to say you are "qualified," and do this for other women. This is especially helpful for women candidates who must demonstrate to voters that they are qualified.

PART III

THE NEW FACE OF LEADERSHIP . . .

CHAPTER 5

POWER WORDS— INTENTIONAL STORYTELLING

"Stories matter. Many stories matter. Stories have been used to dispose and malign, but stories can also be used to empower and to humanize. Stories can break the dignity of people, but stories can also repair that broken dignity."
—Chimamanda Ngozi Adichie,
The Danger of a Single Story

Sometimes truths are so big and so difficult, the audience needs time to process them. This can be unsettling for the speaker. But, know this, that silence you hear is discomfort, and discomfort leads to growth and change. Intentional storytelling is about how to tell your story so you can drive the change you are seeking.

"Be fierce." With those words, Gretchen Carlson concluded her talk to a crowd of professional women and then invited questions. The silence that followed was . . . heavy. Everyone in the room seemed to be processing what they had just heard. Gretchen had shared details of the sexual harassment she had endured during her career in television. She had described the shock of an executive jabbing his tongue down her throat and another who shoved her head into his crotch. It was the threats of Roger Ailes who she said fired her when she wouldn't have sex with him that compelled her to sue the former CEO at Fox News.

Finally, from way back in the room, a woman rose to speak and was asked to move to the microphone so everyone could hear. The woman reluctantly made her way around the tables in the large Washington, DC, hotel conference room. When she arrived up front, she paused and then blurted out, "I'm a survivor, too." Quickly adding, "I had no intention of saying that."

As a speech coach sitting in that audience, I was struck by the contrast in what had just transpired, the difference between Gretchen's speech and the comment from the audience member who felt compelled to come forward. The former journalist's speech was candid but controlled and had a forward-looking message. The lawsuit against Ailes was not the end of Gretchen's story; her fight was just beginning. After the talk, she was headed to Capitol Hill to rally support for legislation that would enable more women to take legal action.

The questioner's unexpected admission evoked audience compassion; heads were nodding as if to let her know #MeToo. It was a show of unspoken empathy for how difficult it is for survivors to come forward. No harm was done, it was just a statement made at a luncheon. And it took courage for her to speak up. Yet she seemed to regret having said anything. The impression left was that if she could do it over, she would have done so differently. While she voiced what others were clearly feeling, she seemed to not feel in control of what she had said.

Let's change that. Let's make sure you are in the driver's seat so you can tell the story you want to tell.

For far too long, women's stories were not considered credible. For inexplicable reasons, they didn't count. Fortunately, the #MeToo movement is having a wide impact. There is more willingness to listen and accept the hard truths about women's lives. Our stories are credible, and they are being taken more seriously.

A cultural shift is underway. Let's keep it going. Women are telling stories that haven't been listened to. And they are speaking up in forums where male voices have dominated—in workplaces, in houses of worship, at town halls, and on the campaign trail.

In 2018, women candidates running at all levels began to change how leadership is defined. In the past, when a woman wanted to show that she had the right stuff for elected office, she sat at a mahogany desk signing documents in a business suit. Now, candidates are more freely sharing their personal stories. They are talking about their entire life experience as moms, daughters, sisters, and partners. In a first, Wisconsin gubernatorial candidate Kelda Roys breastfed her infant daughter on camera. Roys discussed her legacy as a state legislator who had helped ban a chemical found in plastic sippy cups and linked to health problems.[1]

The appeal was a way to break though political discourse crowded with white, male voices. It is also a way to redefine what it means to be qualified to serve. In Chicago, to show her readiness to fight on behalf of others, first-time congressional candidate Sol Flores shared her story of overcoming sexual abuse. In a remarkable ad, Flores pledged to fight as hard in Congress as she did to protect her eleven-year-old self from the man who preyed on her. It's a powerful story because Flores carefully thought out how she described the ordeal and spoke from a place of strength.

What is the story you want to tell? What is the story you need to tell?

Whatever your story, the telling begins with four questions.

4 Ws OF POWER STORYTELLING

1. What's it about?
2. Why am I talking about it?
3. Why should the audience care?
4. What do I want them to do?

1. What's It About?

This question is seemingly simple. At first glance, it may appear too basic to spend much time on. However, if you can't answer this question, no one else will know what your talk is about.

Here's a quick exercise . . .

When will you next speak? Pick a scenario—it doesn't have to be a speech, it could be a staff meeting or a conference call. In one sentence, only one sentence, write down a statement of topic for the subject matter you plan to address.

"I'm going to talk about . . ."

Be sure to respond with a full sentence.

A phrase or a label doesn't provide enough information. For example, if you said, "pay equity," that's too broad. It doesn't convey what aspect of the subject you plan to address—whether it's the legal, political, and/or social ramifications of the subject. Conversely, writing an academic-style abstract that covers the purpose, scope, and results is too much. With a few paragraphs, it's easier to describe what you are going to say. It's more challenging to boil the topic down to its essence. But doing so will bring you greater clarity.

The topic sentence needs to be a complete thought yet narrowly cast. Author Pamela Meyer writes about the pervasiveness of lying in our culture. Lying is a broad topic, so in a TED Talk Meyer described the subject more precisely: "How to Spot a Liar."[2] The specificity avoids vagueness, and the clever wording piques interest, engaging the minds of the listeners. They immediately begin to wonder, "Hmmm, what does a liar look like?" so they're already involved with her subject matter at the outset.

There is always competition for the audience's attention. Whether they're sitting right in front of you or viewing via livestream, it's your job to get their attention. The possible distractions are endless, starting with the smartphone at their fingertips. If you are unable to clearly articulate what it is about, then you are asking the audience to unravel a mystery they may not be interested in or have the time to bother with.

One way to more precisely describe a talk about pay equity is this topic sentence from the American Association of University Women (AAUW), an organization committed to empowering women. A description of one woman's life experience is used to show the severity of the problem for black women:

The gender pay gap shortchanges women like Cheryl Hughes who has lost over one million dollars in her career as an engineer due to the fact that she is African American.[3]

Creative expression of a concept will get the audience's attention.

Make sure your "about" is bite-sized enough for the audience to chew, and tailor it in a way that hooks them.

2. Why Am I Talking about It?

After your "about" has been clearly defined, give them a reason to listen to you.

Pamela Meyer wants her audience to spot liars not because it's a fun party trick or because she works for the FBI. Her aim is to stop the pandemic of deception sweeping the nation by educating people how to recognize lying. Getting at the truth is what motivates her.

So, why do you care about your subject?

The "why you" is the expression of the impetus that is driving you. It is what compels you to stand before the public and take a stand or make a speech.

The impetus may include personal disclosure, but that is not necessary. If you do decide to use a personal experience such as a #MeToo encounter, then it's vital to thoroughly consider how much you want to disclose. Deciding exactly what you will say helps you handle the audience reaction so you are not stunned or dismayed if they do not respond positively. It also helps you avoid saying more than you originally intended.

Dr. Diane Horvath-Cosper is an ob-gyn whose fierce advocacy for patients seeking abortion care has made her a target of protestors who have physically threatened her family. Concern about a shortage of abortion providers is what motivates her to provide the full range of reproductive care. In an interview, she said, "I came to the realization that there would always be people to provide C-sections at three o'clock in the morning. And there were always going to be people to do prenatal care visits."[4] The doctor has thought through how she talks about her decision and desire to provide abortion care.

A well-thought-out impetus story makes it clear that you have skin in the game—a powerful credential. The audience knows you are not up there just mouthing words, paying lip-service to a cause. You're not reading a script prepared by someone in the communications department. You really do care. And that's why you are asking them to get involved. Boston City Councilor Ayanna Pressley, who is a wife and a daughter to formerly incarcerated black men, says her reasons for serving are different from the older, white incumbent congressman she is challenging. Pressley describes her candidacy as an intentional force to dismantle barriers and provide opportunity for everyone.[5]

Once the audience understands your motivation and level of commitment, they are more likely to listen closely to what you have to say and reflect on how the topic is relevant to them.

An executive at an energy company was charged with the task of visiting the company's regional offices to inform the fieldworkers about a new safety policy. It was a tough assignment because the company needed to make changes, and she didn't want to sound like a corporate suit who was pointing fingers. She decided to open her talk by saying that safety procedures were something she had always followed but hadn't really thought about all that much.

However, that changed when one of her co-workers who was also a personal friend was killed on the job. Dealing with the heart-wrenching loss was more painful after she attended the funeral. The wife of the dead co-worker gave her a look that killed, and she suddenly felt like she was a bad guy. She had never been a bad guy and didn't view anyone as such. Her goal was to work for a company she could be proud of.

Your impetus for speaking can serve as the foundation of what you are trying to accomplish. Effectively articulating why you care inspires others to take action. Sharing a core value or belief can be more persuasive than a statistic or factoid. It's not that proof points aren't valuable. They can add support to why you care, but numbers have limitations. Opponents will question studies and present conflicting data. However, it is much more difficult for them to convincingly sway others by attacking your core beliefs.

In 2015, a young immigrant activist made headlines when she asked Pope Francis to step in and help prevent her undocumented parents from being deported. Few will forget six-year-old Sophie Cruz's message at the Women's March in Washington, DC:

> We are here today making a chain of love to protect our families. Let us fight with love, faith, and courage so that our families will not be destroyed. I also want to tell the children not to be afraid because we are not alone. There are still many people that have their hearts filled with love. Let's keep together and fight for the rights.[6]

It's possible to disagree with Sophie on the issue of deporting undocumented people, but it's difficult to argue against the value she places on protecting families. Sophie's "why" captures a moment of truth—she is asking the audience to think about how we treat ourselves, others, and the community around us.

3. Why Should the Audience Care?

Sharing why you care will go a long way in helping the audience to understand why they should care too. But then you must close the deal by communicating how they will benefit from helping you achieve your goal.

"It's not just that you grow local food it is what you grow."[7] Honor the Earth founder Winona LaDuke wants all of us to care about the wild rice fields on the White Earth reservation in northern Minnesota. LaDuke is fighting the genetic engineering of crops because they rob the Anishinaabe people of income from harvesting traditional foods. What the activist tells audiences is that foods like rice, corn, and squash grown from ancient seeds are more nutritious than genetically modified plants. Her argument makes it clear that we should care because doing so is good for our health and because it will help protect the livelihoods of indigenous people.

Appealing to the audience's self-interest is dependent on knowing two things about them. First, who are they demographically? How much do you have in common with them, or how little? Are they young, old, black, white, male, female, trans, economically secure, or economically stressed? Do you come from the same place or hail from different regions, ethnicities, and religions?

Second, what is the audience's relationship with your subject matter? If you want the audience to listen and act on what you say, find out what they need to hear. This doesn't mean you should pander to them. It does mean what you say isn't as important as what the audience will hear and understand. Take time to see your subject matter from their perspective so you can speak from a place of common ground.

Audience's Relationship to Topic

- How much or how little do they know?
- Do they think they know more than you know they do?
- Are they misinformed?
- How controversial is the subject?

Once you understand how they think about the subject and what they care about, it is possible to appeal to their self-interest. Appealing to another's self-interest is a primary way to drive the behavior you are seeking. What motivates you may not be what motivates them. But that doesn't mean that you don't share common goals.

For example, as an advocate working on prison reform, your primary focus might be on creating a criminal-justice system that doesn't discriminate against people of color. Others might support the end goal of reform but for reasons that are different from yours. Their primary motivation may be not social justice but economics.

A study published in the journal *Crime and Delinquency* illustrates the point. It was found that to obtain public support for criminal-justice reform, emphasizing the high cost to taxpayers of incarceration generated more support than citing the high level of racial disparities. Disparity is a critically important moral issue, but using it as a primary message did not increase support for reform.[8] Answering the "what's in it for them?" question is an essential part of being able to persuade an audience whose values are different from your own.

In her role as a Goodwill Ambassador to the United Nations, Emma Watson spoke to a worldwide audience about the need to mobilize men and boys to be advocates for gender equity. Emma appealed to the men in the room to support the HeForShe campaign by showing how gender equity benefits them as well as women.

> Gender equity is your issue too. Because to date I've seen my father's role as a parent being valued less by society despite my needing his presence as a child.
>
> I've seen young men suffering from mental illness unable to ask for help, for fear it would make them look less macho. In fact, in the UK, suicide is the biggest killer of men between 20 and 49 years of age, eclipsing road accidents, cancer, and coronary heart disease. I've seen men made fragile and insecure by a distorted sense of what constitutes male success. Men don't have the benefits of equality either.[9]

4. What Do I Want Them to Do?

A speech or a talk without a call to action is probably a speech or a talk not worth giving. The change you are seeking and what you want the audience members to do will impact how you make the request. Candidates and advocates can make direct, individual appeals. For example, "I need your vote," "Sign this petition," "Donate to the cause," or "Volunteer your time."

For group action, make the task easy to do, and you will get more buy-in and follow-through. At the Women's March, the phone number for the Capitol Hill switchboard was given out repeatedly so the attendees could call their member of Congress to voice opposition to

Donald Trump's executive actions. When to make the call to action is a strategic consideration. Introducing it up front ensures that it isn't inadvertently left out (which is more common than you might suspect).

Another advantage to introducing the action point early on is that it allows you to build buy-in throughout the talk. In May 2017, US Senator Elizabeth Warren delivered the commencement address at the University of Massachusetts Amherst. Unlike so many other addresses, which are filled with empty platitudes, Senator Warren didn't mince words. From the top, she made it clear what she wanted the graduates to do:

> I'm here today to make a pitch for the work that you do going forward. I'm here to ask you to get more involved in our democracy. Some of you are already headed into public service. I'm looking out at future teachers and firefighters, nurses and social workers. Some of you will work directly in government, some will work in nonprofits. And, of course, many of you will work for small businesses. Many of you will start your own businesses. Many of you will join big corporations. But my pitch is for something different. It's to get more directly involved in the democracy of policy.[10]

There are situations when it is powerful to conclude with the call to action. When it is a big one, delivering the point at the end can create a powerful conclusion that generates widespread support. Sometimes what needs to be done cannot be accomplished through the efforts of individuals. Systematic change requires collective action on a large scale.

When Olympic gymnast Aly Raisman spoke at the sentencing hearing of the doctor who was convicted of criminal sexual misconduct by abusing her and over 130 other gymnasts, she would have been fully justified in making a personal plea for justice. Larry Nassar used his position as the team doctor for USA Gymnastics to prey on athletes for whom he was charged with providing medical treatment. In her statement, Aly detailed how the problem was bigger than Nassar. He was able to get away with his crimes because he was protected and enabled by a system. The leadership at USA Gymnastics, the US

Olympic Committee, and Michigan State University (where he had his sports medicine practice) turned deaf ears to the women who spoke out years before he was finally arrested. She said:

> If we are to believe in change, we must first understand the problem and everything that contributed to it. Now is not the time for false reassurances. We need an independent investigation of exactly what happened, what went wrong, and how it can be avoided for the future. Only then can we know what changes are needed. Only then can we believe such changes are real.
>
> Your Honor, I ask you to give Larry the strongest possible sentence, which his actions deserve. For by doing so, you will send a message to him and to other abusers that they cannot get away with their horrible crimes.... And, please Your Honor, stress the need to investigate how this happened, so that we can hold accountable those who empowered and enabled Larry Nassar, so we can repair, and once again believe in this wonderful sport.[11]

Aly took advantage of the platform provided by the sentencing hearing to conclude her remarks with more than a personal call to action for the guilty party to be punished. By laying out the wholesale change needed to clean up women's gymnastics, she made a compelling case for what it will take to ensure the safety of all women competing in the sport. Her testimony made it clear that "empty statements of empty promises"[12] will no longer work for athletes and the people who really care about them.

The 4 *W*s of storytelling are designed to jump-start the writing process. To make it more manageable and less intimidating. No longer do you need to spend time staring at a blank computer screen, wondering how or where you should begin. The process of clarifying your topic, identifying your goals, addressing your audiences' interests, and making an ask provides a strategic road map for your entire talk.

Once you have established why you are up there, what you hope to accomplish, and how the audience will benefit, it's time to start crafting what you will say.

PREPARING POWERFUL REMARKS

The most effective speeches are written not to be read but to be heard. The goal is to write for the ear and not the eye. A text that reads beautifully may not sound good when read aloud. What looks good on paper may come across as dry and uninspiring. For example, compound sentences are fine to read but more difficult for the ear to follow. To capture the listener's ear effectively, be ready to throw out some of the rules you learned in English 101.

Most writing for the eye follows a linear pattern. As "linear" suggests, this approach follows a straight line that starts at the beginning, moves into the middle, and finishes somewhere else. A linear writing style is common in mystery novels that build tension and interest until they culminate in a close when the villain is revealed. In public speaking, this style can be used to entertain an audience in a forum such as an after-dinner talk. An unexpected ending can generate a laugh or create an emotional tug.

When you advocate for a cause or lay out a position on an issue, it is more impactful if the content flow is organized in a nonlinear pattern. Rather than traveling in a straight line from point A to point B to point C, organize your material so that the audience travels full circle. A 360-degree approach ensures that you get to the point quickly and repeat and reinforce it throughout the talk. Repetition is necessary for information retention and to motivate the audience to act.

CONTENT FLOW

Introduction: Tell them what you are going to tell them.
Body: Tell it.
Conclusion: Retell what you just told them.

This basic structure provides the audience with a path and a destination. The listeners want to know where you plan to take them, what they will see along the way, and how long it's going to take to get there. Setting expectations near the opening helps the audience follow along. Chapter 6 provides more details on how to organize content. This next section highlights the top ten mistakes people make when preparing remarks. Avoiding these common errors will help ensure your audience is listening and hears what you need them to hear.

10 SPEECH-WRITING MISTAKES TO AVOID

1. Inability to Edit

Too many presenters try to cram in too much content, and the result is a mess bogged down with details. Saying everything you know about a subject won't make you sound like an expert. It will sound as if you don't know how to prioritize. Avoid giving them a Chinese menu of points to remember, because they will pick only those that most appeal to them. It's more effective to serve up a prix fixe menu with limited choices. If you say less and repeat it with greater frequency, you enhance the audience's ability to retain what you want them to retain.

A general rule of thumb is that people need to hear something at least seven times to be able to recall it. And if you are trying to compel people to take action, more repetition is required.

Further, researchers have found that the amount of information people can retain in their conscious mind or working memory has been shrinking. For example, people can't remember as many numbers as they used to. A study published in the *Proceedings of the National Academy of Sciences* finds that the number is down to three or four digits from seven.[13] Working memory is defined as a more active version of short-term memory. It is the stuff we can pay attention to and manipulate at any one time. It's a much better use of everyone's time to narrow your agenda and develop a few ideas more fully than to contribute to the clutter already in our heads.

2. Passive Voice

A passive writing style can feel slow, even tedious to listeners. Writing with an active voice means the sentences move along. There is energy which creates a sense of purpose. The active voice encourages the listener to follow. The ideas are tighter. The verbs are stronger. The sentences are shorter. Grammarians say it all boils down to the use of active versus passive verbs. In an active-verb sentence, the subject of the sentence does something.

> Active—Stacey won the gubernatorial election. *Yeah!*
> Passive—The gubernatorial election was won by Stacey. *Ho-hum.*

With a passive verb, something is being done to the subject. It sounds like the subject is letting the action happen versus driving it. The passive voice can be more difficult to follow because the sentence structure is less clear; the ideas are vague; and more words are used than are necessary. .

3. Weak Open

The audience doesn't want to hear, "I don't know where to begin, so I'll just start." Or "I didn't prepare anything in particular." With those opening lines, you have already lost them. If you don't preplan and practice the introduction, you risk losing their attention and goodwill right from the get-go.

The opening should be the prologue that sets the stage for the rest of the play. It can be as brief as 30 seconds or as long two or three minutes, depending on the overall length of the speech. Astrophysicist Jedidah Isler hooked her TED Talk audience with this opener about her research into black holes: "My first love was the night sky. Love is complicated."[14]

4. Weak Close

"Any questions?" Sounds like a plea from a speaker who has run out of material. It is not a conclusion that drives home the point you want the listeners to remember or that motivates them to care enough to act. A strong conclusion conveys a sense of wholeness and finality by summarizing the main points. Always preplan the close since it is your last, best chance to ensure you control the buzz in the room once you've finished speaking.

A satisfying way to close is to circle back to the way you introduced the subject matter at the beginning. This is how Jedidah Isler closed her TED Talk:

> This all started as a love story. And it still is. This love transformed me from a curious, stargazing young girl into a professional astrophysicist hot on the heels of celestial discovery. Who knew that chasing after the universe would ground me so deeply to my mission here on Earth. Then again, when do we ever know where love's first flutter will truly take us?[15]

5. Misread Audience

If you neglect to do your homework about the audience, it is more likely you will miss the opportunity to build a connection with them. It's important that you speak to their interests and don't make assumptions about what they know, what they don't know, and what they care about. For example, it would be a mistake for a political candidate to spend a lot of time speaking about her position on reproductive choice before a labor group. The union members want to hear first about her view on raising the minimum wage and collective bargaining.

Be mindful that the use of unfamiliar acronyms and jargon may leave listeners confused. It's best to state the full name of an organization and the acronym initially. If you are speaking to people outside your field, they may not be conversant in the terminology you use with colleagues. This is particularly important for people who work in scientific and technical fields. When speaking to external audiences, be sure to simplify your language and give brief explanations of technical terms. On the other hand, explaining concepts that the audience members are well-versed in will bore them with unnecessary detail and make you appear out of the loop.

6. Stream of Consciousness

Don't be a female broviator. A never-ending stream of consciousness leaves the audience wondering where you are going and how long it is going to take you to get there. Sharing thoughts as they pop into your head may seem like a good idea, but it can try the audience's patience. If you are rambling and scattered, they are not going to listen.

A variation of the stream-of-consciousness issue is reciting lists. Some people organize remarks like a grocery checklist. As they speak, they move from one point to the next as if they are checking off the bread, milk, eggs, and so on. For example, reading a résumé in chronological order is a lazy way to introduce someone. List making can be helpful for organizing your personal life, but it is not a compelling way to present information.

7. Story vs. Data

This is a false choice. The use of both narrative and data can bolster effectiveness but in different ways. A good stat demonstrates that the presenter has done her homework. Further, a factoid from a respected outside source can enhance the speaker's credibility by association. However, most people find it more difficult to remember numbers. They are more likely to recall a compelling story about an individual.

8. Lack of Road Signs

Written communication relies on the rules of grammar and punctuation to help the reader follow the action. With a written text such as a book, the reader has the chapters to indicate the main points. Paragraphs and sentence structure provide clues to the flow. Punctuation helps the reader understand the author's intent. Periods and commas clarify, while exclamation points and question marks add color. Even white space has meaning. The blank space at the end of a chapter gives the readers a chance to pause and reflect before they move onto to the next big idea.

Similar to a book, a talk should be organized so the listener can follow along without visual cues. Once the words are spoken, they are gone. It is up to the speaker to provide structure that is explicit and easy to follow. Verbal and vocal signposts are needed to signal the main points, transitions, and stories, and what's important. An example of a simple verbal signpost is to say, "I'm going to start by providing an overview of our policy goals. Then, I will highlight three pieces of legislation we are working on right now." Also, signal to the audience when you are about to wrap. Use a line that will get their attention: "Before I close, let me leave you with this . . ."

Pauses are an example of an effective vocal signpost. Think of silence as white space on a page. It can signal the end of a main point and a transition to the next point. Changing the rate of speech signals that something different is happening too. Slowing down the speaking pace adds a sense of gravitas to the words; picking up the pace can signal a mood change, such as excitement. There are additional suggestions on how to maximize your vocal effectiveness in chapter 7.

9. Imitation Is Not Flattery

Melania Trump gave a speech at the 2016 Republican National Convention that was well-received and sounded familiar. In fact, it was a little too familiar. It was discovered that she had lifted material from an earlier convention speech given by First Lady Michelle Obama.[16] Trump's speechwriters took the blame for the plagiarism, but the public remembers not who wrote it but who delivered it. It is the speaker's reputation that is tarnished.

Fortunately, there is an online plagiarism detector called Grammarly that can help you avoid Melania's embarrassment. But there is no substitute for being cognizant of history and of what others in your field have said, especially in high-profile venues. When using direct quotes, it is always necessary to cite the source or provide attribution.

10. No Visual Imagery

How dramatic is your writing? Are you using examples and anecdotes to create mental pictures for the audience? Abstract ideas are just that—abstract. Make points more concrete with word pictures, and the audience is more likely to get your point more quickly. For example, the founder of a GIF app has said, "A picture paints a thousand words. By that logic—the average GIF contains 60 frames—then they are capable of conveying 60,000 words, which is the same length as a book."[17]

At the annual Women in Entertainment Power 100 breakfast, the audience could see and even feel the imagery Shonda Rhimes used in her acceptance speech. The television producer and screenwriter was honored by *The Hollywood Reporter* for breaking through the industry's glass ceiling as a woman and an African American. In her remarks, Shonda set the record straight—she had not broken through a glass ceiling.

Rather, she said it was fifty years of other women running at full speed and crashing into a thick layer of glass and falling back that made it possible for her to succeed. Woman after woman running and crashing and falling back. That's what had cracked the glass ceiling.

The remarks were a sensory experience:

So when it was my turn to run, it didn't even look like a ceiling anymore. I mean, the wind was already whistling through—I could always feel it on my face. And there were all these holes giving me a perfect view of the other side. I didn't even notice the gravity; I think it had already worn itself away. So I didn't have to fight as hard. I had time to study the cracks. I had time to decide where the air felt the rarest, where the wind was the coolest, where the view was the most soaring. I picked my spot in the glass, and I called it my target.

And I ran. And when I finally hit that ceiling, it just exploded into dust. Like that. My sisters who went before me had already handled it. No cuts. No bruises. No bleeding.

Making it through the glass ceiling to the other side was simply a matter of running on a path created by every other woman's footprints.[18]

POWER WORD TOOL—THE GRABBER

Now you may ask yourself, How do I write like Shonda Rhimes? How do I talk about a subject like the glass ceiling so it sounds fresh and authentic to me? How do I take my topic and make it come alive? What are the tools I can use to motivate others to listen?

Grabbers help you grab the audience's attention. There are a variety of rhetoric techniques that will ensure your words are vibrant and your ideas stimulating.

Groups of Threes

Groups of three are memorable, and they create a rhythm when spoken aloud. For example: Government of the people, by the people, for the people. She came, she saw, she conquered. Life, liberty, and the pursuit of happiness.

Vivid Examples

The Annie E. Casey Foundation advocates for the closure of juvenile detention centers. The harsh conditions in some facilities were described in graphic detail by the foundation's leader in a TED Talk:

Prisons for kids . . . One hundred young people in a facility built for forty, young people in handcuffs and shackles, rows of isolation cells and in each of those cells a young face staring out because that person had been held in solitary confinement sometimes for weeks. The walls virtually dripped with a pervasive sense of dread, anxiety, tension, and anger.[19]

Alliteration

The repetition of consonant sounds and/or words draws attention to particular lines. And the technique can signal that something is important: That's the truth, the whole truth, and nothing but the truth. Resist, insist, persist, enlist.

Quotes

Quotes are a tried-and-true way to strengthen content, and they can create an affinity with the audience. Quote a respected figure whom you know the audience admires.

A twist that packs a powerful punch is to quote an unlikely source when they agree with you. For example, six months into his papacy, Pope Francis released remarks saying the Catholic Church had grown "obsessed" with gays, abortion, and birth control. And in a speech George W. Bush acknowledged that human activity causes climate change. It's unexpected that these figures made these comments, and that makes it memorable.

Of course, the unlikely quote will garner attention, so it is imperative that it be factually accurate.

Analogies and Metaphors

An analogy is a comparison between two things that can help you explain or clarify a point. An analogy can be used to explain a complex subject with something that is simpler or more familiar.

> "My mamma always said, 'Life is like a box of chocolates. You never know what you're gonna get.'" —Forrest Gump, *Forrest Gump*.

It's time to stretch beyond your comfort zone, just like a caterpillar
   leaving a cocoon.
That's as useful as rearranging chairs on the deck of the *Titanic*.

A metaphor is a figure of speech that describes an object or an
action in a way that is not literally true. To make a point, it equates two
things that are not actually the same.

The audience was dead.
Her spine is made of titanium.
Women face a number of barriers to advancement in the work-
   place: glass ceiling, glass cliff, sticky floor.
A pink wave of women candidates is sweeping into office.

One-Liners

In this case, one-liners refers to well-crafted, well-thought-out ideas
rather than the punchlines of jokes.

Roxane Gay: "It is often women who pay the price for what men
   want."
Jill Filipovic: "If Miss America wants to get out of the sexism game,
   it should probably end Miss America."
Margaret Mead: "Always remember you are absolutely unique, just
   like everyone else."

Leave the joke telling to the professionals. In public speaking, the most
effective humor is drawn from everyday life.

Numbers

Numbers are more powerful when they are put into context. "CNBC
reports that the average bonus compensation on Wall Street is expected

to be $143,462 in 2017." That's a big number, but people can respond by saying, "So what?" You can get more of a reaction if you put the number into a context most people can relate to: "According to the *Wall Street Journal*, the total amount of Wall Street bonus money in 2015 was more than double the salaries of every single minimum-wage worker in the United States." That number is more likely to elicit an emotional response.

Three types of numbers that are easier for the ear to catch:

1. Proportional: Round up or off. "Nearly 60 percent" versus "59.8 percent." "Four out of five dentists recommend..." "Seventy-five percent of people agree..."
2. Startling: "According to the Center for American Progress, in 2013, immigrants contributed $1.6 trillion to the US GDP. That's trillion with a *T*."
3. Relative: Relate the number to something that is visual. "Spokespeople for Friends of the Earth say a single cruise ship dumps 210,000 gallons of human sewage into the ocean every week. That's enough to fill ten backyard-size swimming pools."

Literary and Popular Culture References

The worlds of literature and popular culture include a vast amount of expressions, sayings, lines, lyrics, characters, and phrases that compose an interconnected web of references. Speakers can use the references to illustrate new points by paying homage to readily identified characters or lines.

Make a comparison by using a familiar line from a work of literature: "It was the best of times, it was the worst of times..."

Evoke a beloved author: Movie character Bridget Jones finds romance with a modern-day Mark Darcy plucked from Jane Austen's *Pride and Prejudice*.

Adopt a powerful moniker: On *Scandal*, Olivia Pope's team of
investigators referred to themselves as "Gladiators."

Pull an iconic line from a film franchise: In 2015, Hillary Clinton
concluded a democratic primary debate with an inspirational
message: May the force be with you.

Make a point about entering new terrain: "I don't think we are in
Kansas anymore," like Dorothy did when she started down the
Yellow Brick Road.

Props

An unexpected visual aid will capture audience and media attention,
and often these props can gain a symbolic meaning. For example,
former congresswoman and presidential candidate Shirley Chisholm
once said, "If they don't give you a seat at the table, bring a folding
chair."[20] President pro tempore of the Cincinnati City Council Tamaya
Dennard literally brought a folding chair to celebrate her swearing in.
By doing so, she paid homage to Chisholm.

The 2017 Women's March was a sea of knitted pink hats. The
imagery is an iconic symbol of female power.

When Texas State Senator Wendy Davis delivered an eleven-hour
filibuster on the legislative floor, she wore a pair of pink tennis shoes.
The shoes symbolized the pro-choice community's attempt to outrun
the patriarchy on proposed legislation intended to restrict access to
reproductive healthcare.

Questions

A question is a quick, easy way to gauge the audience's interest about a
subject and to involve them. It is a handy technique to use as an opener,
especially if you are nervous. A question takes the focus off of you and
puts it on the audience. If the audience doesn't respond vocally, just
pretend you meant to pose it rhetorically and answer it yourself. "Why
is it important to overturn Citizens United?" If the audience responds

with silence, provide them with the answer you were seeking. "Because campaign contributions are corrupting democracy."

Questions can be used to invite the audience to agree with you: "Wouldn't you agree that it is important to give middle-class Americans a real tax cut?" And use questions to emphasize previous points: "Tens of thousands of Americans die- from opioid overdoses annually. How many deaths will it take before we finally act?"

In her speech, "The Danger of a Single Story," Nigerian author Chimamanda Ngozi Adichie deploys the art of storytelling to explain the importance of storytelling. She talks about the harm she has seen that comes from reducing human beings and situations to a single narrative—how the people of the continent of Africa can be reduced to one story about pitiable souls, ravaged by disease and civil war. She shares her own journey of awakening. As a child growing up in Nigeria, she wrote about characters who were white and blue-eyed, who played in the snow and ate apples not because she had seen those things but that is what was in books she read by British and American authors. The talk is about the necessity of seeking diverse perspectives and why each of us needs to tell our own story. "The single story creates stereotypes, and the problem with stereotypes is not that they are untrue, but that they are incomplete."[21]

The author concludes by asking the listeners to seek out alternative stories. The call to action summarizes her message and encourages people to open themselves up to stories from many people from different places. "When we reject the single story. When we realize there is never a single story about any place. We regain a kind of paradise."[22]

WELL-SPOKEN WOMEN RESIST, INSIST, PERSIST

Write with a heartbeat.
Stirring words drive action.
Omit wordy words.
Words that elicit sounds, smells, and emotions bring a story to life.

THE POWER INTRODUCTION

1. State the subject matter—tell them what it is about.
2. Share your point of view—why you care.
3. State your goals—tease the call to action.
4. Be clear about why the audience should care—tell them what's in it for them.
5. Hook them—use a grabber.

THE POWER CONCLUSION

1. End on time—leave them wanting more rather than going on too long.
2. Signal that the end is near. Use a line to catch their attention: "In conclusion . . ." or "Let me wrap up with . . ."
3. Summarize the main points—don't throw in new stuff.
4. Share a final thought, the one thing you want them to remember. Illustrate it with a grabber.

CHAPTER 6

POWER WORDS— PERSUASIVE MEDIA MESSAGES

"The stakes are too high for government to be a spectator sport."

—Barbara C. Jordan

Fake news. Alternative facts. Doctored video. Russian bots.

The media landscape is treacherous. The terrain is littered with potholes, detours, and switchbacks. Most damaging—the rubble of lies and misinformation.

For progressive advocates, this landscape requires an approach that is savvy, strategic, and fact-based. Media appearances are not the time to speculate, wing it, or speak off-the-cuff. Well-constructed power messages are necessary to champion equal pay, transgender rights, gun safety, climate-change action, and reproductive freedom.

It's clear. Your voice is needed!

LIES TOLD BY LYING LIARS

"We give the very best information possible at the time," said Sarah Huckabee Sanders.[1] In his first year in office, the *Washington Post* found that Donald Trump made a total of "2,140 false or misleading claims."[2] The amount is even more egregious when compared to the number of lies told by President Obama. Research by the *New York Times* revealed that in Trump's first ten months he told "nearly six times as many lies as Obama did during his entire presidency."[3] The falsehoods, deceptions, and exaggerations don't end there.

The lies started early, and they were not limited to the man in the Oval Office. Without breaking a sweat, presidential advisor Kellyanne Conway offered what came to be known as alternative facts. Conway made up a terrorist attack she called the "Bowling Green massacre" and repeated the lie on national television.[4] At least former White House press secretary Sean Spicer looked uncomfortable when he exaggerated the number of people who watched the presidential inauguration.

In 2015, two antiabortion extremists attempted to discredit Planned Parenthood with a hidden-camera investigation and heavily edited videos. The aim was to stir up conservative opposition to federal funding for the organization's family-planning services. The fanatics were later charged with fifteen felony counts of violating the privacy of healthcare providers.[5]

According to Facebook, 126 million Americans may have seen posts, stories, or other content generated by Russian-government-backed trolls during the 2016 presidential election.[6] The content included anti-Hillary propaganda and false information about where and how to vote, including voting via Twitter.

A power media message is one that establishes your credibility as a knowledgeable and passionate spokesperson and positions you to push back on deceptive and ugly practices. Don't be the talking head with a market-tested script or a hack spreading misinformation. Millennials especially do not appreciate spin and require an approach that is honest, value-based, and authentic.

This chapter builds on the power-word techniques introduced in chapter 5 with a constructive approach that neither relies on incivility nor damages democracy. It provides tools to help you construct proactive, positive messages and deal with obstructionists. Specific techniques will prepare you for all media forums, including live and edited interviews and online appearances.

C3PO MEDIA MESSAGE PRINCIPLES

The C3PO principles are guiding lights in a volatile, crowded media landscape. They help you deftly deal with the limitations of media coverage and the deceptive tactics of extremists. They position you as a credible spokesperson who can be relied upon for a media-savvy, factual quote.

The principles are named for the beloved *Star Wars* droid C3PO, a worrywart who valiantly battled evil forces in the galaxy. Programmed to be an expert on protocol, etiquette, and translation, C3PO is a stickler for detail but guided by a strong moral compass. The C3PO principles are designed to win debates on controversial subjects with conviction and good manners. These principles will ensure that the Resistance prevails.

C3PO Media Messaging

- Credibility
- Connection

- Contrast
- Prioritize
- Oh, Wow!

Credibility

The toxicity in the current media environment is coming at a high cost. A 2016 Gallup poll found only 32 percent of the American public has a "great deal" or a "fair amount" of trust in the mass media.[7] This is the lowest amount recorded since the question was first asked in the wake of the Watergate scandal. At that time, a majority of the public viewed the media as essential to democracy. Now there is a wide ideological gap in who trusts the media for information about the world. In 2017, the Pew Research Center found that Democrats are 47 times more likely than Republicans to support the media's role as a watchdog on society.[8]

The path to credibility starts with telling the truth. Honesty builds trust. It seems so basic that it shouldn't need to be stated, but we are working in an extreme environment. If a large number of people have their own set of facts, it is impossible to have informed, responsible discussion about pressing issues.

You should ground your media messages in arguments that are based on data and research conducted by nonpartisan, independent organizations. Reference the rule of law, constitutional decisions, and science. Cite third-party validators to show widespread support. For women candidates, studies have found that an effective way to bolster an argument is to cite an outside validator who is male. We can take the double standard and use it to our advantage.

Along with establishing your trustworthiness, it is essential to own your expertise. Some reporters and opponents will not take you seriously if you don't take yourself seriously. Articulate your knowledge and bona fides. If you are the leading expert on something, don't hesitate to say so. There's a reason you've been asked to comment, and your perspective brings added value. If this is uncomfortable for you, use the credentialing techniques explained in chapter 4.

It's time to stop minimizing your accomplishments for fear of coming across as "too ambitious," "intimidating," or "self-absorbed." It may feel awkward, like you're bragging, but be ready to take credit for what you've gotten done. Embrace the use of the word "I." Research conducted by the Barbara Lee Family Foundation on women candidates running for governor has found the best way to talk about accomplishments is with a combination of "I" and "we."[9] For example, "I was proud to lead the team that got the project done on time and under budget."

Connection

It can be baffling to keep abreast of all the new media emerging online, from podcasts to blogs. Ten years ago, there were far fewer platforms with less content and more plentiful audiences. But smartphone technology and citizen journalists have spread the content much more widely. Essentially, your potential audience is everywhere. In this dynamic media environment, it is necessary to familiarize yourself with outlets beyond the mainstream standbys like the *New York Times* and NPR. Mobilizing people means reaching out across the ever-expanding media spectrum. Whom do you need to reach and what media are they consuming? The media audience is defined by the outlet, channel, app, or program. The people watching *The View* are different from the ones tuned in to the network news.

Given the wide expanse, it's necessary to focus your outreach on the audience members that are persuadable. In political campaigns, voters are lumped into three broad categories based on ideology. On either end of the ideological continuum are the base voters who agree with the campaign's positions on the issues they care most about. For example, pro-choice voters versus pro-life voters. The people in the middle are the voters most campaigns fight to reach. They are more independent in their thinking and may be open to persuasion, such as voters who support *Roe v. Wade* but favor some restrictions on abortion.

Use the 4 *W*s of storytelling outlined in chapter 5 to understand how to connect with your target audience. Once you know whom you need to talk to and what will motivate them, you can begin to construct a media message.

Contrast

Providing contrast is necessary because you are not speaking into a vacuum—there are other voices pushing oppositional messages at the audience members you need to reach. Contrast messaging isn't about going negative on your opponent like political-candidate TV ads or direct mail. It is about clearly highlighting differences on policy positions and how those differences impact the audience. Messages are more persuasive and impactful when juxtaposed against the shortcomings of the other side.

Being first to define an issue can create favorable headwinds. In 2017, Republicans in Congress passed a tax bill that the nonpartisan Joint Committee on Taxation called the most drastic cut in corporate taxes that would increase the federal deficit by $1.5 trillion over ten years.[10] Conservatives had quickly seized the upper hand in the debate by disingenuously asserting that their proposal was aimed at the middle class. Trump repeatedly claimed it would be a Christmas present for middle-income taxpayers. Independent economists responded that the cuts would actually be "a lump of coal" for the middle class, but the damage was done. Time will tell if voters believe they have actually benefited from the legislation.

Prioritize

Information overload is a crushing problem. Don't allow your passion and depth of knowledge on an issue derail your message. You may think there is much that you must say, but attempting to share everything at once dilutes the message. By trying to say everything, you increase the likelihood that nothing or inconsequential points will be what the audience retains.

How much is too much? The general rule of thumb for interviews is three or four points, maximum. Three or four, no more. With a limited number it is possible to cut through clutter. If you say less and repeat it with greater frequency, you have more control over what the reporter puts in the story. By editing your content, you increase the likelihood that the reporter will use a central message point.

How many message points you can get into an interview can be more precisely determined by the type of interview. If a print reporter is looking for a reaction to breaking news, he or she wants one sound bite about 10 to 20 seconds in length. (This is about the length of a tweet.) With a ten-minute in-studio appearance, the time is divided between you, the host, and possibly other guests, which leaves you with two to three minutes of talking time, so two or three points would be your maximum. Radio and podcasts are the exception to the rule that less is more. Those formats may run twenty minutes or longer, and you may be the sole guest. In that case, you have time to articulate four points and repeat them.

Oh, Wow!

The Oh, Wow! factor is the ability to elicit a strong audience reaction: "Wow, that's incredible!" "YASSS, where do I sign up?" "Hmmm, I never thought of it that way before." "That's so wrong! I've got to do something!" What you have said has touched a nerve, and it cannot be forgotten or ignored.

News consumers are constantly scrolling through email chains, social-media posts, and TV channels while consciously and subconsciously asking themselves the essential question all audience members ask: "So what?" The media environment is competitive, and to be heard your message must grab their attention. The power-word-grabber techniques discussed in chapter 5 are expanded upon in the next section. These techniques provide additional ways to give reporters what they seek—the sound bite.

MEDIA MESSAGING TOOLS

The C3PO principles provide a broad approach to what you say and how you say it. With those principles as a guiding force, it's time to pick up a laser sword and enter the arena. For media interviews, the sword comes in the form of a message-development tool. This tool helps you decide what you must say, what you shouldn't say, and what you don't need to say. The following section outlines three specific types of message tools:

The Issue Message Box provides a template for how to talk about public policy issues when advocating for a cause or a policy position.

The Candidate Message Triangle is a second template designed primarily for political candidates. It can also be adapted for anyone seeking a new position or looking to brand herself. The triangle organizes the key attributes of how and why you are the best-qualified person.

The third tool is the Opposition Message Box, which is a planning tool that both candidates and advocates can use to compare and contrast messages with opponents or the competition. It will also help you anticipate opposition arguments and attacks so you are ready with a counterargument or response.

Power Boxes and Triangle

- Package content
- Simplify complexity
- Create memorable lines
- Have a user-friendly format

Issue Message Box

The Issue Message Box (IMB) is a tool to organize and prioritize your message in media-friendly packaging. The IMB is particularly effective for prepping for news interviews, and it can also help you prepare for any speaking event, including speeches, panel discussions, and meetings. For public-speaking events, the IMB will help you develop and shape the body of your speech. It is an efficient and effective way to come across prepared and polished.

The structure of the box is based on a streamlined version of storytelling so it is desirable to both general audiences, reporters, and news consumers. It is a road map for telling an intentional story. It enables you to educate and advocate by presenting a point of view. Further, the content is boiled down for reporters so you clearly state your position in sound-bite form.

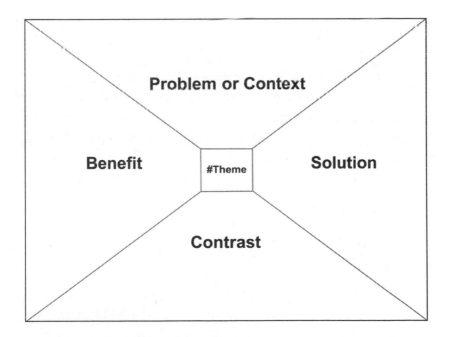

For media interviews, the IMB helps you exert more control over the interview process and the final news story. In interviews you have less control over how your message is received because you need to be responsive to the reporter's questions. And in most interviews the reporter will edit what you say. Rarely is the entire transcript of an interview shared. The IMB packages your message into a format that reporters are attracted to and that they can use. It helps you elevate the most important ideas and deliver sound bites.

Create the Issue Message Box

The development of an Issue Message Box starts with answering the 4 *W* questions introduced in chapter 5: What is my subject about? Why am I talking about it? Why should the audience care? What do I want them to do? The answers to these fundamental questions provide a strategic starting point for the message-development exercise. They narrow the focus of the message topic just as they narrow the statement of topic when preparing for a speech. How you answer these questions will help you frame the topic, address the audience's interests, and articulate the call to action.

With a road map in place, there is a three-step process to developing a media message. The first step is to craft the headline points that tell the entire story you want to tell about the issue. Next, the headline points are illustrated with supporting material. Finally, a theme is selected. The theme is the summary of the story—it is the idea you want to repeat most frequently. It is your version of "Yes We Can" or "Make America Great Again" lines. The idea you want people to remember above and beyond all else.

Step #1—Craft the Headline Points

The box has four headline points that support the theme in the center of the box. Taken together, the headline points tell the entire story. They concisely present your point of view on an issue.

- Frame the issue
- Provide a solution/action point
- Draw contrast
- Offer benefits

Frame the Issue

Framing is a way of defining a problem or a topic. The frame should embody what you value in such a way that it is relevant to the target audience. Speak to the needs and desires of the people you need to motivate. To get the broadest possible support, the frame must be linked to the target audience's existing belief systems and worldview. This means framing the issue so it's about something the audience already agrees with and cares about.

Here's an example of a possible message frame that could have been developed for an actual headline-making news event. In 2015, there was an outbreak of measles at a Disney theme park in California. The outbreak was alarming because measles is a highly infectious disease that remains a leading cause of death for children worldwide. A few years earlier, measles had been eliminated in the United States, so there was confusion about why an outbreak had occurred at an amusement park.

One approach to framing a public-health message about the outbreak would be to target parents. Parents would be a key audience because public safety is threatened when there are groups of children who are not vaccinated.

Measles Outbreak Frame: *Measles outbreaks occur in places where there are unvaccinated people.*

There are always different ways to frame an issue. Getting it right helps you avoid the mistake of only talking to people who already support the issue. Preaching to the choir won't generate new supporters for your position. The right frame ensures that you talk to the people you need to move to your side.

FRAME TECHNIQUES

Be alert to the framing techniques used by conservatives, especially on the religious right. In *Fighting Words*, author Robin Morgan debunks the claims made by fundamental conservatives that their positions on a host of issues originate with our nation's founders.[11] Here are typical examples of arguments used by conservative spokespeople in media forums:

Founding Documents: Gun-rights advocates frame any attempt to control guns as an assault on the Second Amendment.

Morality: Pro-life advocates frame abortion as the taking of an unborn life.

Religion: Conservatives push the religious concept of creationism to argue against teaching the scientific theory of evolution in public schools.

Rule of Law: The Defense of Marriage Act was promoted by opponents of same-sex marriage, or marriage equality.

Patriotism: Proponents for drilling in the Arctic National Wildlife Refuge claim doing so will help make America energy independent.

Provide a Solution

Once the issue or problem has been framed, it is necessary to offer a solution or a course of action. The solution will be more persuasive when supported by facts, data, and research from reputable third-party sources. Share models of success and specific results. People need to know that what you are proposing is grounded in reality and can be achieved. The call to action can be included here.

In our example of the measles outbreak, the solution to preventing future outbreaks is to vaccinate more children. The public-health community moved quickly to get the word out that a vaccine was available and very safe.

Measles Outbreak Solution: *The measles vaccine is effective and very safe.*

Draw Contrast

In public-policy debates, individuals who feel as strongly as you do about an issue will be asserting oppositional arguments. Opponents and skeptics may use tactics to undermine the logic of your argument or create confusion to motivate their base supporters. If these tactics are not addressed or rebutted, they can overpower your message.

Measles Outbreak Contrast: *The best way to protect your children is to get them vaccinated.*

The contrast message on measles needed to be shaped so that it dealt with the claims of anti-vaccinators. Anti-vaccinators believe erroneous information that vaccines are linked to autism. At the time of the measles outbreak, there were growing numbers of parents who were deciding not to vaccinate their kids for fear that the vaccines were dangerous. The public-health community needed to motivate parents who might have been confused by misleading medical advice that was widely circulated online. It was important to treat concerns about the safety of vaccines seriously and not talk down to parents.

A contrast message can be used two ways. First, to respond to the opposition arguments and refute attempts to delegitimize your key points. Second, to lessen the effectiveness of the opposing messages by not waiting to respond and by preempting them. Point out the weaknesses in their arguments with data and facts.

Offer a Benefit

The benefit is the articulation of why the audience should care; this is done by addressing what they stand to gain. Benefits often have a strong moral or ethical frame.

Measles Outbreak Benefit: *Getting vaccinated saves the most vulnerable.*

A public-health message can appeal to the common good. Vaccines not only help the individual children who are vaccinated but also stop the spread of disease to populations who are not able to get vaccinated. There are several groups of people who cannot get vaccines, including pregnant women and children with compromised immune systems, such as those with leukemia.

Step #2—Supporting Material

Once you have crafted the four headline points, the next step is to add supporting material that undergirds and expands upon each of those main points. The supporting points provide different ways to reinforce the headline point. By providing multiple ways to articulate the main points, you are bolstering it with repetition and not overwhelming the audience with too much information. Additionally, you will not sound redundant by repeating one argument only.

The supporting material should be written in grabber or sound-bite form—short sentences or phrases that are colorful and memorable. Reporters use these lines to add color and perspective to their stories. A number of grabber techniques were provided in chapter 5, so please refer back to those.

Here are additional techniques and examples of actual sound bites that reporters used in stories on the 2015 measles outbreak. These techniques also work well for social-media posts.

Grabbers, Soundbites, and Social-Media Posts:

1. Personal Story: "A woman in her fifties who visited Disneyland in mid-December came down with measles but has since recovered." (CNN, January 23)
2. Specific Example: "People who ate at La Mediterranee restaurant in Berkeley between 6:45 and 10 p.m. on Feb. 20 could

have been exposed to the measles." (*Los Angeles Times*, February 27)

3. Startling Stat: "Each person infected with the measles will transmit the disease to 12 to 18 other people." (*Forbes*, January 20)
4. Relative Numbers: "July 2015: Measles kills first patient in 12 years." (*USA Today*, July 2)
5. Clichés: "The uptick in measles cases is a wake-up call." (NPR, March 16)
6. Cultural Reference: "The misery of a measles outbreak at the Happiest Place on Earth is an irony even the most jaded epidemiologist could do without." (*Wired*, January 26)

This opening paragraph from a *Washington Post* story on the outbreak illustrates how journalists will often use a combination of the grabber techniques to make their writing more compelling:

Sometime in early December, somebody who probably caught measles abroad visited one of the Disney theme parks in California and perhaps sneezed. That's all it took. That and the fact there are a lot of people walking around California who have chosen not to be immunized against measles.[12]

Step #3—Craft a Theme

The Issue Message Box is complete when you have a theme. Hashtags are the perfect embodiments of a theme; #BlackLivesMatter, #MeToo, and #ItGetsBetter are examples of powerful themes that crystalize the "why" of a movement or campaign. The theme may come to you at any point in the message-development process. It's generally best to avoid trying to start by identifying a theme, because you can get stuck. Know that you need a theme, and, as you are brainstorming the headline points, be open to ideas for it and be alert for phrasing that will capture it concisely.

For a public-health message in our example, #VaccinesWork is a possible theme. It would help spread a broader message about the importance of all vaccines. The most salient themes have an action component, such as #BringOurGirlsHome. This particular hashtag became a rallying cry about the disappearance of 276 Nigerian school-girls who were abducted from their homes by the terrorist group Boko Haram.

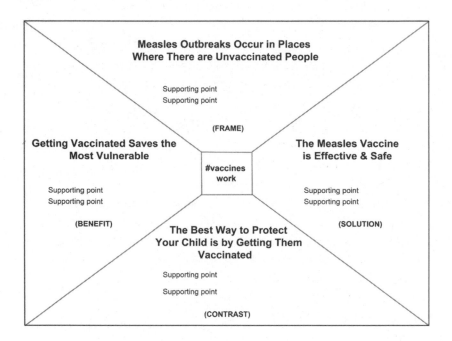

Candidate Message Triangle

The Candidate Message Triangle (CMT) is intended for anyone who is vying for a competitive position, such as a political candidate seeking public office or a prospective employee applying for a job. The triangle can also be used to help you develop a personal brand. The triangle has three headline points and a main theme.

The first headline point is designed to define who you are and articulate your core strengths. The second point focuses on what you intend to accomplish once you achieve the desired position. Use this point to show how you relate to the audience and how you can deliver results for them. Finally, the third point provides clarification of why you are the best woman for the job. Draw comparisons between your track record of success and the competition's vulnerabilities or weaknesses.

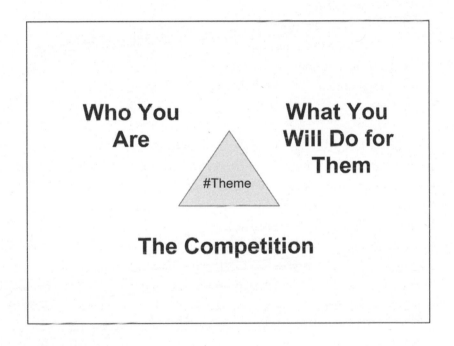

Who You Are

- Experience
- Accomplishments/Results
- Motivation
- Familiarity with the audience
- Why they should support you

What You Will Do for Them

- How you can relate to their problems
- Position on key issues
- Problem-solving ability
- Vision for the future

The Competition

- Professional weaknesses
- Lack of experience or qualifications
- Temperamentally unsuitable
- Out of step on values

The Candidate Message Triangle can serve as the framework for a political candidate's stump speech. As you develop the three headline points, think about the specific "asks" you need to make. What kind of help do you need from the voters to run a successful campaign and to be elected? Be as specific as possible.

One way to work in the call to action or the ask is to make it a central part of the "What You Will Do for Them" side of the box. For example, "I'm running as a strong pro-choice, pro-family candidate, and I need your support. Your contribution today of $100 will help ensure I can defeat the incumbent, who consistently votes against women and their families. He voted to defund Planned Parenthood and voted against paid family leave, pay equity, and raising the minimum wage. I care about the issues that will provide health and economic security to women and their families. With your help, I will represent you and the issues you care about."

Below are the Candidate Message Triangles used by the Democratic and Republican Party nominees in the 2016 presidential election campaign. These examples illustrate how the two candidates defined themselves, presented their agenda for the future, and articulated the weaknesses of one another.

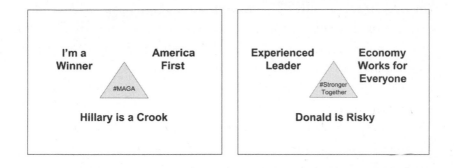

The triangle can also be used to help you package and present your unique personal brand. A personal brand will establish you as a trustworthy, credible spokesperson, which is a valuable asset during a period when audience members report less trust in major institutions. For the first time in nearly twenty years, an annual survey found that trust in government, media, business, and nonprofit organizations has declined—"the general populations did not trust the four major institutions 'to do the right thing.'"[13]

Crafting your personal brand can also make it easier to pitch yourself as a thought leader or newsmaker to media organizations. Many people feel uncomfortable pitching themselves as experts, but media bookers and program producers are looking for spokespeople with a clear point of view. The triangle will help you control your story by uniting your areas of interest and passion around a central theme. It will ensure that you decide what you want people to know about you and that you are able to put the focus on your special talents and tell your story in a positive way.

Opposition Box

> *"If you know the enemy and know yourself, you need not fear the result of a hundred battles. If you know yourself but not the enemy, for every victory gained you will also suffer a defeat. If you know neither the enemy nor yourself, you will succumb in every battle."*
>
> —Sun Tzu, *The Art of War*

The ancient philosophy of Chinese strategist Sun Tzu provides timely guidance on how to prep for forums in which you will need to contend with an oppositional message. Sun Tzu focused his preparation and resources on achieving victory with the least amount of conflict. He achieved this by disrupting enemies psychologically rather than attempting to destroy them physically.

The Opposition Box, or the Tully Message Box, is a strategy tool to arm yourself with intel on the other side's tactics and messages. This box was first developed by a political consultant named Paul Tully, who helped elect many progressive Democratic candidates to office at all levels. It allows you to compare and contrast your message points with the opposition's. The comparison reveals how you match up; it identifies weaknesses in your messaging; and it helps you anticipate their vulnerabilities. It is particularly useful when preparing to face off in live interviews with multiple guests, in candidate debates, and at town hall meetings on controversial subjects.

The Opposition Box or Tully Message Box is an effective way to game out the back-and-forth you can expect from an opponent. It crystalizes the key points you want to make and helps you anticipate what your opponent will say. This ensures that you are ready with a response and will not be caught off guard or get sidetracked, especially if your opponent has lied about you or has used other deceptive tactics.

Quadrant 1: What you say about yourself
Quadrant 2: What you say about your opponent
Quadrant 3: What your opponent says about him or herself
Quadrant 4: What your opponent says about you

Here is an example of an Opposition Box from the 2016 presidential campaign. The example lays out how Hillary Clinton self-described and how she talked about her opponent, Donald Trump. Similarly, Trump had a few lines he used repeatedly to describe himself and lines he used to describe his opponent.

Hillary on Hillary

Experienced Leader
Grandmother, Daughter
Stronger Together
I'm With Her

Trump on Trump

Make America Great Again
America First
Build a Wall
Winning

Hillary on Trump

Donald is Risky
Lacks the Temperament
Sexist, Racist
Bully

Trump on Hillary

Crooked Hillary
Liar
No Stamina
Not Presidential

HOW TO USE THE POWER BOXES AND TRIANGLE

Ideally, you would develop a message box or triangle in the early stages of a campaign or when you launch a new project. For example, if your organization is releasing a report or study, the message box should be ready to go on the day the report is issued. If you are a candidate, the triangle message is the basis of your stump speech and should be ready for the announcement. As the campaign evolves, the triangle or box should be tweaked or adjusted as needed over time. Updating the headline points and revising the supporting material ensures that the message remains relevant.

Quick Prep Tool

In those situations when you don't have months, weeks, or even hours to plan, a box or triangle can be a guide to quickly prepare. Reporters often call experts or involved parties and want a response to breaking news or a trending topic. The box gives you a way to pull your thoughts together so you can give a substantive answer and meet a deadline. The headline points distill your message down to a few sentences, which enables you to formulate a mini story. There may not be enough time to craft supporting material or a theme. That's okay, though, because the reporter probably has time only for a brief reaction.

Message Discipline

The design of the boxes and triangle prioritizes the most important pieces of information in the headline points. When you create the templates, use a larger font so the headline sentences jump off the page and are easy to see. During an interview, begin answers by using the headline points first because together they tell the complete story. As the interview continues, you can drill down into the supporting material to reinforce the headline points. The theme should be used repeatedly throughout the interview. It's a good way to set the stage at the beginning; repeat it during the interview to reinforce your message; and end with it to clarify the takeaway point.

The message tools can be shared by a team of spokespeople in addition to the main newsmaker. If the team works together on developing the message, there will be across-the-board buy-in on the key points. Additionally, the entire team will be on message, that is, using the same messages. Reporters notice inconsistencies in messaging, so it is important that the choir sings from the same song sheet.

Improves Delivery

The boxes and the triangle are functional, portable, and sharable. Everything you want to say is on one sheet of paper or is clearly visible on a computer screen. No more thumbing through pages of talking points or cumbersome three-ring binders. No more trying to decipher messy notes. The easy-to-read layout will help you see and remember what you want to say.

The one-page layout also promotes brevity and discipline because you have distilled what you need to say into a tight package. This allows you to efficiently hit points during the interview. The tight packaging ensures that you won't ramble or drone on with long answers that the reporter will need to edit.

On the drive to the studio or before you hop on the telephone, pull out the message box or triangle and review it aloud. Avoid reading from the box in a robotic fashion. A few minutes of practice immediately prior to the interview will ensure that your delivery sounds fresh and that the most salient points are at the top of your mind. An effective practice routine is to have a colleague or staff member help you warm up by posing questions to you. In chapter 9 there are more prep tips for specific types of interviews.

Powerful media messages start with a message box or a triangle. These tools help you package what you want to say in an accessible narrative that frames a problem and lays out a progressive solution. Power messages do more than inform and educate about a topic. Power messages present your point of view in a context designed to elicit an audience response, whether individual or collective.

WELL-SPOKEN WOMEN RESIST, INSIST, PERSIST

Credibility starts with fact-based messaging.
C3PO principals guide the way to credibility.
Message boxes or triangles prioritize essential points.

CHAPTER 7

THE NEW LOOK AND SOUND OF LEADERSHIP

"I just threw up on international TV. And it felt great."
—Samantha Fuentes, Parkland student, recovering to
finish her speech at the 2018 March for Our Lives

"**Y**ou look like you've got a great idea."

"You sound like you know what you're talking about."

These are the types of compliments women need to hear more of. Let's collectively say good-bye to "she's too this" or "she's too that." That way space is freed up for "She looks and sounds like a leader."

That's the new look and sound of leadership. Along with power words, we all need our own power moves and power sounds. Our own ways of working the stage, directing the meeting, or leading the campaign.

View the power moves and power sounds as techniques to help you present your best self. The techniques are a starting point. This isn't about fitting into a mold. There isn't one right approach. Good technique and the spark of your personality is the foundation of a polished performance. It's about knowing how to use purposeful movement and an expressive voice to enhance your authentic self.

POWER MOVES

Hands raised high in an exuberant power pose, Amy Schumer literally jumps with joy as she moves to center stage. Beaming ear to ear, she claps along with the crowd, fueling the kickoff of her comedy set. Amy and her sisters in comedy are excellent role models for owning a speaking space.

Are you a space consumer or a space saver? Generally, men are space consumers, hence the phrase "manspreading." They eat up space by holding themselves erect, pumping up the chest, and spreading arms and legs. Women tend to be space savers. We move aside for others, hold gestures tight to the body, and cross our legs. We are more likely to shrink rather than expand onstage. What's so fabulous about comediennes is that so many of them blow those stereotypes out of the water.

What is your body language communicating? Have you thought about it? Do you face the room or turn away slightly? Do you subtly try to hide behind a table? Is your posture off balance? The power moves will help you stop shrinking and start expanding. The well-spoken woman's Stand Up approach is designed for both in-person and on-camera appearances.

WELL-SPOKEN WOMEN STAND UP

Sure Stance
Targeted Eye Contact
Animated Hands
Natural Facial Expression
Directed Movement
Upper-Body Motion
Purposeful Performance

Sure Stance

When Leslie Jones strides onto a comedy stage, she does so with the gait of warrior who has slain a dragon. Taking full advantage of her six-foot frame and WNBA wingspan, she reaches out to embrace the audience's roar of approval. Without uttering a word, Leslie signals who's in charge and that the evening ahead is going to be a wild ride.

Looking like a leader starts with standing like one. For your next presentation, get started on the right foot by changing up your foot stance. Don't stand with your feet shoulder-width apart, because this locks the knees. Rather, position one foot slightly in front of the other, about two or three inches apart. Experiment to figure out which foot you prefer to place in the forward position. Pick whichever one feels more comfortable. Point your toes straight ahead.

Next, stand up straight with your body weight resting on the back leg. Your knees will be looser, you will feel more relaxed, and you will look less rigid. When your knees are locked, nervous tension can run up your spine and settle in your neck and shoulders. With your feet in place and with your weight on the back leg, position your face forward to the audience.

To complete the sure-stance position, imagine that there is a string attached to the lower part of your spinal column. The string extends up your spinal cord, through your neck, and out the top of your head. Project the string straight up from the crown of your head into the ceiling. Next, drop your shoulders back slightly. Don't stick your chest out. Just drop your shoulders back with your arms loose. If you raise your hands to waist level, this will cause your shoulders to drop. The shoulder drop is the secret to projecting confidence.

At this point, if there is movement in your body, it will be forward because your body weight is on the back leg. Again, this movement keeps your knees loose, and it is interactive because you are moving toward the audience. This stance prevents you from swaying side to side or nervously shifting your body weight from one foot to the other.

Try this in front of a mirror and see how confident you look. These tips create a sure stance, the stance of a champion. The champion stance will ensure that you look confident even if you feel nervous or uncomfortable. The stance allows you to mask any uncertainty you may feel.

For standing TV interviews or press conferences, follow the suggestions outlined above. Be sure to avoid positioning your feet shoulder-width apart, because rocking back and forth will be exaggerated on camera and you may appear nervous. Be sure to position one foot in front of the other so that if there is movement, it is toward the camera. Leaning in will look and feel interactive.

Targeted Eye Contact

Targeted eye contact is direct, steady, and sustained. It signals trustworthiness, sincerity, and seriousness. Directly looking at the audience draws them in, creating a connection. The people in the room will feel recognized and validated. It is essential to establish eye contact at the very beginning and maintain it during the talk.

Poor-quality eye contact can blow your credibility in a matter of seconds. It is amateurish to look down at notes while saying, "Hello, everyone, thank you for inviting me." It's like when you meet someone one-on-one and she looks away when you shake hands. The sideways glance creates a negative first impression. Similarly, the audience wants you to look them in the eye.

Establish Eye Contact

Good eye contact is your visual hello. At the onset, establish eye contact by taking a second or two to look directly at the audience. This can be difficult because adrenaline may be pumping, which causes you to break eye contact and to speak too quickly. Resist the impulse to race ahead and instead take a moment to greet them properly.

Use a deep breath to counteract the adrenaline rush, and use the key target to look at the audience. The key target is usually a spot on the wall in the back of the room, like a light-switch plate. With an audience of more than twenty people, the key target is the spot straight in front of you, slightly above the head of the person seated farthest away. Directing eye contact on the key target means you aren't looking at any one person. But to the audience it will appear as if you are looking at everyone.

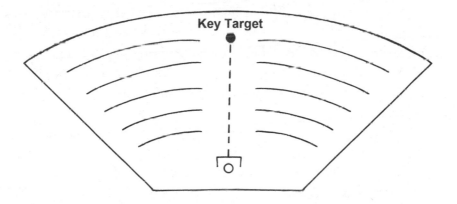

Focusing eye contact on the key target will improve your posture because it raises your chin slightly. Hold your eyes on the spot long enough to greet the audience. For example, "Hello, everyone. It's good to be here." Return to the spot anytime during the presentation when you have an important point you want to share with everyone. Likewise, use the key target at the conclusion. This ensures that everyone feels as if they are included in the wrap-up. It works best when there are more than twenty people in the room. The key target is also usually the location where cameras are positioned if the event is livestreamed or videotaped.

With a smaller group, it may look odd to the audience members if you direct your eye contact at a spot on the back wall. They will be wondering what you are looking at. With fewer people, you can begin by looking at the person who introduced you, or, if there was no introduction, address the most senior person in the room initially. As you continue talking, you will want to establish eye contact with individuals in the room as described in the next section.

Maintain Eye Contact

Kathy Griffin rarely breaks eye contact in a fifty-minute set. Her head is up, her eyes on the room, constantly gauging the audience's reaction—are they keeping pace with her high energy? Did they get the joke? Or are they confused? Looking at them provides real-time feedback on how you are doing. Are they paying attention or have you gone on for too long? If they no longer return eye contact, they may be bored or lost. That's a sign to ask them a question to reengage, or to begin to wrap up it up.

Once you've established eye contact with the key target, the quadrant system ensures that you bring in everyone in the room, no matter the audience size, whether twenty or two thousand. The quadrants system helps you target eye contact at individuals seated around the room. Implement the quadrant system by mentally drawing a line across the middle of the room horizontally and vertically to divide the room into four sections, or quadrants. Number each section of the room.

Start by turning toward the first quadrant and talking to one person seated in it. Then, move on to quadrant two, again looking at one person. Work your way around the room in a clockwise fashion. When you look at one person, keep your eyes steady on that person until you finish the sentence or thought. Avoid looking away midsentence.

After you've moved around all four boxes, go back to the first one. This time, look at a different individual seated in the area. Same thing for quadrant two; look at someone else. This way, you won't get stuck making too much eye contact with one person, which can quickly become uncomfortable for you and for the person you keep looking at. Once you are able to look at one person at a time, you don't need to keep looking around the room using the clockwise pattern. The quadrants are used to ensure you hit all areas, but the clockwise movement isn't the key to maintaining eye contact. What is key is holding eye contact steadily on one person at a time.

Eye-Contact Don'ts

- Head down during greeting
- Constantly turning your head side to side
- Rapid eye darts around the room
- Body turned to the projection screen
- Searching the heavens or staring at the floor
- Head buried in notes

Finish the Thought Exercise

In one-on-one conversations, eye contact is constantly broken so we don't come across as if we are trying to stare down the person we are talking to. In front of an audience, you don't want to cheat by scanning the room or looking from one person to the next too quickly. Another common mistake is to look down at your notes to get to the next point before you've finished delivering a sentence. For the big ideas, it's important to maintain steady, direct eye contact on one person or the key target until the end of the sentence.

State the following sentence aloud twice. The first time you say it, drop your eyes to look at your feet when you hit the word "steady."

"The most important public-speaking technique is steady eye contact."

Did that feel as if you were speaking with conviction?

Read the sentence again and, this time, hold your eyes on a key target directly in front of you.

"The most important public-speaking technique is steady eye contact."

Now that looks convincing. Hold your eyes up until the end of the sentence. That way, your eye contact shows you believe what you are saying.

On-Camera Eye Contact

Steady eye contact is crucial to looking credible on-camera. Where you focus your eyes depends on the type of appearance. For media interviews with a reporter, look directly at the questioner. Avoid glancing away while speaking, because breaking eye contact is exaggerated. If the camera catches you looking up, you appear to be searching the heavens. Looking off to the side appears shifty, and looking down can seem uncertain. Steady eye contact on one spot establishes your credibility with the viewer. Direct your gaze at the reporter's face; it isn't necessary to eyeball them. You can look at an earring or a necktie knot or the third eye (middle of the forehead) if that is less distracting.

Satellite Interviews and Webcasts

With satellite interviews, online presentations, and video conferences, look directly at the camera. In those formats, you may be alone with the camera—there is no questioner or live audience. Look directly into the center of the camera lens. The principle of steady eye contact remains unchanged. Aim your eye contact straight at the camera lens—not above, below, or to the side. Hold your eyes steady on the camera while you are talking. When you pause, it's okay to break eye contact by looking down. This will appear reflective, as if you are collecting your thoughts.

ANIMATED HANDS

Most people talk with their hands when they are telling a story. They use gestures to show how big the fish was or how far the ball went. Researchers at the University of Alberta have shown that "moving your hands around helps you recall parts of a story—the gestures help you access memory and language so you can tell more of a story."[1] In situations when you are nervous, it can be difficult to get the language out; moving your hands can prompt the words.

Hand gestures can be welcoming. The movement literally opens you up so you look more accessible to the audience. For an example of how to get your hands in the act, watch Samantha Bee on *Full Frontal with Samantha Bee*. She literally hands off her points to people in the studio audience. When she delivers her standing monologue, she gestures consistently, keeping her hands at waist level. This looks better than repeatedly raising and dropping your arms.

All movement should be smooth and round. Avoid quick jabs with your hands. Encompassing gestures start at the shoulder—use your entire arm and slowly extend your hand out to someone. By using the entire arm, you avoid looking like an angry *Tyrannosaurus rex* flailing its tiny arms.

As discussed earlier, holding your hands at waist level improves your posture. There are two other hand positions that are not distracting. First, arms hanging loosely at your sides. This is a neutral position, but it can feel awkward when you are nervous. Another option is to hold one hand at waist level with the other hand hanging at your side. Having one hand up and one hand down gives you something to do with both hands. If you have a pocket that you can easily slide your hand in and out of, it's okay to put one hand in a pocket. However, putting both hands in your pockets will look causal or sloppy.

How Not to Talk with Your Hands

- Arms crossed in front of your chest
- Arms military straight at your sides
- Hands tapping the lectern
- Fiddling with a pen or shuffling papers
- Jerky karate chops
- Wild, over-the-head, chimpanzee-style arm swings

On-Camera Hand Gestures

The worst-possible thing to do on-camera is to hold yourself perfectly still. Sometimes people are nervous or worried about doing the wrong thing. As a result, they hold themselves motionless, projecting the proverbial deer-caught-in-the-headlights look. The frozen look telegraphs anxiety. In daily conversation, people interact by using hand gestures and head and shoulder nods. This movement will also look natural on-camera.

Use hands gestures as you do in person to underscore key points and to externalize excess energy. However, your hand movement needs to be contained so that your hands don't bob in and out of the camera frame. Keep the gestures in an imaginary "hand box" that is centered at the top of the chest. The parameters of the hand box are below the chin, between the shoulders, and above the top of the bra. Use one hand or two, but keep the movement inside the box.

Resist the temptation to reach a hand out to the camera as if you are about to wave to your mom like athletes do after they've scored a big point. Rather, hold your hands or hand about six inches or so away from the chest. Initially, this positioning may feel tight since the placement is different from how we gesture during regular conversation. With practice, it will feel comfortable.

Natural Facial Expression

Your facial expression should match the words coming out of your mouth. Look like you are happy if you say you are. This sounds obvious, but it is not unusual for people to start a presentation by mouthing the words "I'm pleased to join you" with a less-than-happy or even grim expression. They are often concentrating too much on what they are going to say and not thinking about what their expression is communicating.

Some faces are naturally more expressive than others. *SNL*'s Kate McKinnon, for example, can morph from Attorney General Jeff Sessions to Hillary Clinton to actress Gal Gadot. Use facial expressions to signal confidence. Men are rarely, if ever, told to smile, and you may resent being asked to do so. But an open-mouthed smile at the beginning of a talk sets a positive tone. A closed-mouth smile may look like a smirk. A tight-lipped smile can be perceived as an attempt to mask anger. A twisted smile may convey sarcasm. The smile isn't about being happy or wanting to be accepted. A wide smile shows that you are comfortable and in control.

A confident expression at the beginning can mirror the expression you would like the audience to reflect back to you. Psychologists say that mirroring is a way to bond, and we do it instinctively. The most obvious forms are the yawn and the smile. If you see someone yawn, you are likely to yawn in the next thirty seconds. Similarly, a purposeful smile allows you to set a positive tone.

If your subject matter is grim, a smile can appear flip or disrespectful. Should you be responsible for delivering bad news, use steady eye contact and a neutral facial expression. This will help you convey the seriousness of the situation.

"RESTING BITCH FACE,"
OR BOSS LADY EXPRESSION?

Some people use a limited range of facial expressions. Generally, men in leadership positions smile less and use fewer facial expressions. When women don't smile, they are not viewed as leaders and are called out for having "Resting Bitch Face" (RBF.) If you have RBF, when you are at rest, your natural expression is slightly sullen or annoyed rather than neutral. This expression isn't intentional, it's just the way some people appear.

Scientists say both men and women have RBF, but it has been deemed unacceptable for women.[2] Rather than describing a woman as forceful or commanding, RBF is an insult used to imply that the woman is unpleasant or nasty. It makes us wonder, Why are women expected to appear happy all the time? How many men are advised to smile?

If you have RBF in person, it will likely be exaggerated when you are speaking on-camera. You may appear to be scowling because of the way the camera technology flattens facial expressions. It will seem counterintuitive or feel fake to smile, but on TV everyone needs to be slightly more expressive.

It's up to you, and you may elect to own your RBF. In that case, give them your best Wanda Sykes scowl and tell people RBF is your boss-lady expression.

Directed Movement

People are reading your body language before you begin speaking. Your first impression will be not what you say but how you enter the room, climb stairs to the stage, or walk to the head table. Plan your first impression in advance, particularly if you feel anxious. Don't set a negative tone by slinking against the wall with your head bowed, eyes on your feet.

Give the audience a full-body visual greeting that projects confidence. Your walk should be intentional, with your head slightly tilted up, shoulders dropped back, and arms swinging loosely. Turn your body as you walk across the stage so more of your front faces the audience rather than your side. A slightly quickened pace—not rushed, but not a stroll—conveys energy and enthusiasm. Walk as if you are the commander in chief.

Waist Turns

Standing stock-still will feel uncomfortable and look unnatural. Most people do not stand motionless in everyday conversation. Rather, they turn and face the person they are talking to. Use this same movement when you're giving a talk.

Let's revisit the eye-contact quadrant system to add another layer of technique. When you look at someone who is seated in a quadrant, don't just turn your head or eyes in that person's direction. Turn from the waist and face him or her straight on. With your loose-kneed stance, you can step into the turn. Turn so your shoulders are squared toward the person at whom you are looking. Then turn to the next quadrant as you look at the next person. The waist turn eliminates excessive neck movement. If you feel your neck turning, that is a signal that you need to get your body moving. This is the secret to appearing conversational.

Behind a Lectern

Lecterns are generally used for more formal occasions, such as keynote addresses, debates, or press conferences. It is there to hold a microphone, speech notes, and/or a glass of water. It is not there to prop you up or for you to try to hide behind. When speaking from behind a lectern, some presenters develop tunnel vision as they lapse into lecture mode. Grasping the sides of the lectern, they clamp down, shoulders bunched with tension. Any movement is limited to neck turns or eye darts.

The lectern is the ultimate example of staging bias. Most lecterns are designed and built to be used by men. The height of the average male in the United State is 5 feet 10 inches. The average height for women is 5 feet 4 inches. That is significant because the top of the lectern hits a man at about waist level so it is possible for the audience to view most of his upper body, including hand gestures.

For a woman, the lectern may cut her off right around the neck, which diminishes her stature. If you are shorter than five feet six, consider purchasing a small podium to stand on. The technical name for a small, portable one is an "apple box" and they are available online. Apple boxes are inexpensive, are lightweight, and come in varying heights.

The best way to interface with the lectern is to rest your fingertips on the edge in front of you, as if you are playing the piano. With your hands at waist level, your shoulders will drop back, improving your posture. Avoid standing too close to it. Give yourself some wiggle room by backing away about eight inches or so.

Freestyle

If you are standing without a lectern, be aware of your position on the floor relative to the audience and how you use the floor space. The way to control your movement is to make it purposeful and not random. Use movement the way Wanda Sykes does. She walks causally and comfortably onstage. When she wants to drive home a killer line, she punctuates it by stopping. She delivers the punchline while holding herself motionless.

A way to get comfortable with this is to use the "three-star" technique. Envision three stars on the floor laid out in a triangle shape with the center star pointing toward the back of the stage or the wall behind you. Position yourself on the center star so that when you initially move, you walk to one side of the triangle toward the audience. You want to walk closer to the audience because that movement is more interactive than walking away from the listeners. When you arrive at a star, stay a while—a few sentences or paragraphs—before you move to another star. This prevents you from pacing. As you walk, be careful not to turn your backside to the audience. This requires walking a little sideways or backward if you are returning to the center star. This may feel awkward, but it will look better and is easy to do once you practice a couple of times.

Upper-Body Motion

Standing posture presents a more dynamic presence and can give you more control over the room. Some forums are set up so you need to remain seated, such as panel discussions or testimonies. The key to an interactive presence while seated is to tilt forward in the chair from the waist. This posture will position your head so it is closer to the audience. If you lean back or slump in the chair, your knees will be closer to them.

Tilt forward from the waist two or three inches. Always keep your shoulders dropped back. If you relax back in the chair or slouch, you can appear disinterested or intimidated. Avoid crossing your arms and legs as if you have been stuffed into a middle seat in the back of an airplane.

There are three different options for what to do with your legs. What you do depends on your height, what you are wearing, and the type of chair you're sitting in. If your feet touch the ground comfortably and you are wearing pants, try the runner's position. Just like it sounds, place one foot slightly in front of the other on the ground as if you are about to take off in a 100-yard dash. This position allows you to balance your body weight forward on your feet.

If you are wearing a dress or a skirt, it is more "ladylike" to cross your legs at the knee. Don't forget to sit up and lean forward. If you are shorter in height and/or wearing a dress or a skirt, try crossing your ankles and pulling both feet straight under the chair. This position will reduce the leg shot, showing less thigh and more skirt. It will help ensure your feet touch the ground, and it works well when the chair lacks support.

There are two good options for your hand placement when you are not gesturing. (1) Rest one hand on each leg about midway down your thigh, with your fingers closed. (2) Place one hand on top of the other on one leg. Both are quiet hand positions, meaning they are not distracting to the viewer. Avoid gripping the armrests, because you will appear as if you are strapped into an electric chair. Don't rest your elbows on the armrests, either, because doing so will cause your posture to slump.

When you are seated behind a table or desk, put your hands and forearms on the table in front of you. Position your forearms so they form the letter *V* on the top of the furniture, with your hands at the apex of the *V*. Just placing your hands on the table will appear meek. Be sure to use the *V*, because if you place your arms parallel to your body, it is more likely that you will slouch or hunch your back. With your forearms in the *V* position, place one hand on top of the other. Avoid interlacing your fingers, because you may clench them tightly or fiddle with your fingers or rings.

Director's chairs and bar stools are too high for the average woman. Legs dangle, skirts hike up, and shoes fall off. Scaling them is like trying to reach the peak of Mount Everest. Once you reach the top, your ability to use good posture is inhibited by the fact that your feet don't touch the floor or that little rung at the base.

One solution is to wear pants rather than a skirt or a dress. A skirt that is long enough while you're standing may reveal too much thigh when you're seated. A streamlined pencil skirt will not allow you to cross your legs, thus forcing you to focus on holding your knees together so nothing is exposed. Another solution is to stand when it is your time to talk, this way, you can concentrate on what you want to say rather than on what your legs are doing.

Purposeful Performance

The Stand Up techniques help you develop a polished stage presence that is central to a purposeful performance. They help you create a connection with the audience with engaging body language. Some of the techniques will initially feel awkward and forced. That's understandable; you need time to figure out what works best for you. Experiment by trying out different techniques in front of a mirror. Then videotape yourself and see how it looks.

With practice, these techniques will become second nature. Muscle memory is developed through repetition, so eventually you will move without having to think about what you are doing. This frees you up to focus on sharing your experience, knowledge, and issue expertise. The next chapter has additional tips on the right way to practice your performance.

POWER SOUND

Say it like you mean it.

Chelsea Handler is emphatic—unequivocal in her opinions and always forceful in her delivery. She delivers a call to action with choppy, declarative (often profane) statements. Chelsea's voice sounds powerful. For most presenters, the voice is an under-utilized tool. Most put little thought into the overall quality of their sound and their level of expressiveness. Maximizing the full range and capability of your voice will ensure it is a power tool.

Audiences take in speakers on three levels—they listen to the words, they watch the body language, and they hear the voice. The tone of your voice matters as much as power words and power moves. In some forums, such as on a podcast or on the phone, it's the best tool to express how much you care.

Turn your voice into a power tool by learning how to operate it. Most tools look more complicated than they are. Basically, you need to know how to turn power tools on and off. And when to adjust speed, volume, and capacity. The voice is no different. The overall quality of your sound can be controlled with the following: pace, pitch, pause, pronunciation, and projection.

5 VOCAL POWER CONTROLS

Pace

The pace is how quickly or how slowly you speak. An ideal speaking pace is a conversational rate. The rate is one the listeners can follow, and it gives the presenter time to think and breathe. A conversational rate is approximately 140 to 170 words per minute. This is about the rate broadcasters use to deliver the news, so it is one that is familiar.

Clock yourself by reading aloud for 60 seconds, and then use the word count function on the computer to see how many words you said. It is important to read aloud. Most people read more quickly when they don't have to audibly articulate the vowel and consonant sounds. If you use more than 170 words when reading aloud, you are a fast talker. At this speed, it is more difficult for listeners to keep up. If you are below 130 words, you are a slow talker. Your normal rate is dragging, and the audience may become impatient.

Pitch

What is your natural pitch? Is it high or low on the musical scale? There are two general pitch ranges: chest voice and head voice. The chest voice resonates in the top part of the chest. It produces lower tones that can convey control, confidence, and expertise. A head voice will have a higher pitch. A higher pitch can express energy, excitement, and enthusiasm. Your pitch may be somewhere in the middle.

Pause

Not talking can be powerful.

Margaret Cho is a master of the pause. Her spot-on timing makes you want to laugh. She uses the silence to create curiosity—*What's coming?* The continued silence builds tension and then *zing*—she hits you with the funny line. There's no fear of the silence, it's a hook.

Pauses are not just for setting up one-liners. Most speakers do not pause frequently enough. And when they do pause, they don't pause long enough. A standard pause is 2 to 3 seconds in length. Count it out: "One Mississippi, two Mississippi, three Mississippi." This is not wasted time. The audience has a moment to reflect on what was just said. Remember, they are likely hearing your speech for the first time, and they need time to absorb the meaning of your words. While the audience is reflecting, you can think about what you want to say next or take a breath if you are nervous. Or, if it's available on a lectern or tabletop, you may take a sip of water.

Projection

Most voices have a wide volume range, from barely audible to booming. Sarah Silverman uses the full range of her voice. She will drop it to whisper level to bring the audience in, and the next instant she is at full volume. Are you on the quiet side, the loud side, or somewhere in between? If you are naturally soft-spoken, consider requesting a microphone when speaking to groups larger than twenty-five people or when speaking outside. If you are a loud talker, listeners can feel like you are shouting at them needlessly, and they will quickly grow tired of it. Modulate the volume so you don't overwhelm them. It's not uncommon for a presenter to begin with a high-volume level because they want to sound energetic or passionate. Using a mid-range volume is more effective because it allows you to build to a crescendo, as is explained in the following section on inflection.

Pronunciation and Enunciation

Pronunciation is the way a word is spoken. Social, cultural, and regional differences create interesting variations. For example, southerners are said to speak with a drawl; Midwesterners, a twang; and some Bostonians, with dropped *R*s.

Enunciation is the clear articulation of word. It's been said, "When in doubt, mumble." But don't risk sounding like your mouth is filled with marbles or that you don't know what you are talking about. Mumblers are more likely to be regarded as less decisive and as poorly informed. Mumbling is the vocal equivalent of not looking someone in the eye.

VOCAL COMPLAINTS

When the host of NPR's *Fresh Air*, Terry Gross, first started out in radio, she was told her voice sounded "hissy." It turns out the problem wasn't her voice but the low-quality microphone at the local radio station. This is not an isolated incident. NPR has found that its listeners are more likely to complain about the way women sound than how men do. And its older listeners are most likely to express disapproval of the way younger women talk.[3] Public-radio personality Ira Glass's voice has a vocal-fry quality or a sound that is hard and nasal. Listeners describe his voice as distinctive, but women with the same vocal-fry sound are described as annoying.

THE WAYS PEOPLE TELL WOMEN TO SHUT UP

- "Just calm down."
- "You sound shrill."
- "I feel like you are lecturing me."
- "Why are you shouting?"
- "Your laugh is a cackle."
- "Your voice sounds like a twelve-year old."
- "You remind me of my nagging wife."

ARTICULATE YOUR INTENTION

Now that you have an overview of the fundamentals, it's time to expand the range of how to use your voice. Audiences interpret what is said according to how it is said and the way it sounds. The Power Control techniques listed above enable a presenter to provide clues regarding their feelings about the topic at hand. The way a word is stressed, or when inflection is added, can change the meaning of a sentence. Here is a twist on a classic illustration.

In Chelsea Handler style, read the following sentence aloud, stressing the first word, "I":

"**I** didn't say he stole the election."

Read this way, it sounds as if you are not accusing him, but someone else may have raised the accusation.

Now read the sentence again, this time stressing the second word, "didn't":

"I **DIDN'T** say he stole the election."

Now, it sounds like you are denying that you made an accusation.

Continue with this pattern, stressing each subsequent word within the sentence:

"I didn't **SAY** he stole the election."

This could suggest that you wrote an article about how he stole the election.

Notice how the meaning of the sentence changes depending on which word is emphasized. If you repeat the sentence seven times and stress a different word each time, the meaning changes each time.

As you can see, inflection is a powerful vocal tool. You can change the meaning of the words simply by stressing them or not. Without any inflection, you risk having a monotone sound. Droning on using one note at one pace will lull the audience to sleep. Variety, variety, variety will keep them alert.

Most presenters worry about overdoing it with the voice when, in fact, they are nowhere near being on overload. Below are instructions for how to use inflection and other power tools to amp up your sound. Along with the standup comediennes, Senator Elizabeth Warren knows how to use power sounds to wow a crowd. The following are excerpts from her 2017 Netroots Nation speech.[4]

POWER TOOL TECHNIQUES

1. Inflection

Add inflection by raising or lowering your pitch on key words. If your normal speaking voice has a lower pitch overall, raise the pitch slightly and the word will stand out. If your overall pitch is higher, then you will want to do the opposite. Lower the pitch a note or two on key words. Raising volume slightly on stressed words adds interest, but be careful not to shout.

"Any other bankruptcy **NERDS** in the house?"
"We can care about a mom who's worried that her kid will get **SHOT** during a traffic stop."

2. Extend One-Syllable Words

Extending the pronunciation of a small word gives the word gravitas and makes the sentence stand out. Drag out the sound of the one-syllable words in bold.

"... my friend **A-N-D M-Y-Y** hero John Lewis."
"The real threat is **A-L-L-L** of you."
"**B-I-G Y-A-W-N**."

3. Exaggerated Pronunciation

Exaggerate the pronunciation of multisyllable words. Each syllable in the words highlighted below is stressed.

"... protected from **DE-POR-TA-TION**."
"... millions are **STRUG-GLING** ..."
"... corporate money is **SLITH-ER-ING** through ..."

4. Dramatic Volume Drops

Change the volume in unexpected ways. Try raising the level in the middle of a sentence. Or build to a crescendo at the end of sentence. The volume should slowly and deliberately rise as you reach the end of the sentence.

"We wanted **A MOVEMENT** and now look around ..."
"Me, I've been shouting **ABOUT THIS CRISIS** from every rooftop I could find for years ..."

"For a lot of our fellow citizens, the system is rigged now, and it has been rigged **FOR A LONG, LONG TIME**."

Avoid having your volume trail off at the end of sentences. This will sound like you are running out of energy. If you find this happening, it may be that your sentences are too long and/or you are not breathing properly.

5. Repetition on Purpose

Repeat sounds, words, or phrases.

"These fights matter. These fights matter."
"We're not going back to the days of being lukewarm on choice. We're not going back to the days when universal health was something Democrats talked about on the campaign trail but were too chicken to fight for after they got elected. And we're not going back to the days when a Democrat who wanted a seat in Washington first had to grovel on Wall Street."

6. Clipped Sentences

A series of short sentences can help you build to a call to action.

"We will not. We shall not. We must not. Allow anyone to turn back the clock."
"This fight is the fight Americans are counting on us to win. This fight is my fight. This fight is your fight. So, let's go win it!"

The ability to use these vocal-power techniques is possible when you have prepared your remarks in advance and know what you are going to say. With written remarks, you are not talking off the top of your head, so you can practice when and where you add inflection or extend a key word. The next chapter outlines how to prepare the text so it will help you maximize your sound.

AVOID REPETITIVE PATTERNS

Your use of the power-tool techniques should be intentional rather than a bad habit or a nervous tic. Some people use patterns that distract, and oftentimes they are unaware of it. However, the audience notices quickly. From your own experience, how long can you listen to someone who constantly "ums" and "ahhs"? It doesn't take long before the audience tunes out the offending speaker.

Repetitive, extraneous noise is the most common bad habit. Here are the other vocal faux pas that signal uncertainty, anxiousness, or unpreparedness:

- Filler Words: "You know," "like," and "actually" are often overused.
- Up Speak: Sentences that should be declarative sound like questions.
- Nonstop Conjunctions: Nearly every sentence is strung together with "so," "but," "and," or "or."
- Endless Sentences: The thought goes on and on and on and on.
- Laughter Punctuation: A giggle is used as punctuation at the end of a sentence.

POWER OUTFIT

When going on-camera, it's time to brace yourself for the fashion police. Helene Cooper, who is the Pentagon reporter for the *New York Times* and a frequent Sunday-morning talk-show guest, has learned to ignore viewer commentary about her clothing choices: "You have the worst wardrobe of all the newscasters, male or female, on all of the networks and cable channels."[5] Helene has found that it doesn't matter what she wears, someone will not like it and will let her know.

An acclaimed photojournalist was taken aback when a makeup artist at RT (Russian Television) asked: "Do you want hair extensions for your in-studio interview?" The photographer wasn't sure how to respond, so she tentatively replied no. A liberal commentator on Fox was offered a version of the Jerry Seinfeld puffy shirt and false eyelashes. She said yes to the eyelashes but no to the shirt. It seems studio personnel at RT and Fox want their women guests to have a certain look.

Deciding what to wear is more than a vexing question. Research on media coverage of women political candidates found that descriptions of their appearance hurt them at the polls. It didn't matter whether the description was positive, negative, or benign. A survey of voters conducted by the Women's Media Center and She Should Run revealed that that "in close races, sexist coverage on top of the attacks that every candidate faces can make the difference between winning and losing."[6] If your appearance does become a focal point, it is important not to ignore the commentary. Either you or a surrogate should call out sexist language.

"My relationship with brick-and-mortar shopping is, in general, unpleasant. I can't remember a time in my life when I could go to a physical store and find a variety of things in my size that excited me and fit my personal style," said Lindy West.[7]

The unpleasant aspects of shopping can be magnified when you know your choice will likely be criticized. It's easy to pick the wrong thing or to be confused about what will look good and be comfortable under hot lights or when standing at a lectern. For both the fashionista and for those who view clothes as an afterthought, there are options that will help keep the attention on the message, not the heel height or hemline. The following guidelines will help ensure that you don't fall prey to shopping faux pas, overly eager stylists, creepy TV executives, or sexist comments.

Test Drive the Outfit

1. Public speaking is a physical activity. In some scenarios, you need to be able to stand for long periods, walk comfortably, sit, and move your arms.
2. Clothing choices should be practical. Pockets are handy for notecards, tissues, throat lozenges, or a clicker.
3. A waist band or jacket pocket will hold a microphone power pack.
4. A good fit, no matter your size, will be more comfortable.
5. Accessories like bracelets can be noisy, and large rings can be visually distracting.
6. Shoes should not pinch or cause blisters.

Wardrobe Malfunctions

1. Slightly short skirts can ride up when you're seated, exposing your thighs.
2. Wrap and slit skirts fall open.
3. Fidgeting with clothes might be perceived as nervousness.
4. A low-cut blouse will reveal cleavage when you tilt forward in a chair.
5. Button-front shirts can gap at the bust line.
6. Tucked-in shirts bunch, wrinkle, and dampen with perspiration.
7. Light-colored clothes show stains, perspiration, or dark-colored underclothes.
8. Dangling metal earrings catch the light.
9. Microphones pick up clinking bracelets.
10. Long necklaces draw attention to the bust.

Seven Go-To Pieces

1. A contemporary suit with pants or skirt in a solid, flattering color.

2. A three-quarter-sleeve or long-sleeve dress with an A-line skirt.
3. A sheath dress with a matching jacket.
4. A tunic-length blouse that covers your rear end, in a solid, flattering color.
5. A fitted but not tight cardigan sweater that can substitute as jacket.
6. A solid denim shirt for causal or outdoor events.
7. Comfortable shoes for parades and rallies.

CAMERA-READY

What looks good in person may look different or not so good on camera. The camera technology and lighting change the way clothing colors, patterns, and fabrics show up. Digital technology magnifies skin discolorations; perspiration will gleam; and hair can appear to conceal your eyes. Even if you never wear makeup, there are three items you should use: a liquid foundation for your face, powder to absorb shine, and lipstick in a matte finish—not shiny or glossy. If you have dark circles under your eyes, you may also want to add concealer.

Be aware of the background of the studio set or interview location. If the backdrop is light in color, a beige top and light skin blend in. Many TV news programs have busy, multi-colored backdrops, and at the bottom of the screen text constantly scrolls. In that scenario, a simple, dark-colored top is the best choice. On some programs, you may appear on split screen with other guests, so a brighter, solid-color top will stand out.

Best Choices for On-Camera Appearances

1. Solid, rich blues and purples are universally flattering colors. They match all skin tones.
2. Avoid patterns like checks and stripes, which create a moiré effect, meaning they appear to move.

3. Necklines appear lower—crew or boatneck tops are safe choices.
4. Natural fabrics with rough or bumpy textures look better than shiny ones, which can reflect light.
5. Headscarves in solid, complexion-flattering shades are best.
6. The two-eyebrow rule: If the viewer can't see both of your eyebrows, your hair is likely casting a shadow across your eyes.
7. Contemporary, flattering haircuts are preferred. Avoid outdated styles.
8. Wire-rim, rimless, or light-colored eyeglass frames are better for on-screen appearances. Dark, heavy frames cast shadows. Have a nonreflective coating put on the lenses.

REDEFINING THE LOOK AND SOUND OF LEADERSHIP

One of the tropes of public-speaking coaching is the advice to "just be yourself." However, it's hard to be yourself when you know that everything you say and do is put under the microscope of audience scrutiny. This is a conundrum faced by all women leaders, especially the progressive women candidates I've worked with. We've spent many years trying to figure out how they can demonstrate that they have the right stuff without, as the pollster Celinda Lake would say, coming across as the type of woman who would bring a briefcase to church.

The way women are presenting themselves in the 2018 election cycle is different. We used to think the way for a woman to show that she was a leader was to adopt a business-executive look. Candidates are putting themselves out there in ways they were afraid to in the past or had been advised not to. Women on the campaign trail are saving the black blazer and pumps for debate day and donning rainbows scarves, baby carriers, and tennis shoes. These optics are breaking through a political environment crowded with old, white men in gray suits and redefining what leadership looks and sounds like. I hope the change is permanent, and I hope it empowers all people to be themselves.

WELL-SPOKEN WOMEN RESIST, INSIST, PERSIST

STAND UP for stage presence.
Build vocal gravitas with power sounds.
Well-dressed is well-spoken.

PART IV

SHE SPOKE IN ARENAS FAR AND WIDE . . .

CHAPTER 8

PREPARATION IS QUEEN

*"Everyone wants to be Beyoncé. But you don't wanna
put in the work."*

—Cookie Lyon, *Empire*

It takes work to sound like yourself. Those who make it look casy have workcd the hardest. Case in point, Mindy Kaling's commence-ment speech at Harvard Law School in 2014:

> Even though I have no idea why I was asked to speak here today, I prepared a speech very carefully. The way that any good Dartmouth-educated graduate would. I drank a 40 of Jägermeister. I called my dad to see if he could get me out of it. But, he could not. I tried to hire a college freshman to write it for mc in exchange for a $200 gift card to Newbury Comics. That didn't work out.
>
> Finally, seeing that I absolutely had to do this and couldn't get out of it, I rolled up my sleeves. Sat down at my computer. And ... tried to buy a commencement address off of movingcom-mencementspeeches.com. My credit card was declined. So, I had to write the thing myself.[1]

Mindy Kaling's feigned approach to preparation probably isn't too far off the mark from your own occasional attempts to cut corners. We've all looked for ways to circumvent the work. However, writing in a style as personable and effortless as Mindy's requires real effort. Blood, toil, tears, and sweat might be an overstatement. But most speakers experience some degree of hair pulling before the content is ready to share.

So how much effort does it take? The amount of preparation time is a one-to-one ratio. What that means is for every minute you plan to speak, you need to have spent at least an hour preparing.

PREP EQUATION

1 hour of prep for every 1 minute of talk

The prep equation is meant to shock and awe. Some people will invariably roll their eyes and say, "You must be kidding!" The ratio may strike you as beyond the realm of possibility given the multitasking you are already doing with home and work responsibilities. But it's not an exaggeration, and it helps dispel the notion that the best speakers were simply born with the talent. While natural ability may be a factor, it is not the main reason the best succeed.

Take comfort in knowing that the people who are top-level speakers make the magic happen through hard work and the assistance of others. There's no pixie dust. Let me pull back the curtain and assure you that high-profile public figures have teams—coaches, writers, schedulers, and stylists. The bulk of preparation time is taken up with the strategic planning, writing, rewriting, and rehearsal. Team members think through every aspect of every speaking event.

Preparation is truly queen. This chapter breaks down how to prepare step-by-step. The process begins with gathering the logistical and event information so you can tailor the talk to the audience and the occasion. There are specific suggestions on how to lay out a speech text or notes to aid delivery, and how to design visual aids to emphasize what's most important. Practice tips will help you maximize rehearsal time and take the edge off your nerves.

UNPLUGGED BUT NOT UNSCRIPTED

Preparation starts with advancing the speaking event and gathering information about the audience so you know what's expected of you. Then you can begin the process of writing the remarks, developing visual aids and other support materials, and scheduling rehearsal time.

Pose the following questions to event organizers in advance so you can gauge how much time and effort will be required to prepare. Find out how much flexibility there is with the agenda and your speaking slot. Are the organizers willing to modify the event so that it works with your schedule and is well-suited to your speaking strengths?

RESEARCHING THE EVENT

1. Who is hosting the event, and what is the purpose?
2. What do they want you to talk about? If needed, is there flexibility with the topic?
3. At what time will you speak and for how long? Can the length be adjusted?
4. When and where will the event take place?
5. Are there other speakers on the program?
6. Who will introduce you? Is it possible for you to write your own intro?
7. Are they planning a question-and-answer period? Will there be a moderator to assist? Can the Q&A session be modified?
8. Will media be present? If so, can the coverage be limited?
9. Will the event be livestreamed or recorded?

LOGISTICS

1. How large is the event space, and how is the seating arranged?
2. How far away is the audience seated?
3. Is a speaker's lectern available? How tall is it?
4. If seated, what type of chairs are they planning to use? Can this be changed?
5. What type of microphones are available?
6. Is there rehearsal time? When can A/V equipment be tested?
7. What's the best way to share handouts or other takeaway material?
8. Do they need your bio, headshot, and/or topic blurb?
9. Is there a break before you speak so there is time to set up after previous speakers?
10. Is food being served while you are talking?
11. If outside, what is the contingency plan for bad weather?

The reconnaissance and logistical questions help you decide whether to accept an invitation and ensure you meet the expectations of the event planners. They also inform what you will need to prepare and how much time will be required for your preparation. Being realistic about the commitment from the outset helps you avoid last-minute crunch time and feeling overwhelmed as the speaking date draws near.

It's also necessary to gauge who will be in the room and why they are there. Chapter 5 focused on techniques to articulate why you care about the subject matter and how it is relevant to the listeners. Here are some additional questions to drill down on the audience's interests and expectations. With a thorough understanding of them in advance, you will be better able to motivate them.

WHO ARE THEY AND WHY ARE THEY THERE?

1. What is the demographic makeup? Female/male, young/old, urban/rural, black/white, liberal/conservative, and economically secure/insecure?
2. How familiar are they with your topic? Are they peers, supervisors, or subordinates?
3. Are they experts or nonexperts in your field?
4. What is your relationship to them? Are you meeting for the first time or are they well-known to you?
5. Do they have an opinion of you? Have you spoken to them previously?
6. What is their attitude about the subject matter? Are there areas of disagreement? Are they skeptical? Are they misinformed?
7. How does the subject matter impact their decision-making?

TOOLS TO POWER DELIVERY

Along with the message boxes in chapter 6 and the power moves and power sounds in chapter 7, there are power tools that will signal to the audience you are a professional who came ready to deliver her best. The use of well-laid out notes and well-designed visuals can boost your performance and ensure the audience takes away the most salient points.

The speaker who uses prepared notes will give a better talk than someone who is struggling to decipher handwritten scribbles. A speech text should be formatted differently than a standard document. Standing at a lectern with the lights dimmed, a 12-point font may not be legible. Last-minute changes added in the margins and crossed-out lines can trip you up.

There are options for how to lay out the remarks. There is no one right way. What you decide will depend on your level of experience, the type of speaking event, and what works best for you. Find out how the stage will be set up. Will there be a lectern for notes, or will you be seated? Is a teleprompter an option?

Some people tell themselves they will memorize the talk, but that adds needless pressure. A good way to make a mistake is to rely on memorization. If your mind goes blank, you are up there with no backup. Memorizing a speech can also result in a monotone delivery style because the presenter is focused on the getting the words out in a certain order rather than concentrating on the meaning behind the words.

FULL-TEXT SCRIPT

A full-text script is a good approach for more-formal events and for longer presentations. A full text is not meant to be read word for word. What's key is to lay out the copy so it's legible and so it's a guide for strong delivery. Reformatting the pages ensures that you are able to see the words and make eye contact with the audience. If you use standard-sized printer paper, you will need to stand at a lectern. It is too cumbersome to hold paper that size in your hands.

Full-Page Formatting Tips

1. Increase the font to size 16 or larger so each line is shorter. This reduces the need for your eye to scan long lines of text.
2. Adjust the page margins so that the words appear at the top of the page and stop about two-thirds of the way down. A large margin at the bottom keeps you from having to dip your head down to see the last lines.
3. Use a familiar font and use upper and lower case. AVOID ALL CAPS BECAUSE IT IS MORE DIFFICULT TO READ.
4. Break lines and paragraphs for pauses. For example:

"Whatever you choose,
However many roads you travel,
I hope that you choose—not to be a lady.
I hope you will find some way to break the rules
And make a little trouble out there.
And, I also hope that you will choose to make some of
    that trouble
On behalf of other women.
Thank you. Good luck.
The first act of your life is over.
Welcome to the best years of your lives."
                    —Nora Ephron, commencement speech,
                                    Wellesley, 1996

5. Don't have a single line jump from one page to another. Always finish sentences on one page.
6. Add delivery reminders in parenthesis so you don't read them aloud. For example, (PAUSE).
7. Number the pages. The longer the talk, the more likely it is you will wind up with out-of-order pages. Heaven forbid you should drop them on the way to the lectern.
8. Use slightly heavier paper stock. It is easier to handle when you're nervous and your hands are sweaty. You can grab and move individual pages.
9. Never staple the pages together, because they become more cumbersome to turn.
10. At the lectern, start with the first two pages laid out in front of you like two pages of a book. Then, simply slide one page across from left to right. That way you avoid flipping the pages, which is visible to the audience.

THE OUTLINE

When well-versed in the subject matter or for a shorter talk you may elect to use an outline approach to notes. An outline helps you remember the flow of the content, key points, important details such as names and stats, and stories. It provides the flexibility to easily add or subtract material. Many speakers start with a full text and then move to an outline when they feel confident with what they want to say.

Note cards will work for a full text as well as for an outline. Cards can help you look and feel more "in the moment" and connected to the audience. Card stock is stiffer than regular paper and easier to hold. Use them when a lectern isn't available.

Tips for Note Cards:

1. Use either 3×5 or 5×8 cards. Smaller cards will slip into a jacket pocket.
2. Use one main heading or idea per card.
3. Write clearly or use a larger font.
4. Only use one side of the card so you don't have to flip them over.
5. Always number all cards.
6. Practice aloud with the cards to figure out if you need additional prompts for transitions or stories.
7. For accuracy, jot down stats, names of organizations, and anything that is difficult to remember.
8. Avoid waving the cards when gesturing.
9. Hold the cards flat in one hand, and they are nearly invisible to the audience.

SOFTWARE APPS

Delivering a speech to a large group while looking down at a cell phone can be distracting to the audience members. Holding the phone can look and feel awkward, limits gestures, and can be a barrier between you and them. Interfacing with the gadget breaks your connection with the people in the room as you attempt to find your place on a small screen. For them, it's a bit rude to watch a presenter scroll through page after page. Some presenters have found themselves in the embarrassing position of having a phone ring midway through a talk. A better choice is to add speaker notes to a visual aid, such as when you are using a slide deck like PowerPoint. Reminders about what you want to say can be added at the bottom of the slides that are only visible to the speaker. Be careful not to try to jam too much into the limited space.

There are a growing number of apps for smartphones and note-pads that perform a variety of different functions to help you prepare for speeches and/or manage stage fright. Teleprompter apps are available for smartphones and notepads. The notepad apps can be useful if you want to produce video of yourself. The teleprompter attaches to the front of a camera so you can look directly into the camera while reading a script that rolls across the screen. Similarly, phone apps allow you to add a text overlay to the screen so you can read a script on the screen.

Smartphone apps can record you while you practice and log a script of what you said. The app will tell you when you paused and how many "ums" you used. There is a virtual-reality app that creates a 3-D experience as if you were in a room with an audience. It is designed to replicate a speaking venue with a lectern and rows of people watching you speak. You may also listen to guided-meditation apps before a talk to help calm your nerves.

VISUALS AIDS

Relegate text-heavy slides to the dustbin. The presenter who uses visually outdated slides risks putting the audience to sleep with ideas that look dull and drab. If you're on a program with other speakers using clean, dynamic images with simple text you by comparison will appear lazy and lackluster.

Don't begin the writing process with a slide-deck template. Decide what you are going to say first and then chose the visual that supports the message. No matter what type of visual you choose, the bottom line is they are aids. The presenter should drive the presentation. Don't allow visuals to become a crutch.

Well-designed visual aids can add a big impact for the viewer. Memes, photographs, art, animated GIFs, and video break through clutter to capture the audience's attention and sustain it. Pictures create a richer experience by providing additional information and context that supports what you are saying. Good interface with strong visuals makes the presenter appear more professional and relevant to the audience.

The more technically advanced the talk, the greater the need for practice. Hollywood producer Michael Bay learned this the hard way when, at the 2014 Consumer Electronics Show, he fled the stage after only 60 seconds before a jam-packed auditorium. Bay initially claimed that the teleprompter operator messed up. But later he admitted that he couldn't continue because he hadn't rehearsed, wasn't familiar with the stage setup, and didn't know anything about the fancy TV he was there to pitch.

Choose a visual that complements your speaking style and is well-suited to the speaking venue. Below are some advantages and disadvantages of different types of visual aids.

PRESENTATION SOFTWARE—SLIDE DECKS

1. Suitable for meetings, conferences, and training workshops.
2. Political candidates should avoid using them because they can feel too canned.
3. Easy to use.
4. Standard templates limit creativity for text.
5. Possible to add video and photographs.
6. Design to look like highway billboards—easy to read at 55 mph.
7. Avoid heavy text and unfamiliar fonts.
8. Compatible with most A/V setups.

INTERNET-BASED SLIDES

1. Suitable for more-formal events such as keynotes, conferences, and board presentations.
2. Allows online collaboration and sharing with others.
3. Add video, audio, animation, and 3-D effects to boost attention.
4. Ability to create interactive exercises with audience.
5. Built-in timers aid pacing.
6. Interface can be tricky, requiring more practice time.
7. Some programs pull in live tweets or blog feeds.
8. May not be compatible in some offices or conference-room setups.
9. Ability to edit on a smartphone.

ERASABLE BOARDS AND FLIP CHARTS

1. Low-tech alternative suitable for training workshops and smaller groups.

2. Allows you to take notes on audience comments.
3. Great for brainstorming exercises.
4. Creates an "in the moment" feel.
5. Smaller sizes are portable.
6. Difficult to see in large rooms with large audiences.

PROPS

1. Suitable for most venues.
2. Memorable: Scientist Jill Bolte Taylor held an actual human brain in her hands to discuss the stroke she suffered.[2]
3. Adds unexpected element: Author Amy Tan revealed her creative muse to be the Yorkshire Terrier hidden in a bag onstage.[3]
4. Can be used to demonstrate a task or product.
5. Requires more prep time.
6. Must thoroughly rehearse.

PREPARATION MEANS PRACTICE

> *"You criticized me for preparing for this debate. And, yes, I did. Do you know what else I prepared for? I also prepared to be president."[4]*
>
> —Hillary Clinton

Approach practice in an organized fashion. One way to establish a regimen is to emulate what athletes do to build on core strengths and minimize weaknesses. Like sports, the act of public speaking requires mental and physical exertion. Innate ability is just a starting point— the athletes who are the most disciplined and work the hardest achieve more in the long run. Venus and Serena Williams own the tennis courts because of natural athletic ability plus years of disciplined workouts and top-level competition.

WELL-SPOKEN WOMEN AT WORK

Author Malcom Gladwell generated controversy when he wrote that it takes ten thousand hours of practice to become an expert at anything. Scientists say excellence isn't dependent on a set number of practice hours. Rather, improvement comes through a combination of factors including practice time, how you practice, and innate ability.[5]

There is agreement that people have a tremendous ability to improve performance when they train the right way. And when they keep at the work of getting better—whether it be for a few hours or a few thousand. Everyone has the potential to make progress over time.

Beyoncé scheduled eleven-hour rehearsal sessions to get her one-hundred-member band into formation for her 2018 Coachella performance.[6]

Lady Gaga said she spent her entire life preparing for the Super Bowl LI halftime show.[7]

Eleanor Roosevelt gave 1,300 speeches while First Lady.

For her Supreme Court nomination hearings, judge Sonia Sotomayor spent days undergoing intense grilling in mock hearings and met privately with over seventy senators.[8]

Viola Davis wrote a fifty-page biography of her Oscar-nominated character, Mrs. Miller, for her sole scene in *Doubt*.[9]

Where you are now is not where you can be. The real pros know there is always something that needs more work. They don't make the mistake of telling themselves there is nothing left to learn. To get better, they work at getting better. Along with skill building, practice helps you anticipate possible pitfalls so you can be ready to manage them.

LEARN FROM PRACTICE

Once a near-final written draft of the talk is ready, it's time to practice so you can test how it sounds. With the words in place, you can make decisions about how to best express a point. It is difficult to add vocal power when speaking off the cuff or in the heat of the moment. Practicing aloud with written remarks greatly enhances your ability to deliver them well.

Anyone who has ever told a story knows that most stories improve with repetition. It's difficult to nail the details on the first telling. Decisions need to be made about what content is necessary to drive the story and what is extraneous. Practice helps you avoid rambling.

This is especially important when talking about personal subjects such as #MeToo, gun violence, or abortion stories. It is necessary to decide in advance how much to tell and what to leave out. You need to know how to handle what makes you vulnerable so you can avoid becoming overly emotional in front of an audience. There still exists a double standard on displays of emotion. When a man sheds a tear, he is praised for being human. For women, it's a sign of weakness.

The best approach to practice is to videotape yourself. For videotaping, a camcorder on a tripod will ensure you avoid shaky-cam footage. Small tripods are also available to fit smartphones. Ideally, you will run through the presentation in its entirety or do a mock practice interview. Then playback the tape to review the content, vocal quality, and nonverbal techniques. The following summary is a handy guide of what to look and listen for when you review the tape.

POWER MOVES

- Steady eye contact
- Good posture
- Interactive body movement

- Open hand gestures
- Welcoming facial expression

POWER SOUNDS

- Rate of speech
- Amount of inflection
- Use of pauses

POWER WORDS

- Call to action is clear
- Open and close are compelling
- Concrete ideas
- Purposeful storytelling
- Jargon-free language

If you don't have time to videotape the entire talk, taping even a few minutes will still make a difference. Focus on the first three minutes to ensure a strong open and transition into the first main point. Audiences remember best what they hear first. Rehearse getting to the theme or a main point quickly—try to do it in the first 30 to 90 seconds. Concentrate your remaining practice time on delivering a memorable close. Audiences remember second-best what they hear last. If video isn't an option, stand in front of a mirror and say the words aloud. Or make an audio recording.

LEARN FROM GAME TAPES

Reviewing video from an actual speaking event is also an efficient way to promote continuous learning and to gain a more accurate assessment of how you are doing. Whenever possible, ask the event organizer for a copy of your talk. Real-life performances are opportunities to gauge both how you did and how the audience reacted.

It's a good idea to do a post-event assessment immediately after you leave the stage. However, you probably haven't come down from the performance high and may not be able to fully assess how it went. Your perception may be too negative if you were nervous or if something minor went astray. Or it could be inaccurate if you were unaware of a delivery tic that was distracting to the audience. Waiting a couple of days to review video with fresh eyes will round out your initial perception.

Seek out feedback from colleagues and people who will provide constructive criticism. Develop a written feedback system so you can solicit comments from a range of people. Logging the feedback will enable you to chart progress over time. A review of past notes prior to the next event will serve as a clear reminder of what skills need attention. This prevents you from repeating mistakes as well as builds on what you have learned.

PREPARATION CALMS NERVES

"But I am happy that I'm nervous. I care, is basically what that means."[10]

—actress Jane Krakowski

Being nervous can also suck.

Let's face it: there are few emotional and physical experiences more depleting, frightening, or confidence-shattering than the discomfort and mental torture that can accompany talking in front of others.

For most people, making the time to prepare the content and rehearse can go a long way to reducing the level of anxiety they experience. The degree to which you are nervous is impacted by the Self-Awareness Quotient factors discussed in chapter 2. Your responses to the questions about the SAQ factors provide answers to why and when anxiety is most likely to strike. For the occasions when your stress levels spike, there are specific techniques to calm your nerves.

Physical and mental relaxation exercises can help ensure anxiety doesn't zap the joy out of a speaking event. These exercises can be performed beforehand to relieve the physical symptoms of the fight-or-flight response. Having a set routine of warm-ups will quiet your pounding heart and deepen your shallow breathing. During the talk, these techniques will also ensure that you are able to keep anxiety at bay.

BEST WAYS TO RELAX

Deep Breathing

Proper breath support is key to staying in control. Rapid, shallow breathing in the chest can impact the quality of your voice. Standing onstage and hearing yourself speak in a false falsetto like Minnie Mouse can be an out-of-body experience. A modified yoga breath will slow your racing heart and allow you to control your speaking pace and pitch. Take a deep breath in through the nose, hold it for two or three counts, and then audibly exhale through your mouth. Repeat this slowly as many times as needed.

Use the deep breaths while you are waiting your turn to speak. You can even use a less exaggerated version of the breath while you are talking. During a pause, take the breath in and hold it for a second or two, and begin talking as you exhale. No one will notice what you are doing, and you will be able to modulate your sound.

Body Movement

If anxiety makes you jittery, you need to expend the excess energy before you go onstage so it doesn't build up. Slowly walk down a hallway and swing your arms back and forth across your chest. Take long, purposeful strides. For some people, power posing is a favorite technique. Power posing is standing in positions that elongate your limbs and make you larger, like Wonder Woman's famous stance or the warrior pose in yoga. Focus on stretching the muscles in your back so they are loose and relaxed.

When seated before it's your turn to you speak, it's possible to relax nearly every muscle in your body. Lean forward in the chair while holding onto the armrests to stretch out your back. When you lean back, shift your body weight from one cheek to the other. Or, slowly cross and uncross your legs. More tension can be released with simple ankle turns. Slowly, deliberately turn your ankle five times in one direction and then five times in the other direction. Exercise both ankles.

Neck and Shoulder Turns

While standing, drop your arms at your sides and slowly roll your shoulders back to open and expand the chest. Repeat several times slowly. Drop your chin to your chest and roll your head side to side 180 degrees. Avoid rolling your head in a circle because this may strain your neck.

Jaw Opener

Slowly scrunch the muscles in your face, squeezing them into the middle around your nose. Hold for a second or two, then slowly release and open your jaw. Work the muscles in your jaw by slowly sliding it back and forth. Open your eyes wide, hold, and release.

Mental Release

While you are working through the physical warmup exercises, you can negate worry and self-doubt by practicing positive visualization. Positive visualization is another technique utilized by athletes as well as stage-performing artists. Oprah Winfrey uses affirmations—positive goal statements spoken aloud—to push herself to the next level.[11] Many athletes use mental imagery that involves all of the senses. They smell the ball leather, feel the sweat on their neck, hear the crowd cheer.

Positive visualization directs mental energy to the execution of proactive movements. Athletes feel themselves going through the motions of hitting the ball, crossing the finish line, making the shot. This technique is well-suited to gearing up for any type of public-speaking event. Mentally visualize yourself delivering the speech the way you want it to go. See yourself walk confidently to the front of the room, hear yourself warmly greet the audience, watch their heads nod encouragement, soak in the applause at the end. The exercise helps you develop and hold a visual blueprint of how you want the speaking engagement to go, step by step.

At the same time, the technique refocuses your thoughts away from all the possible negative outcomes that drag energy and create bad feelings. It's about replacing negative self-talk with positive self-talk. When doubts creep in, remind yourself about the preparation steps you've taken to ensure the talk goes the way you want it to. Tell yourself what you are going to do and how you are going to do it.

DEALING WITH ANXIETY TRIGGERS

There are potential problems that may trigger anxiety or increase your level of physical discomfort. When you feel the onrush of stage fright, keep in mind that what you are experiencing onstage is different from what the audience is experiencing while they watch you. They may not be aware of the stress you feel unless you telegraph it to them. If you are in a large room standing several feet away, they likely will not see the perspiration or the tremble. Drawing attention to your distress focuses everyone's attention on a negative.

In a smaller room with people in closer proximity, your discomfort may be more apparent. You may want to acknowledge the nerves, and you can do so in a way that encourages the audience to root for you. For example, "I'm feeling a little nervous because what we are talking about really matters to me." Everyone gets nervous, and people will empathize with what you are going through, especially if you put a positive spin on it.

Rather than dwelling on what could go wrong, here is a list of the solutions to prevent or alleviate any problems.

The Problem	The Solution
My Voice Quivers	Deep breathing before speech to warm up vocal cords. Drink room-temperature water. Pause during talk to breathe.
Cotton Mouth	Put a small piece of a throat lozenge in back of mouth. Use an OTC dry-mouth product. Or try slowly and firmly biting down on the back of your tongue to generate saliva.
Profuse Sweating / Hot Flash	Dress in thin layers. Have a tissue to blot. Stay hydrated.
Blushing	Focusing on it can increase intensity. Accept it and focus outward on what's happening around you, not on yourself.
Can't Breathe	Pause to breathe—3 seconds for a deep breath. Have a preplanned question for the audience. While they are responding, take a deep breath.

I Forgot What I Want to Say	Go to the next point in your prepared notes or message box. Audience will not know unless you tell them.
Technical Glitches	Arrive early to test equipment. Calmly acknowledge the issue and have a plan B teed up.
Heckler	Ignore. See chapter 4.
Audience Is Flat	Recognize it's probably not you. Cut the talk short or involve them by asking a question.
People Think I'm Not Qualified	Credential yourself. See chapter 4 for ideas.
Talk Too Fast	The eye-contact quadrant technique in chapter 7 will slow you down. Deliver an entire short sentence to one person without looking away. Then pause and turn to someone else.
Can't Answer a Question	Use a pivot technique covered in chapter 9. *Here's what I can tell you . . .*

YOU GO, GIRL!

Well-spoken women achieve success over time. There really is no such thing as an overnight success. Every individual starts in her own place and moves at her own pace.

Becoming well-spoken is a process of setting goals, seeking assistance, and accepting failure along with success. Improvement comes when you make time to prepare, rehearse your message, deliver before an audience, analyze feedback, and refine your technique. As Beyoncé says, "I can never be safe. I always try and go against the grain. As soon as I accomplish one thing, I just set a higher goal. That is how I've gotten to where I am."[12]

Every time you stand up to speak out, you have the opportunity to learn something new. Here are four proactive steps for your learning journey.

1. Do to Improve

The way to build public-speaking skills is by doing. This guidebook provides tools to help you work on technique, but nothing can substitute for real-life experience. If you are a beginner or experience stage fright, make the first steps smaller ones. Ask a question during a panel discussion. Volunteer to do an introduction. Give a brief thank you at the office going-away party. Attend a Toastmaster meeting to practice and get feedback from other aspiring speakers. The organization has chapters around the country that provide a supportive, learn-by-doing environment.

If becoming a media spokesperson is your goal, don't wait for an invitation to be a guest on MSNBC. Start getting ready now by seeking out radio interviews and podcasts. There is less pressure when you aren't on camera. Branch out to local cable programs and edited television interviews. Get experience under the lights and in the studio to ensure your first live, national appearance is a breakout moment.

Seek out opportunities to talk at social gatherings. Book club is a chance to offer a brief summary of plot twists and turns. Deliver a toast at your friend's shower. Lead your family in prayer at the next holiday gathering. The pressure is less intense in familiar settings. And friends and family will be touched by your thoughtfulness.

2. Get Yourself Some Coaching

"You can't be good all the time. You need to be good when it's time."[13] That's the advice Céline Dion gives to aspiring vocalists. The multiple-Grammy winner still works with a vocal coach to keep her instrument in shape. It's important and often necessary to invest in personal and professional growth. A speech coach can pinpoint strengths and areas of improvement to build skills more quickly. Speechwriters can add extra sparkle and depth to content. Vocal coaches and speech therapists are experts who can improve your sound and aid with stuttering or other speech disorders.

Professional consultants can provide a fresh perspective and give frank advice that some leaders need to hear. My goal as a coach is to provide constructive feedback in an unthreatening manner. And I often work with communication teams to help ensure the top spokesperson has everything she needs for a major appearance.

3. Reach Back and Lift Up

As you climb, be sure to pull others along. Within your organization, work to build an atmosphere where everyone's confidence can flourish. Institute your own version of the amplification technique deployed by the women in the Obama White House. Amplify good work by letting a colleague know she has done well on the spot. "Atta girls" go a long way. Deserved praise gives people a more accurate sense of how they come across, fine-tuning their self-awareness.

"I have two words to leave you with tonight ladies and gentleman: inclusion rider."[14] Actress Frances McDormand educated a whole lot of people with the conclusion to her rousing acceptance speech at the 2018 Oscars. She was referring to a contract provision that allows A-list actors to stipulate that diversity be reflected in personnel on camera and behind the scenes. When you are seated in a room where decisions are being made, look around the table. Are you the only woman? Are there any people of color? Ask yourself, what can I do to make this group more inclusive?

4. See the Good

Give credit when it's due, especially to yourself. Public speaking is hard work. You know you will hold yourself accountable when something goes wrong, so give yourself credit when things go right. Say good-bye to the imposter syndrome. Say hello to "I done good."

My favorite power pose is the one where you take your right hand, lift it high above your head, then reach down and pat yourself on the back.

WELL-SPOKEN WOMEN RESIST, INSIST, PERSIST

Preparation = Confidence.
The right tools build a strong foundation.
Mental and physical prep deplete stage fright.

CHAPTER 9

MEDIA INTERVIEWS AND DEBATES

"Sometimes when someone is making an idiot of them-selves, especially on live television, it's just better to let them go ahead."

—Cecile Richards, *Make Trouble*

It's 3:00 p.m. on a Friday; the phone rings, and it's a producer at CNN who would like you to be a guest on a weekend show.

A reporter from the *New York Times* has emailed and needs a quote right now for an online story.

C-SPAN will air a candidate debate forum, and it will be the first live broadcast appearance with your opponent.

Before you say no or start to panic, hold on a second. Ask yourself, "How will this help me achieve my goals?" Media opportunities provide an excellent way to get your message to a target audience. Put aside the excuses not to do it. Think proactively about what you need to do to get ready.

What it takes to prepare will depend on what type of appearance it is and your experience level. Is it a brief telephone interview or a longer in-person session? Are they asking you to be live in the studio or can it be done via video chat from your office? Will there be multiple guests on a podcast, or is it a one-on-one with a boldface cable network host?

The prep regimen for any media scenario involves three steps: (1) understanding the format; (2) preparing tools for handling questions and opposition arguments; and (3) rehearsing delivery techniques in mock practice scenarios. The following interview and debate guidelines will help you say yes to opportunities without hesitation and with confidence. Specific tips are provided for edited and live interviews, talk shows, satellite and video chats, and candidate debate forums.

THE INTERVIEW FORMAT

Always gather information about the reporter, the media organization, and how the content will be used before agreeing to the interview. Don't assume that you know what the reporter is looking for or how the information you provide will be used. Every request should be evaluated to ensure that it is the right fit for achieving your goals.

These questions help you gauge whether to do the interview and what it will take to prepare:

1. What is the topic of the story? Ask the reporter to be specific about their angle.
2. Who is the reporter/what is their style? If unknown, do a search. Read past articles or listen to the program.
3. What is the media organization? If it's unfamiliar to you, look them up.
4. Will the interview be live, live on tape, or edited?
5. How long will the interview run?
6. Will the content appear online, on air, in print, or a combination?
7. Who are the other sources?
8. On talk shows, will there be other guests? Will you appear simultaneously?
9. What is the reporter's deadline?

When to Say No

There are a few situations when the best decision is to decline an interview request.

- You are not the appropriate spokesperson.
- The timing is not right on a strategic level.
- The topic is a "hot potato" that doesn't lend itself to a productive discussion.
- There is not enough time or information to prepare for tough questions.

Requests from extreme conservatives and alt-right groups like Breitbart News Network, Fox News, and Sinclair Broadcasting need to be weighed carefully. Groups that report biased content and promote overtly racist and sexist points of view operate in fact-free zones. Fox News host Sean Hannity, who self-describes as an "opinion journalist," told the *New York Times* that his show hinges on a "nostalgia for an America he feels is slipping away."[1] Evaluate each program, host, and interview subject to make a strategic decision about the pros and cons of attempting to engage audience members that may not be persuadable. Your experience and skill level should also factor into whether or not it makes sense to deal with media outlets that peddle scare tactics, propaganda, and extreme right-wing commentary.

Once you've evaluated the request, more often than not you will make the decision to proceed with the interview. If you do need to decline a request from a reputable news organization, explain why to the reporter. If the topic isn't in your area of expertise, suggest a like-minded colleague as a substitute. This provides an opportunity for another progressive spokesperson to weigh in. And it keeps you on good terms with the reporter for future coverage.

HANDLING QUESTIONS

The bulk of interview prep time and energy should be focused on what you plan to say and how to convey it. The message box and triangle templates provided in chapter 6 provide a step-by-step guide. For topics that you want to address proactively, start creating message boxes now so you are ready when a reporter reaches out to you. That way, when the call comes in, your prep time will be limited to minor tweaks that reflect the news cycle. And you will have time to craft a sound bite tailored to the interview request.

With the message ready to go, the next step is anticipating the questions. Most questions can be predicted in advance. For example, if you are a candidate running for office, the most commonly asked question is, "Why are you running?" Be ready for the seemingly easy questions; the softballs are the ones interviewees tend to whiff. The Candidate Message Triangle helps you give a substantive answer in sound-bite form.

The types of questions generally follow a pattern. Most interviews begin with open-ended ones such as, "Tell me about that . . . Why do you think that happened? How did that make you feel . . . ?" Skilled reporters will start with easy questions to give you a chance to warm up and—they hope—to let your guard down. Ana Marie Cox summed up the technique she used as the Talk columnist for the *New York Times Sunday Magazine*, "I let the subject exhaust that line of conversation, like an owner tiring out a dog on however long a walk was needed to make them more pliable and relaxed once they returned home, to the conversation I really wanted to have."[2]

Expect the reporter to move on to more challenging questions: "What went wrong? Do you agree with that . . . ? What should have been done differently?" Reporters frequently phrase their questions with a negative premise, "Why didn't you see the problem? Who's to blame?" "Would you say that was a mistake in judgment?" Be careful not to respond by repeating the negative premise. State your proactive answer so you don't respond defensively to questions that are phrased negatively.

At the end of the interview, there usually is a chance to summarize. The reporter will ask, "Is there anything else you would like to add? Is there something else I should have asked you? What else should I know?" These questions are great opportunities to share your message of change right off of the message box.

COMMON TYPES OF QUESTIONS

1. *What if . . . ?* Hypotheticals should be called out as such. Stick to the facts.
2. *Third-party or unknown source.* Only respond to statements or claims you know to be true.
3. *Wouldn't you agree . . . ?* Don't agree when you don't. Restate why you disagree.
4. *Ranking or choice.* Don't be limited to narrow choice. You can respond with "None of the above," and give your own answer.
5. *Personal opinion.* It's never obligatory to share your opinion, especially if you are speaking on behalf of an organization.
6. *Cheap shots.* Call out pettiness, set the messenger straight, and bridge to your message.

Questions will often relate to the news cycle or the trending topics of the day. You must be up to speed on breaking news when doing live interviews. In the 2016 presidential campaign, Libertarian candidate Gary Johnson was ticking up in the polls until he appeared on morning television. When asked about the refugee crisis situation in Aleppo on MSNBC's *Morning Joe*, a blank expression crossed his face and he had to ask, "What is Aleppo?"[3] His inability to respond to a question about the headline-dominating situation in the Syrian city stalled his campaign's momentum.

At the 2018 Golden Globe Awards, most attendees wore all-black outfits to show solidarity with the #MeToo movement. This led to a refreshing change in the pre-show questioning on the red carpet. The standard—"What are you wearing?" Was replaced with: "Why are you wearing black?" *Will & Grace* star Debra Messing didn't fumble but drove home the point she wanted to make about gender equity when queried by *E! News*: "Time is up and we want diversity and we want intersectional gender parity. We want equal pay, and I was so shocked to hear that *E!* doesn't believe in paying their female co-hosts the same as their male co-hosts."[4]

Debra seized the opportunity of live television to express a view that the *E! News* director was not able to edit out. The power of the live interview is whatever comes out of your mouth goes straight into your mother's ears. And everyone else's. Debra successfully furthered the Times Up agenda because she was prepared with an on-message response that criticized the network broadcasting the interview. Her daring comment ensured other media would pick it up, expanding the coverage.

Don't expect the reporter to know everything about the subject or to ask all of the right questions. Provide them with background information about the issue prior to the interview and, where appropriate, follow up with an e-mail after it's over to reinforce and substantiate your key points. Depending on the reporter's experience and level of understanding of the subject matter, they may not know what to ask. Don't wait for questions about what's on your message box. Those questions may never come, and, before you know it, you might hear, "Thanks—I've got what I need." You must inject your message points into the dialogue early and often.

STAYING ON MESSAGE

The pivot technique can be used to transition from off-track questions to the content of your message box. This technique isn't about ducking the question. Skilled reporters don't let newsmakers off the hook that easily. It is necessary to be ready with answers to tough questions. The viewing public expects a response to questions that are germane to the issue. Talking heads who talk right past the question lose credibility quickly with independent-minded news consumers.

To anticipate questions off the beaten path, review what the reporter has written in the past and how their news organization has covered the issue. Some questions will be based on what the reporter has heard from skeptics, opponents, or conservative talking points. They will ask for your response to the other side.

Use the pivot technique to respond to challenging queries and to steer the interview toward what is important. The AATM approach outlined below ensures that you are responsive but also don't get stuck on a line of questioning that is off message.

AATM

Anticipate the Question: Advance homework prepares you for tough questions.

Answer Directly: Give a brief, preformulated response to the tough question.

Transition to Message: Transition to the message.

Message: Land and end on the message box.

For most people, the transition to the message is initially difficult. It can feel uncomfortable to change the subject. Having preplanned transition phrases and practicing with them will ensure a smoother delivery. An all-purpose transition phrase is, "Here's what I can tell you . . ." It works because it sounds positive, forthcoming, and concise. Here are some variations of the all-purpose phrase.

Here's What I Can Tell You . . .

- Let me answer that question this way . . .
- Your question raises an equally important point that needs to be addressed. . . .
- The question doesn't directly address what I'm hearing . . .
- I wouldn't characterize the situation that way. What I would say is . . .
- That comes up frequently; it reminds me of a story . . .
- Let me tell you why your question is an important one . . .

Most reporters are familiar with the concept of pivoting and may try to get you to say something off message by asking you the same question repeatedly. Feel comfortable giving the same answer. Don't allow the reporter to wear you down and put words in your mouth. If the reporter becomes frustrated, calmly say that you don't have anything to add, then repeat what you want the audience to hear.

The pivot technique has its limitations and should not be viewed as a panacea, especially in live broadcast interviews. If a reporter has a tough but fair question, attempting to dodge it by using the pivot may cause audiences to believe you are hiding something or are grossly unprepared. There is no substitute for anticipating a challenging but reasonable question and being ready to respond with a direct answer. Telling it straight is the way to ensure your credibility remains undamaged.

PREP FOR SPECIFIC FORMATS

Edited Interviews

Print, radio, television, and online interviews are most often edited. Usually, a reporter is calling to get a response to breaking news. Reporters are working under tight deadlines and often only want a sound bite from you. Therefore, it's not unusual for the reporter to contact you when their story is near completion. They may be looking for a specific response. If what they want you to say is on your message box, then this will be a quick conversation.

1. Give the interview your undivided attention. When talking on the phone, don't try to multi-task by reading email or driving a car. Listen carefully.
2. Lead with your strongest sound bite. The reporter may be in a hurry. Radio and TV reporters will need to edit the tape. They may not have time to playback the entire interview.
3. Consider everything you say and do to be on the record.
4. Keep the overall interview length brief—fifteen to twenty minutes is plenty of time and will prevent you from wandering off message.
5. Notify the reporter if you are taping the interview.
6. Keep your answers short and simple. Use jargon-free language.
7. Don't respond to third-hand or unseen documentation. Ask to see it or hear it before responding.
8. On radio and TV, avoid using the reporter's name since they will need to edit it out.

LIVE TV, CABLE, OR RADIO IN-STUDIO

The first rule is to watch or listen to the program to get a sense of the overall tone, the host's style, and the types of questions typically asked. No two programs or interviewers are alike. Sitting down with TV host Megyn Kelly is different from joining Kathie Lee Gifford. Megyn honed her style as a corporate defense attorney, whereas Kathie Lee is a former actress.

The biggest mistakes made during live interviews are being too technical or long-winded. Even Judy Woodruff, host of the venerable *PBS NewsHour*, doesn't want you to launch into the minutiae of arcane policy matters. Woodruff will have substantive questions, but she's hoping you can simplify complex policy and translate legislation so the viewer will understand and be interested.

1. Treat pre-interviews on the phone as the real thing. It's an audition, and not everyone makes the cut.
2. Greet the technical crew. They can help with mics and camera angles.
3. Make a strong first impression with a confident smile and a friendly hello.
4. Lead with an on-message answer to frame the conversation. Don't expect the host to be a mind reader or to ask the right question.
5. If you are surprised by a question and don't know the answer, resist the temptation to speculate or guess. It's better to transition back to your message: "That's an important point, and what I can say about it right now is . . ." (See the above list of transition phrases.)
6. Use a conversational rate of pace.
7. Sit up, lean forward, keep hand gestures in the camera frame, and maintain steady eye contact on the questioner.
8. On longer-format radio or podcast programs there is time to give longer answers.
9. If audience questions are taken, plant a question with a colleague or supporter that you want to answer.
10. If questions are biased, call that out and respond on message.

LIVE TV OR CABLE WITH MULTIPLE GUESTS

Some live television and cable talk shows resemble mosh pits with guests talking over one another and elbows flying. The opposition will likely try to get a rise out of you, so avoid falling prey to their tactics that are intended to throw you off balance. Some program hosts are known for being antagonistic. Most of the time, it's not personal. It's okay not to like the question, but separate it from the questioner. Keep your private views about the questioner and other spokespeople private, and stick to the message box.

1. Stay Calm

Be ready to roll with the punches. This doesn't mean allowing people to roll over you by interrupting you or mansplaining. What it does mean is keeping calm, cool, and collected. And not taking the bait from opponents who might try to set you up or losing your temper by personalizing something another guest says. An angry or inappropriate outburst will be replayed and used against you long past the interview. For reminders on how to deal with bullying tactics, see chapter 4.

2. Talk to the Real Audience

Never lose sight of the real audience, which is the viewer. The program host is the conduit you use to reach the media consumer. Don't try to convince the host or argue with another guest. Always talk to the people who are watching or listening.

3. Be Ready to Interject

When the first question doesn't go to you, be aware that the clock is ticking. Use a nonverbal to signal the host that you have a counterpoint. Try shaking your head no while an opposing guest is talking. Or look directly at the host, nod your head, and raise your hand slightly to indicate that you want to talk. If the signals are ineffective, use the host's name and refer to the viewers. For example, "Mary, if I can add something. What the viewers might not know is that . . ."

If the host doesn't respond to your attempts to interject, you can use the techniques described in chapter 4 on how to break into the dialogue. There are also techniques for how to hold the floor if someone tries to talk over you.

4. Anticipate Challenges

Expect challenging questions from the host and attacks from opposing guests. They will test your strengths and exploit your weaknesses. The Opposition Message Box described in chapter 6 is designed to help you anticipate these challenges. An opposition attack can be preempted by raising a weakness in your argument with an explanation of why it's not important. Be ready to flag the weakness in the opposition's position and describe how what they propose will be harmful to the viewing audiences, for example.

5. Call Out Opponent Tactics

Some conservative commentators will attempt to disrupt your game plan by raising outrageous, off-topic points. For example, on CNN, spokesperson Symone Sanders was debating Trump mouthpiece Jeffrey Lord on Republican attempts to repeal Obamacare. Lord asked Sanders "to think of President Trump as the Martin Luther King Jr. of healthcare." Symone cut him off mid-statement, saying, "Let's not equate Dr. Martin Luther King Jr., humanitarian and Nobel Peace Prize winner, with the vagina-grabbing president, Donald Trump."[5]

Symone, who is a veteran of the talk shows, was quick on her feet and forcefully shut down the bizarre rationalization. Her response is an example of how researching the opposition's messaging and tactics pays off. Lord is a vocal Trump booster and repeatedly used race-baiting tactics during the campaign. Symone couldn't have guessed that Lord would make the comparison to the Reverend King, but she was aware of his offensive track record.

6. Push Back on Questions

Some TV hosts are better prepared than others. Some will raise insightful points and press on substance. Others may not have a grounding in the topic, and their questioning suffers. Don't feel as if you have to accept the premise of a reporter question. If the question is biased or inaccurate, flag it as such. Push back on a reporter who repeats lies for the sake of achieving balance: "That is false and a disservice to your viewers." When reporters accept untruths, they are asking their audience members to do the same. Assert that the audience deserves better.

7. Use the Pivot

When you need to redirect the dialogue, the AATM technique and the use of transition phrases will help you get the conversation back on track.

SATELLITE AND ONLINE VIDEO INTERVIEWS

In these scenarios, you are usually alone with the camera. A satellite interview is frequently conducted from a remote studio location with a camera, and you hear the questions through an earpiece called an IFB (interruptible foldback). The earpiece allows you to hear what is being said on the air and sometimes what is happening in the director's control booth.

Online video conversations can be done on a computer in your office or home, and you may need headphones to hear the questions. These interviews are an opportunity to weigh in on breaking news even when you can't travel to a studio. Take advantage of the convenience by creating a professional-looking environment. The video and audio quality can be improved if you use a camcorder that you feed into the computer rather than using the computer camera itself. If the only lighting in the room is overhead fluorescents, consider purchasing supplementary professional lights that fill in shadows and help you look more natural.

Set up your shot and find the best angle for your face and lighting. Position the camera so it is level with your eyes. If you are using a computer camera, you may need to raise or lower the height of the monitor. If the camera is shooting down at you, it diminishes your stature; and if it is shooting up, too much of your neck will show. Don't sit too close to the camera, because this will distort the picture and make your head look larger than normal.

Keep the backdrop simple. A blank wall is better than distracting clutter such as personal photographs, loud art, or busy wallpaper. A well-organized bookcase is a safe choice. Or create a camera-ready graphic with an organization logo.

Video Chat How-To

1. Position the camera at eye level.
2. Avoid wearing white ear buds.
3. Choose a neutral backdrop.
4. Brighten the space with light from the sides and below.
5. Turn your body slightly away from the camera and turn your head back square for a more flattering angle.

CANDIDATE DEBATES

On a debate stage, the candidate's job is to be the candidate. The primary responsibility is to articulate the response to one question: Why should the voters pick you and not your opponent?

A debate stage provides an unparalleled opportunity to define your candidacy, provide contrast with opponents, and demonstrate leadership. But only if you are prepared and feeling confident. Don't allow yourself to become distracted by the competing demands placed on your time from the campaign and your personal life. Avoid last-minute cram sessions by working with the campaign team to chart a plan early on. A well-organized and well-executed prep regimen ensures that you deliver a performance that creates positive buzz for polls, fundraising, and media coverage.

The campaign team should lay out a strategy for handling debate requests. What is the purpose of the debates, and what are the overall goals? Whether, when, and how many debates are accepted is best determined by assessing the candidate's strengths and weaknesses. Is the candidate a first-timer who will need more time to familiarize herself with key issues and develop policy positions? Or is she an incumbent who has a track record to defend?

Is the candidate a compelling speaker, and in what forums does she shine? Debate formats can vary widely. In primary campaigns, most are multi-candidate events that more closely resemble joint appearances rather than actual debates. The format is set up so that the candidates do not engage one another directly but rather give brief opening and closing statements and respond to a few questions. Often, the topics for the questions can be predetermined.

In general elections, the forums tend to be more traditional, one-on-one encounters, although third-party candidates may also be present. Town-hall-style debates with relaxed time limits and questions from voters are popular. An experienced moderator is necessary to enforce time limits and ensure balanced questioning. Researching the opponent's strengths and vulnerabilities must be done to anticipate attacks and formulate counterattacks.

The staffer with the strongest negotiation techniques should be tasked with securing what will benefit the campaign and what the candidate needs to perform at her best. All agreements should be in writing. The campaign should consider every detail of the format and venue to be negotiable. Is there a day, time, or place preference? How much time is allotted for questions and answers—will some be thematic?

The following questions will help the campaign negotiate a format that is best suited to the candidate.

Debate Format Questions

- What day and time will it be scheduled?
- How long will it run?
- How many candidates will participate?
- Will there be a single moderator?
- Will there be a panel of questioners?
- Will the candidates question one another?
- Will there be audience questions?
- Will there be a theme to the questions?
- What is the length of answers and rebuttals?
- Will there be follow-up questions?

- Will candidates stand or sit?
- Are the candidates allowed to walk around the stage?
- Will there be media coverage?
- What are the camera angles, and will there be reaction shots or split screens?
- What does the backdrop look like—is it busy or plain?
- Are the candidates allowed to have paper and pen onstage?

Debate Messaging

The goal of any debate is to frame the campaign as a choice and make it clear why you are the right choice. It is important to be knowledgeable on the issues the voters care about. But debates are not a test of how much data and information can be crammed into the answers. What's key is the ability to give clear, concise responses that highlight your experience and provide contrast with your opponent.

The message templates presented in chapter 6 will help you prepare for candidate forums. Showcase your experience and qualifications with the Candidate Message Triangle. It is important to share specific examples of your accomplishments, lay out an agenda for the future, and say how you will achieve results. Voters assume that male candidates are qualified, but you need to demonstrate that you are ready to lead.

Summarize your strengths and weaknesses as well as those of your opponent by using the Opposition Message Box. This box will help you anticipate the opponent's attacks and be strategic about how you respond with a rebuttal or counterattack. Initiating an attack can come across as too aggressive. It's usually best to lead with your positive agenda focused on voter concerns.

Be prepared to have your positive attributes come under attack. In focus groups, voters generally give women candidates high marks for characteristics such as honesty, integrity, authenticity, and empathy. One tactic used by opponents is to try to knock women off these pedestals of credibility and character. Professor Kelly Dittmar has found that this strategy has a negative impact on women candidates "It hurts. And it hurts more when women fall from high pedestals. Building up the stereotypes places women higher up, and if they are perceived to violate the norms, they have farther to fall."[6]

An example occurred in the 2012 US Senate campaign between Elizabeth Warren and Scott Brown. In the debates, Brown repeatedly attacked Warren's credibility by alleging that she claimed to have Native American ancestry when she applied for a teaching job earlier in her career. Brown accused Warren of not being who she said she was and of trying to take advantage of a status that didn't apply to her. Warren denied the allegations and focused on Brown's votes against working families. The attack against Warren remains a consistent talking point for conservatives; Donald Trump resurrected it with his "Pocahontas" name-calling.[7]

The Issue Message Box gives you a way to prepare substantive responses to the top voter issues you need to address in the race. Most campaigns hinge on a short list of key issues, such as jobs and the economy, education, healthcare, taxes, and budget.

Structure your answers to questions about issues so that you first frame the issue with a statement of your values. For example, "I believe that access to healthcare is a right and it's the government's job to ensure everyone has access to high-quality, affordable care." This broad framing helps voters understand your core value and how it may be different from what your opponent believes.

Once you have positioned your answer with a value frame, then transition to a specific accomplishment or what you plan to change. Again, it is important for you to demonstrate your qualifications. Tell the voters about results and how those results positively impact their lives. If you don't yet have a track record on an issue, you can share a policy idea that will solve a problem affecting voters. If there is enough time, you can add a story about someone in the district or a personal experience.

GOTCHA DEBATE QUESTIONS

A student questioner at a 2007 CNN debate asked Hillary Clinton if she preferred "diamonds or pearls." The student had a preplanned question about nuclear-waste storage but the TV producers forced her to ask the silly question.[8]

Voters tend to ask better questions because they want to focus on bread-and-butter issues. Reporters try to throw candidates off message. Here are some tricky questions to be ready for:

1. Can you tell us one thing about your opponent that you admire?
2. What's your favorite movie, book, or song?
3. What is an example of an issue on which you've changed your position?
4. Is there a past vote or position that you now regret?
5. Who is the leader of Ukraine? (Be ready for a pop quiz on world leaders or little-known countries.)
6. (In a primary.) If you lose, will you endorse your opponent?
7. Where do you disagree with Democratic Party leaders?
8. Which comic-book villain are you? (CNBC presidential debate, 2015.[9])
9. What's your greatest weakness? (This seems easy, but if the response isn't serious, you will appear disingenuous.)
10. Yes or no, do you support trade with China? (Lightning rounds that are intended to elicit one-word responses over-simplify complex subjects.)

Debate Rehearsal

The campaign team needs to structure practice sessions that are productive and don't exhaust the candidate's energy or dampen her confidence. Use early practice rounds as opportunities for the candidate to read through messaging aloud and work on developing themes and sound bites. The candidate needs time to process the information and get comfortable articulating what she wants to say. During this period, the team can be developing a list of likely questions and anticipating opponent messages and attack lines. The schedule should permit plenty of time for the candidate to ask questions to the prep team and have a back-and-forth on message content.

Closer to a scheduled debate, arrange for mock-debate practice scenarios that replicate the actual format, including the stage set up with furniture, moderator, questioners, and the opponent. The mock scenario should duplicate the overall length and flow. Rehearse the opening and closing statements to ensure you stay within the time limits. The response time to most questions is generally between 60 seconds and two minutes. All responses and rebuttals should be timed. In some formats, these are as short as 15 to 30 seconds.

Run the mock scenario without interruptions so the candidate has a feel for the length of an actual debate. If it's a one-on-one encounter, the candidate can practice handling opponent attacks and her rebuttals. The final prep sessions should focus on polishing answers and fine-tuning delivery techniques.

Keep the debate prep team to a small group of advisors. Consultants and advisors talking over one another or giving conflicting feedback will not be conducive to productive sessions. If the team is not unified in the advice given to the candidate, this can cause her to have doubts about strategy and may negatively affect her performance on debate day. The practice sessions can be taped, and written feedback can be solicited from trusted, knowledgeable strategists.

Debates generate media coverage, and many, including down-ballot races, are carried live on cable television or online channels. To ensure a polished performance, see the delivery techniques for on-camera appearances outlined in chapter 7. A debate is not the time to lash out in anger at an opponent or to appear defensive about a policy position. The rehearsal sessions were the time for the debate team to push the candidate on her vulnerabilities so any underling emotional responses can be worked out before hitting the debate stage.

In the town hall debate in the 2016 presidential campaign, Donald Trump appeared to be stalking Hillary Clinton while she was speaking. In her memoir, Hillary said it was incredibly uncomfortable as she could literally ". . . feel him breathing down my neck. My skin crawled."[10] Later, she expressed regret about not calling out his tactic, and she said that she felt she had over-learned the lessons of staying calm, "biting my tongue, digging my fingernails into a clenched fist, smiling all the while, determined to present a composed face to the world." Hindsight is always 20/20, and in her book, Hillary shares what would have been a strong retort, "Back up, you creep. Get away from me. I know you love to intimidate women, but you can't intimi-date me, so back up."[11]

Trump's outrageous behavior on the debate stage was a low point in the history of presidential debates. The lack of civility dealt a blow to public discourse and showed disrespect to his opponent and the voters. At the same time, it frees women from a double-bind that may have constrained them. In the past, women had to be concerned that if they pushed back too strongly, they would be labeled as strident. Moving forward, it's important for women to stand up for themselves. If you are surprised by an opponent with an unsavory attack or underhanded tactic, in the moment call out the bad behavior using direct but non-inflammatory rhetoric. The campaign team will have time backstage to formulate a full-blown response that they can use during post-debate interviews.

Debate Best and Worst Practices

Worst—Type A Overachiever

Yes, it is possible to be over-prepared. The debate stage is not the time to channel the Tracy Flick character portrayed by Reese Witherspoon in the movie *Election*. Type A overachievers are the smartest people in the room because they've worked diligently to memorize all of the answers. Memorization leads to a rote delivery style and focusing on what a candidate knows versus why it is important to voters. Reciting a litany of issues Al Gore–style will never be as compelling as a story about overcoming a personal challenge or a plan to drive change.

Worst—Wallflower

To control the stage, you must own the stage. The pre-debate negotiations are not the time to be reticent or timid. Know what you need in order to perform at your best. Do you prefer to sit or stand? Don't agree to stools or movie-director chairs. How high is the lectern, and is it transparent? What color is the backdrop? Do you want water, a notepad, or note cards onstage? Demonstrate that you are the voters' biggest and best advocate with the power-move and power-sound techniques outlined in chapter 7.

Worst—Take Me as I Am, Damn It

Don't allow the unfair and disproportionate attention paid to the appearance of women to cause you to dig your heels in about what to wear. What you stand for should matter more than your clothing, but the double-standard exists and a wardrobe choice can potentially turn off voters. If your dress or hair is dowdy, you may be dismissed as outdated. You may think that black nail polish and low-cut blouses are fashionable, but you should expect snide remarks from voters and media commentators that detract from your important message.

Best—Pitch-Perfect

What do you want the social-media post that goes viral during the debate to be? Prepare so you have a line that frames the debate showcasing why you are the best choice. The frame should be a contrast message that highlights why you are ideally suited to lead and why your opponent is not. Be ready to get this idea in during the first five minutes by having it in the opening statement or pivoting to it in the first question. Look for opportunities where it fits in without sounding forced. And circle back to it in the close.

Best—Most Qualified

The debate stage is not the place for humble pie. Voters want to hear more from women candidates about their qualifications. Rhode Island's state treasurer, Gina Raimondo, described how her business background and financial acumen enabled her to fix a state pension system in crisis. Hammering away on her track record of providing retirement security for thousands of families ensured she bested her debate opponents and was elected governor. Take credit for real results, and voters will believe you are qualified.

Best—The Good Sport

There is no crying in baseball, and there is no whining on the debate stage. Expect that things will go wrong, like the moderator skipping a question or mistiming an answer. On-stage complaining will sound petty. Better to let minor mishaps go so you can focus on getting to your message. Campaign staff members should alert the media to any dirty tricks or breeches of debate rules by the opponent or their campaign.

Best—Look and Sound Like a Leader

On the day of the debate, schedule a lighter load of activities. Feeling rested and refreshed will power your onstage performance. Have a regimen for handling nervous anxiety, including the physical relaxation exercises and positive visualization techniques described in chapter 8. Keep your meals light and drink plenty of water to keep your vocal cords healthy.

WELL-SPOKEN WOMEN RESIST, INSIST, PERSIST

Every interview is different, know what you are getting yourself into.

Write your dream headline and prepare to deliver it.

Use the debate to define yourself and draw contrast with your opponent.

CHAPTER 10

KEYNOTES, PANELS, INTRODUCTIONS, AND AWARDS

"This little light of mine, I'm gonna let it shine."

—folk song

There are certain events where pulling out the stump speech, a slide deck, or even a message box will not be enough. Special occasions deserve special treatment. Some events are a chance to create a big impact.

Such a moment took place at the 2018 Golden Globe Award ceremony. Upon receiving a lifetime achievement award, Oprah Winfrey used the platform to lift the Times Up movement and speak against inequity in the entertainment industry and beyond. The acceptance speech was an emotional showstopper. The crowd was on its feet as Oprah declared that a new day was on the horizon.

> Which brings me to this—what I know for sure is that speaking your truth is the most powerful tool we all have. And I'm especially proud and inspired by all the women who felt strong enough and empowered enough to speak up and share their personal stories. Each of us in this room are celebrated for the stories we tell. And this year we became the story . . .[1]

Timeless speeches don't happen by accident. A big moment takes the right speaker, at the right time, with the right message. The magic happens when the presenter seizes the chance to make it happen. Oprah exemplified the life lesson that luck is when preparation meets opportunity.

The magic can happen for you too. Here are best practices to help you be well-spoken at special forums including keynote addresses, protests and rallies, and panel discussions. Guidance is also provided on how to make a winning introduction and on how to graciously accept an award.

UNCONVENTIONALLY SPEAKING

In politics, the Olympics of oratory is the stage at the major party conventions. Hundreds of speakers gather for the single purpose of electing the next leader of the free world. In 2016, Hillary Clinton broke through an iron-clad barrier when she took that stage as the first woman to accept a presidential nomination. It had been thirty-two years since vice presidential pick Geraldine Ferraro graced the stage as the first woman on a ticket for either major party.

Political-convention organizers had long barred women from speaking. Susan B. Anthony asked to address women's suffrage, but her request was ignored by the leading parties. Ever expedient, the activist accepted an invitation from the Populist Party in 1894: "For forty years I've been laboring for the success of the women's enfranchisement and I always said for the party which first endorsed whether ... Republican, Democrat, or Populist I would wave my handkerchief."[2] Though she had campaigned for the vote her entire life, the suffragist would not live to see the passage of the Nineteenth Amendment.

It was the irrepressible Ann Richards who summed up the paucity of women in her 1988 keynote: "Two women in 160 years is about par for the course."[3] Another Texan congresswoman, Barbara Jordan, had been the first granted a coveted slot. Richards made an indelible mark when she branded the first President Bush with the zinger, "Poor George, he can't help it. He was born with a silver foot in his mouth." The element of surprise and the lower expectations that accompanied the speech catapulted the speaker who was little-known at the time into the stratosphere, and she would go on to be elected governor of Texas.

KEYNOTE ADDRESS

A major speech such as a keynote at a professional conference, policy forum, or political convention is not the occasion to do a deep dive on information sharing. It is the time to present a significant idea—what is the change you seek, and how will it be achieved? "If there is one message that echoes forth from this conference, it is that human rights are women's rights. And women's rights are human rights."[4] At the 1995 World Conference on Women held in China, Hillary Clinton put the plight of women and girls on the world's agenda. She used her keynote to set the tone for a broader dialogue and to unify the audience behind a common purpose. More than twenty years later, the former First Lady's message remains a rallying cry for women around the globe who strive for equality, respect, and dignity.

The most powerful keynotes are a testament to the power of words and the fortitude of the people who deliver them. The words are long remembered because they mark a turning point. What is said changes the way people think about something. Such a speech can change the life of the person who gives it. And the lives of people who hear it.

Speeches that exert a potent hold on people employ writing techniques that bring a sense of urgency to the call to action. Urgency is different from being alarmist. The point is not to be a doomsayer but to inspire people to take action on the change you seek. Language grounded in arguments for change that arise from personal experience, historical events, and literary texts is powerful and uplifting. These types of references add the authority of tradition and the weight of positive association.

> *"I had crossed the line. I was free; but there was no one to welcome me to the land of freedom. I was a stranger in a strange land."*[5]
> —Harriet Tubman, a conductor on the
> Underground Railroad who led slaves to freedom

Here are some techniques to elevate the scope and depth of your writing.

ELEVATE THE WRITING

1. Foundational Documents

Sentiments from historic documents elicit feelings of patriotism and unity. Examples include the Declaration of Independence ("Life, Liberty, and the pursuit of Happiness") and the US Constitution ("We the people . . ."). A patriotic song can have the same effect, such as the amber grain and purple mountains in "America the Beautiful."

Religious texts such as Bible verses and teachings from the Quran convey spiritual beliefs and faith in a god. Sharing philosophical ideas or personal reflections helps people understand how and why you believe certain things and can prompt deeper insights. Melinda Gates reaffirmed her commitment to family planning at an important point in her life. "There is something about turning fifty. It is kind of funny, but you can see the end of your life, you start to realize you are on the back half of life. And so I look there and say, 'Well, what do I want to get accomplished in the next thirty years?' And, by gosh, I better make sure I'm doing that."[6]

Use references to the rule of law to show that it is an ideal that democratic governments should strive to uphold.

> *"Sentencing a political opponent to death after a show trial is no different than taking him out in the street and shooting him. In fact, it is worse because using the court system as a tool of state repression makes a mockery of the rule of law."*[7]
> —Human rights lawyer Amal Clooney
> criticizing the Egyptian court system

> *"The key to peace is the rule of law. The key to rule of*
> *law is impartial judiciary. And the key to an impartial*
> *judiciary is the participation of women."*[8]
> —Sandra Day O'Connor, the first woman justice
> to serve on the Supreme Court

2. Cultural References

Evoke lines from a beloved theater production, such as Lin-Manuel Miranda's sentiments about immigrants getting the job done in the musical *Hamilton*.

"We shall overcome." Lyrics from protest anthems reverberate because they reflect upon the injustice of racism and misogyny. The civil-rights movement has a rich soundtrack, from Billie Holiday's "Strange Fruit" to Beyoncé's "Formation."

3. Personal Observation

> *"We had violence directed at us by the growers them-*
> *selves, trying to run us down by cars, pointing rifles at*
> *us, spraying the people when they were on the picket line*
> *with sulfur. . . . We had a lot of violence definitely. And*
> *then I was beaten up by the police in San Francisco."*[9]
> —United Farm Workers leader Dolores Huerta
> on what it was like to be on the front lines
> of a labor strike

At the Democratic National Convention in 2016, First Lady Michelle Obama called on the nation to remain vigilant about progress on race and spoke from her perspective as mom-in-chief.

> That is the story of this country, the story that brought me to this stage tonight. The story of generations of people who felt the lash of bondage, the shame of servitude, the sting of segregation. But

who kept on striving and hoping and doing what needed to be done so that today I wake up every morning in a house that was built by slaves. I watch my daughters, two beautiful, intelligent, black, young women playing with their dogs on the White House lawn.[10]

4. Contrast

A way to bring an idea into sharp focus is to contrast it with what it is not. There are a number of ways to show vibrant contrast—problem/ solution, us/them, forward/backward, present/future, yes/no, the thrill of victory/the agony of defeat, or David versus Goliath.

5. Anchor in a Meaningful Location

In 1939, Marian Anderson was the image of bravery as she stood alone on the steps of the Lincoln Memorial to sing "My Country, 'Tis of Thee." Anderson had originally been scheduled to sing at Constitution Hall, but the Daughters of the American Revolution denied her entry, citing a whites-only policy.

In his second inaugural address, President Obama noted the places where historic struggles for civil, gender, and gay rights took place.[11] He named Selma, Stonewall, Seneca Falls.

A meaningful location can be any place that has special meaning to you, such as a community park, a homeless shelter, or a house of worship.

> *"This is where I got my start in activism. Right here, in this building . . ."*
> —Charlene Carruthers, national director
> of the Black Youth Project 100,
> referring to a special place on the campus of her
> alma mater, Illinois Wesleyan University

6. End on Hope

Paint a picture of how things can be. Show the audience the top of the mountain. Take them to the other side. Oprah concluded her Golden Globe remarks by looking to the future:

> So, I want all of the girls watching here, now, to know that a new day is on the horizon. And when that new day finally dawns, it will be because of a lot of magnificent women. Many of whom are right here in this room tonight. And some pretty phenomenal men. Fighting hard to make sure they become the leaders who take us to the time when nobody ever has to say "me too" again.

DELIVERY

The length of a keynote is typically around twenty minutes, but Oprah said what she needed to say and had the audience on their feet in less than nine minutes. The speaking pace is more important than its length. A hectic pace will exhaust the audience, and a sluggish one will bore them. Variability in your speaking rate will keep them attuned. Purposefully slowing down the pace adds gravitas to what is being said and can build intensity. Picking it up can feel energetic and forward-looking.

It can be difficult to hit the right pace and energy level at the beginning if you are speaking to a large crowd, especially when nervous. Surging adrenaline can cause any speaker to rush, literally leaving them breathless—and leaving the audience wishing the speaker would slow down. Inexperienced presenters often mistakenly believe they need to do more than they should to be seen and heard. There is a compulsion to shout to be heard above the din or to over-gesticulate in order to be visible on a massive stage when standing before lots of people. The microphone and jumbotron screens are there to enhance the speaker's stature.

Michelle Obama's speech at the 2016 Democratic Convention provides an excellent example of how to control the delivery. When the First Lady walked across the stage to the lectern, she was purposeful and energetic but not hurried. Arriving at the lectern, she took time to embrace the audience's reception. She blew kisses and waved to individuals in the crowd, giving herself a chance to breathe. The physical greeting lasted a full 40 seconds. She "settled in" at the lectern by getting herself physically set. Both hands were placed on top of it so she could claim the space without clutching the lectern.

As she began to speak, acknowledgments were foregone. She dove in, "It's hard to believe that it has been eight years since I first came to this convention to talk with you about why I thought my husband should be president."[12] There is no need to signal to the audience that she is starting with a story, no need to say, "Let me start with a story." The audience is smart; they are in sync with her. The speaking pace is relaxed; the pauses are healthy; yet there is no shortage of energy.

TELEPROMPTERS

The stage at the Democratic Convention is equipped with a large teleprompter screen positioned directly in front of the speaker. It is several feet wide and high, and it is set several rows back from the stage, but the words displayed on it are easy to read because of their size. This placement and large font size help ensure that the speakers don't appear to be reading word for word.

Most speaking venues will not have a large, jumbotron-sized teleprompter. The most common types are presidential paddles and confidence monitors. Presidential paddles are most often used at formal events when the speaker is standing at a lectern. Two sheets of glass are positioned on either side of the lectern and the speech text scrolls across the glass panes.

This setup can be tricky because the speaker needs to be able to transition smoothly from one paddle to another. A common delivery mistake is to only turn the neck or shift the eyes back and forth. This movement makes it obvious that the speaker is reading. It takes practice to learn how to make the movement look natural and comfortable. The trick is to use the power move technique of turning your body from the waist, which is described in chapter 7.

Confidence monitors are commonly used at conferences, conventions, and events like TED Talks. A confidence monitor looks like a large television screen and is usually positioned a few inches off the floor. The monitor placement frees the speaker to be able to move around the stage. However, if the speaker stands too close to the monitor, it will look as if she is staring at her feet.

If you plan to use a prompter or monitor, it is essential to rehearse with the equipment in the room in which the talk will be given. That way, you can become comfortable with the setup. Practice ensures that the tool doesn't become a barrier between you and the audience. Or a crutch you are overly dependent upon.

MOMENT OF REPOSE

The backstage space at big events can be a hectic scene with headache-inducing noise. If you are nervous or an introvert, you may need to find a quieter space to take a moment of repose before you hit the stage lights. If the green room is filled with other presenters waiting for their stage turn, a quiet bathroom or an empty hallway may help you escape the hubbub and provide a place to calm pre-speech jitters. Give yourself a chance to warm up mentally and physically. Do a power pose or two, take several deep breaths, and rehearse the opening aloud.

REHEARSAL TIME

A big speech requires more prep time. The one-to-one equation recommended earlier—one hour of prep for every one minute of speaking time—will not be enough. The writing process for a major address needs to start several weeks, if not months, in advance of the event. The following checklist provides an overview of a typical schedule when getting ready for a big talk.

KEYNOTE SPEECH PREPARATION PROCESS

1. Research event and audience.
2. Answer 4 *W* questions (what's it about, why you care, why they should care, what's the call to action).
3. Identify the main idea or theme and develop supporting points.
4. Write the introduction and conclusion.
5. Review the first draft and revise.
6. Create visual aids, if any are to be used.
7. Read through aloud to check for overall length and flow.
8. Make revisions to edit for time and strengthen transitions.
9. Complete ongoing read-throughs to edit wordiness and difficult phrasing.
10. Format speech text for delivery—full text or outline.
11. Videotape rehearsal with playback and review.
12. Final revisions to content—polish humor and stories.
13. More videotaping to focus on delivery technique—power moves and sounds.
14. Final tweaks to speech text or notes.
15. Speech day.

PROTESTS AND RALLIES

The Women's March in 2017 made history as the largest peaceful gathering for change in the United States and around the world. The collective voice of a march is impossible to ignore. One voice can be talked over, dismissed, or shouted down. When a multitude come together to speak as one, the message resonates far and wide.

Participating as a speaker can be an exhilarating and grueling experience. Long periods of waiting, foul weather, bad food, and restroom shortages are the price for a few minutes onstage. But that moment can be well worth the trouble. At the 2018 March for Our Lives, the student speakers successfully spoke with one voice about their vision to prevent future gun-violence tragedies. The absence of politicians ensured that the event theme was not hijacked by personal agendas or individual egos. The handful of celebrities who performed didn't overshadow the students but rather praised their bravery and celebrated their resilience.

Before you attend a large-scale march or rally, consider the following. As you prepare your remarks, keep the big picture in mind. What is the event's purpose? How do your goals and/or the goals of your organization align with that purpose? How can your individual voice complement the larger message?

What is your role at the event? How can you use that role to amplify the larger theme and further the work of your organization? Are you a featured speaker, an introducer, or a brief greeter? If you are a headliner, the rally is an opportunity to demonstrate leadership and your message should focus on a big idea. If you are not well known, this is a chance to put yourself and your organization on the map. And to show solidarity for the bigger cause.

PROTEST/RALLY MESSAGE

Keep It Short

Even if you are a featured speaker, you are one of many on the program. The event organizers have gone to a lot of trouble to pull together an agenda, so stick to your slot and time limit. Movie producer Michael Moore went on so long at the Women's March that Ashley Judd nearly had to rip the mic out of his hands to get him to stop. Buoyed by the exuberance of the crowd, Moore launched into a rambling comedic routine. When it was clear he was going well over his allotted time, Ashley walked onstage and cut him off midsentence by asking the crowd to thank him.[13]

A rally is not the time to grandstand, detail a laundry list of policy initiatives, or provide an exhaustive history of your organization. Women's March co-chair Gloria Steinem's powerful call to resist division clocked in under ten minutes. A three-minute time slot may not seem like a lot, but it can be plenty of time if you are prepared. Use the Issue Message Box template to tell your advocacy story.

Get to the Point

What is your take on the event's theme? Use your time onstage to share your unique point of view about what is at stake and why you care. Actress and daughter of Honduran immigrants America Ferrera built on the theme of unity and one America by saying that immigrants are America and they are here to stay.

> We march today for the moral core of this nation, against which this president is waging a war. He would like us to forget the words, "give me your tired, your poor, your huddled masses yearning to breathe free." And instead take up a credo of hate, fear, and suspicion of one another. But we are gathered here and across the country and around the world today to say, "Mr. Trump we refuse."[14]

Call to Action

The primary purpose should be to advocate and motivate. What is the one thing you want the audience to do? Be clear. Be specific. Make it easy to do. And repeat it. For example, a phone number to call or a text message to send. Or a petition sheet to sign that's being circulated. Or a website for more information.

Use a chant or call-and-response to motivate the crowd. The best interactions with the audience are succinct, meaningful, and rhythmic. A simple message can be used to unite the audience in a collective activity.

The call-and-response is a tradition in black churches with the preacher calling and the congregation responding. The Ferguson Response Network's action resource has examples used in the wake of the killings of Michael Brown, Freddie Gray, and Eric Garner.[15]

> Call: We marchin'.
> Response: We marchin'.
> Call: To justice.
> Response: To justice.
> Call: For our sisters.
> Response: For our sisters.
> Call: And our brothers.
> Response: And our brothers.
>
> Call: Hands up!
> Response: DON'T SHOOT!

WOMEN'S MARCH CHANTS

- Love Trumps Hate.
- Say it loud. Say it clear. Immigrants are welcome here.
- Education not deportation.
- Pussy grabs back.
- Black Lives Matter.
- Muslim rights are human rights.
- My body. My choice.
- No justice. No Peace.
- Love not hate. Makes America great.

Expect Program Changes

The program agenda is an unwieldy beast the event producers are wrestling to stay on top of. Expect your speaking slot to change as technical glitches cause delays, other presenters arrive late, or some people run on too long. Many events have set time limits and benchmarks to hit. The headline speakers are scheduled to maximize media coverage. Park permits have start and end times. If you run over, there are real costs in time, money, and impact that hurt the greater cause.

Statement Clothing

What you are wearing can send a powerful signal: Pink pussy hats are an iconic symbol of feminism. An all-white or purple ensemble evokes images of the suffragists. At the March for Science on Earth Day 2017, scientists wore lab coats to advocate for more federal funding for scientific research and for action on climate change.

Stick to the Script

If you go rogue with your remarks, that can detract from the overall message of the event. The media will pick up on the most negative or outrageous statements and replay them endlessly. Anti-women commentators tried to paint the Women's March as a violent protest based on one off-message comment. When Madonna said she had thought an awful lot about "blowing up the White House," conservative pundits attempted to demean all marchers and dismiss the event as a fringe protest.[16]

Delivery Tips

- Don't be offended if your speaking time is changed or cut short.
- Don't yell into the microphone; ask an on-site tech person for advice.
- Don't be distracted if the crowd is not listening, you are being recorded by thousands of smartphones and media cameras.
- Prepare notecards on heavy stock paper to withstand wind and rain. There may not be a lectern for larger paper.
- Get on and get off the stage quickly. Don't waste time with a long introduction of yourself, and don't linger with multiple thank-yous.
- Make sure your statement clothing includes walking shoes and weather-appropriate gear.

PANEL DISCUSSIONS

Panel discussions and moderated conversations don't have to be mundane, run-of-the-mill question-and-answer sessions. Most are forgettable for one reason: The moderator didn't do their homework.

Panels that are well-run look, feel, and sound like a lively conversation with something at stake. The moderator's job starts well before the day of the discussion. It begins with reaching out to the panelists to discuss goals and objectives. Possible questions should be shared and feedback elicited from each panelist. That way, the panelists are familiar with the other speakers, know how they fit into the group, and can then plan accordingly.

At the start of the discussion, the moderator should frame the conversation by briefly stating the objectives. Introductions of each panelist should be brief and personalized. No reciting of résumés. The best moderators ask questions that focus not on the what and how but on the why. They don't waste precious minutes asking about things that are already known. They include what the panelists want to talk about.

Journalists often make good moderators because they are accustomed to asking questions that draw out the people they are talking to. They ask open-ended questions that focus on memories, emotions, and characterizations that prompt more personal and revealing responses: "How did that decision impact your family?" "What was most surprising about what happened?" Broadcaster journalists are also good at keeping an eye on the clock and do a good job of holding panel members to time limits.

The moderator's final task is to be ready to wrap up. A stimulating conversation deserves a better conclusion than, "That's all we have time for." Additionally, you don't want to be caught short ending on a down note with everyone walking out discouraged. That can happen when the flow of the conversation lands on a grim or depressing topic and time runs out. Be ready with a final question that will ensure a brief, forward-looking answer from each panelist. That will ensure everyone leaves with something positive.

How to Be an Excellent Moderator

1. Select panelists who represent diverse opinions and backgrounds.
2. First question should be thematic rather than "Tell us what you do."

3. Get all the panelists involved at the top with a question that can be answered briefly.
4. Listen to the responses.
5. Follow up on something just said. For example, "Tell me more about that."
6. Demonstrate interest in the speakers by knowing something special about them.
7. Weave unexpected bio tidbits into questions.
8. Ask some questions that will elicit short and long answers to break up the pacing.
9. Involve the audience by taking their questions.
10. Don't have each panelist answer each question—it creates a lifeless, repetitive pattern.
11. Sit with the panelists rather than standing apart or at a lectern.
12. Watch the clock. It's your job to make sure one speaker doesn't hog the speaking time.

How to Be an Excellent Panelist

1. Respond to the moderator's request for background information.
2. Recognize that your speaking time will be limited. Plan to have two or three points that you will elaborate on if you have time.
3. Be ready to credential yourself if necessary.
4. Have an easy-to-implement call to action.
5. Research the other panelists so you know what they will address.
6. Always be ready to ditch some of your prepared remarks when other speakers run over their allotted time.
7. Volunteer to speak first. This allows you to tee up what you want to discuss.
8. If another speaker steals your best material, feel comfortable revisiting the point by saying, "I want to reinforce what a previous speaker mentioned because it's important. . . ."

9. Don't feel as if you have to respond to every question, particularly if you have nothing new to add.
10. Listen to what other people are saying so you don't repeat verbatim what was just said.
11. When you're talking, begin your response by looking at the questioner. As you continue to talk, you can turn and look at the audience to engage them.
12. Avoid scanning the audience. Use the eye-contact techniques outlined in chapter 7.
13. Use active listening skills when not talking. Sit up and forward in your chair. Turn slightly to the person who is speaking.
14. Never send a signal that you are bored or have more-important things to do by looking at a phone or a watch.

THE ART OF INTERJECTING ON A PANEL

The moderator and the panelists can work together to ensure the event is a lively conversation and not a mundane back-and-forth. Chiming in is a good way to ensure the conversation is upbeat and proactive.

Pay a genuine compliment as you sense the speaker is wrapping up her thought.

- Jane's insights are so valuable, and her legal expertise so crucial. We also need . . .
- Aiesha is raising the bar with her leadership. Another innovation I've seen is . . .
- We are fortunate to have Joanna's wit and wisdom driving this effort. Her energy inspires me . . .

Use the improv technique of "yes, and" to build on someone's point.

- While we are on this topic, let me add . . .
- Nina is raising an excellent point, and what I've seen that works is . . .
- What Jane just said reminds me . . .

Involve the other panelists and/or audience members.

- I would be really interested to hear what Aiesha has experienced.
- Ask a question to the audience, "Raise your hand if you have experienced a similar situation."
- Pose a rhetorical question to the audience, "What would you do, if this happened . . ."

Employ the following delivery techniques for interjecting in a friendly way.

- Politely flag an interruption, "Sorry to interrupt, but what Jane said is key, and I'd like to suggest . . ."
- Indicate to the moderator that you have something to add with a visual cue such as a head nod or a slightly raised hand.
- Reach out with one hand to the person who's talking and look them directly in the eye, "Nina, I'd like to share. What I've seen is . . ." If they are seated close to you, you can also lightly touch the speaker's forearm, as you would a friend, to indicate you have something to add.
- Use the speaker's name, "Joanna, if I may say . . ."

INTRODUCTIONS

A well-spoken introduction sets the stage for what's to come. It primes the audience with the speaker's qualifications and passion for the topic. It helps ensure the speaker gets off on the right foot and that the audience is ready to listen. However, not all introductions are created equal. Introductions of women speakers fail when the speaker relies on clichés or outdated notions. The three most flagrant violations are using sexist titles; commenting on appearance or attire; and mentioning marital status, gender, or age.

Give Her Her Due

Two women physicians at the Mayo Clinic thought they were hearing a pattern at medical conferences when women doctors were introduced. It seemed the women were introduced by colleagues on a first-name basis. "Let's welcome, Amanda." But, when their male colleagues where introduced, they were called "Dr. So-and-So."

It turns out their perception was accurate. A study showed that the double-standard introductions were really happening in situations where it mattered.[17] In "ground rounds" women physicians were less likely to be introduced by their professional title when men were doing the introducing. Ground rounds are meetings where doctors, researchers, and medical students present medical issues for discussion.

The Little Lady

"Not only is she beautiful, but she also happens to be an expert in her field . . ." When do you ever hear a man's appearance described when he is introduced? The mention of physical appearance undermines professional qualifications. References to size are particularly offensive, such as, "Sally, shows that big ideas can come in small packages." Or, "It's hard to believe such a tiny person could accomplish so much."

Lady Doctor or Young Thing

A reference to gender is outrageously irrelevant and comes across as sexist. The word *male* doesn't precede a title such as *professor, lawyer,* or *doctor.* The gender-neutral title, if there isn't a professional or academic one, is "Ms." Referencing the age of an adult woman can be pointless and demeaning. "Wanda is young but has many accomplishments . . ."

IT'S MY PLEASURE TO WELCOME . . .

Most people who make introductions don't set out to sabotage the speaker. But they do make mistakes. They may rely on an out-of-date résumé, misstate the topic, or mispronounce your name.

The introduction that relies on the use of a cliché is weak: "The next speaker needs no introduction." This sounds like the introducer didn't take time to prepare. Another lazy approach is the introducer who reads a résumé in chronological order.

A surefire way to ensure you are happy with how you are introduced is to write it yourself. The person who's making the introduction will be grateful to be relieved of the task of drafting what to say. If you have a tricky name, be sure to spell it phonetically. When you are asked to introduce someone, the first question you pose to the speaker should be "How do I pronounce your name correctly?"

The introduction is not a trivial task. A thoughtfully prepared and well-delivered one reflects positively on both you and the speaker. Impressive introductions whet the audience's appetite; establish why the speaker was chosen, and set the speaker up for success. Here's how to deliver an outstanding intro.

Highlight the Speaker's Expertise

Use an introduction as an opportunity to boost the speaker's stature. An amazingly easy way to do this is to describe her as qualified. This is particularly helpful for women candidates. Research conducted by the Barbara Lee Family Foundation found that voters assume that men are qualified when they run, but women have to prove they are ready.[18] For example, you can give a woman a boost by simply using the word *qualified*: "I'd like you to meet Jane Smith, who is running for city council and who is the most qualified candidate in the race." Similarly, candidates should introduce themselves by saying, "I'm Jane Smith, and I'm qualified because . . ."

Make It Distinctive

The best introductions are personalized and convey something unknown about the speaker. Momentous occasions when prestigious honors are bestowed on luminaries provide rare opportunities to see masters at work.

Viola Davis had the unenviable task of introducing screen legend Meryl Streep when she was honored with a lifetime achievement award at the Golden Globes in 2017. How does one sum up a career that is a standout in its field? How does one adequately acknowledge the accomplishments of a living legend? How does one talk about someone whom they personally admire and who is beloved by millions? Viola showed she was up to the task.

> She stares. That's the first thing you notice about her. She tilts her head back with that sly, suspicious smile, and she stares for a long time. And you think, "Do I have something in my teeth or does she want to kick my ass?" Which is not going to happen. And then she'll ask questions: "What did you do last night, Viola?" *Oh, I cooked an apple pie.* "Did you use Pippin apples?" *No, I didn't use Pippin apples, what the hell are Pippin apples? I used Granny Smith apples.* "Did you make your own crust?" *No, I used store-bought crust, that's what I did.* "Then you didn't make an apple pie, Viola . . ."
>
> She is an observer and a thief. She reveals what she has stolen on that sacred place, which is the screen. She makes the most heroic

characters vulnerable; the most known, familiar; the most despised, relatable. Dame Streep . . .

I see you. And you know, all those rainy days we spent on the set of *Doubt*, every day my husband would call me at night and say, "Did you tell her how much she means to you?" and I would say, "Nah, I can't say anything, Julius. I'm just nervous. All I do is stare at her all the time." And he said, "Well, you need to say something. You have been waiting all your life to work with this woman—say something." I said, "Julius, I'll do it tomorrow." "Okay, well, you better do it tomorrow, because when I get there, I'm going say something." I never said anything.

But, I'm gonna say it now: You make me proud to be an artist. You make me feel that what I have in me—my body, my face, my age—is enough. You encapsulate that great Émile Zola quote that if you ask me as an artist what I came into this world to do, I, as an artist, would say, I came to live out loud.[19]

Viola didn't fall into the trap of hyperbole and empty platitudes. Her introduction was remarkable for its simplicity, its personalization, its intimacy. In less than four minutes, she didn't overplay her role but set the stage for the honoree.

HOW TO INTRODUCE YOURSELF

1. Say hello and state your name clearly and slowly.
2. Explain what you do in one sentence.
3. Tell the audience what the topic of the talk is.
4. Give an example of why you care about the topic.
5. Share what you have in common with the listeners.

ACCEPTING AN AWARD

The trick to accepting an award is to give an acceptance speech that makes people glad you received the honor. Be heartfelt and genuine as you accept recognition for your leadership, volunteerism, groundbreaking research, contributions to a field, or fundraising efforts. Acknowledge the organization bestowing the honor and the contributions of the people who made it possible. Be sure to mention family members who provided love and support while tolerating your absences away from home. Tell the audience what the honor means to you with a personal story.

Practice so you don't get weepy onstage. No one wants to sit through a soppy mess or endure an outburst. A moist eye is expected, but if you are prone to tears, your emotion may derail you. An overly emotive display can be misinterpreted by those who are looking to find fault. Write your remarks and rehearse them so you will be able to channel emotion into a passionate, clear-eyed statement.

EXCELLENCE IN THE CATEGORY OF ACCEPTING AN AWARD

Be Gracious

Avoid inadvertently insulting the award presenters by rushing off the stage. Recognize that if you're uncomfortable in the spotlight, you may try to downplay the occasion. But if you are too humble or self-deprecating, the audience can feel as if you have trivialized the honor. Avoid, "I don't deserve this." Or "There are others who have done so much more."

Rather, express gratitude for the honor. And voice your appreciation for the people who helped make it possible. The recognition of your talent, contribution, or dedication is coming from people who share your commitment to the cause. At the time she received the Presidential Medal of Freedom, Gloria Steinem said, "I'd be crazy if I didn't understand that this was a medal for the entire women's movement.... It belongs to Shirley Chisholm, Bella Abzug...so, many more."[20]

Make an Appeal

Pakistani education advocate Malala Yousafzai is the youngest person to be awarded the Nobel Peace Prize. At the age of seventeen she had already been a leader in the fight to educate girls for years. And she had demonstrated through her own heroic struggle that children and young people can contribute to improving their own situations. Malala used her Noble lecture to make an appeal for governments to devote resources to education rather than funding wars.

> Dear brothers and sisters, the so-called world of adults may understand it, but we children do not. Why is it that countries which we call "strong" are so powerful in creating wars but are so weak in bringing peace? Why is it that giving guns is so easy but giving books is so hard? Why is it, why is it that making tanks is so easy, but building schools is so hard?
>
> We are living in the modern age and we believe that nothing is impossible. We have reached the moon 45 years ago and will soon land on Mars. Then, in this 21st century, we must be able to give every child quality education.[21]

Speak for the Unheard

In 2014, Laverne Cox accepted her Logo Trailblazer Award on behalf of the cast members of the television program *Orange Is the New Black*. Laverne used the award ceremony as an occasion to tell the untold stories of trans women like Monica Jones, who was arrested for nothing more than walking through a Phoenix neighborhood while trans; and

Sylvia Rivera, a transgender community leader who faced opposition within the LGBT community and who had been present at Stonewall, an antigay riot in New York City.

> Sylvia Rivera, so many years ago, warned us about becoming a movement that was only for white, middle-class people. And forty-five years later the most marginalized of our communities are still struggling. Trans, LGBTQ people of color, and working-class folks are fighting for their lives. People are fighting for dignity in prison, particularly people who are trans. As we celebrate this show and this historic moment forty-five years since Stonewall, I want to encourage us to ask what more can we do to honor the legacy of Stonewall and the trailblazers that made it possible for us to be here.[22]

Acknowledge the Team

Convey heartfelt gratitude to those who were there along the way by skipping the platitude about working with a "great team." Be specific, and it will be memorable. At her Soccer Hall of Fame induction, Olympian Mia Hamm said her life has been a collaborative effort of family, fans, sponsors, and coaches. To her teammates, she said: "There are times when you're playing, when you're not at your best. There are times when you're at your best, and you carry the team. But, when you are not at your best, they carry you. And, let me tell you, I have been carried much more than I ever carried."[23]

The Funny Side

Humor drawn from everyday life can draw the audience in and show them the speaker doesn't take herself too seriously. Engineer Karen Panetta was honored by the Anita Borg Institute for founding the program Nerd Girls to encourage girls to pursue careers in engineering and science. During her speech, she recounted what first motivated her to learn about computers.

While in high school, Karen took a computer-generated career-assessment exam to help her choose a career. The assessment report showed she was best suited to be a schoolteacher or cosmetic saleswoman. Her best friend, a boy who scored lower than she did in math and science, was told he could be a university professor or engineer. Karen said she was upset about the results even though, "It was well-known, regardless of gender, if you were a professor, you would have to wear a lab coat, grow facial hair, and sacrifice all personal hygiene."[24] When Karen complained to the guidance counselor, she was told "computers don't make mistakes."

A big moment onstage can create a lasting impact. The stage can be stadium with a crowd numbering in the thousands. Or it can be an intimate space—a room of dedicated souls. The impact comes when the speaker is ready to stir deep emotions, capture the shared energy, and drive the listeners to take action.

Women are taking to stages large and small to change the conversation in this country. At marches and rallies, in auditoriums and studios, in basements and community centers, we are adding our narratives to the dialogue about equality, justice, and fairness. We are raising our voices to organize, protest, advocate, and celebrate.

We are preparing for our standing ovation.

WELL-SPOKEN WOMEN RESIST, INSIST, PERSIST

Magic happens with the right speaker in the right moment.
A big event is the time for a big idea.
Raise your game with stellar writing.

PART V

NOW YOUR STORY IS THE ONE TO TELL

EPILOGUE

"Experience has taught me that you cannot value dreams according to the odds of their coming true. Their real value is in stirring within us the will to aspire."
— Sonia Sotomayor, *My Beloved World*

And so we come to the end of this how-to,

Yet your journey must continue.

It's been a whirlwind time to be writing about women speaking out to drive change.

So much is happening. It's like being in a real-life *Wonder Woman* movie, but even better. There's not one super action hero, there are thousands and thousands of women battling bigotry and injustice.

REAL-LIFE WONDER WOMEN

More than thirty thousand women pledge to run for office nationwide. *POW!* Take that, patriarchy!

#MeToo stories break the silence on sexual harassment. *SHAZAM!* Take that, abusers!

Black women voters say no to a white nationalist, making their votes decisive in the election of an Alabama Democrat to the Senate. *BAM!* Take that, disgusting creep!

The Times Up movement unites celebrities and activists to fight abuse and harassment.

KAPOW! Take that, division!

Student activists stand up to the NRA and march for their lives.

BOOM! Take that, gun lobby!

A tidal wave of attention is being paid to what women have to say. It seems every day there's a new story. It's almost overwhelming, so here's the good news and the bad about what lies ahead.

The good news: The attention is long overdue. Abusers are being held accountable. Mansplainers and broviators have been put on notice. Manels are not viewed as a given. Sexist, racist trolls are called out. Tremendous role models provide inspiration.

The bad news: The power gavel is still held by people who do not accept change.

A sobering reminder of the challenges that remain occurred at a routine school-board meeting in January 2018. A middle-school English teacher who dared to question a proposed raise for a school superintendent was evicted and handcuffed at a community meeting in Vermilion Parish School District outside of New Orleans. Deyshia Hargrave had done nothing except ask why the superintendent was slated to get a nearly $30,000 raise when teachers in the district had not received a pay increase in ten years.

It was a fair question and one that deserved an answer. But the school-board president, Anthony Fontana, who cut her off and ordered her evicted, likened the teacher to "an unruly student" and "a poor little woman."[1] The treatment was heavy-handed and unjustified. But it should not deter you.

Let it inspire you.

If you've gotten anything out of this book, it's that speaking out is imperative. It is about resisting, persisting, and insisting our way to equity. You have a voice, and you can use it. And when you do, you help yourself and a whole lot of other women.

The guidance in this book has been tried and tested. It works! Put it into action: Answer the "why" to make your purpose clear. Prepare message boxes to succeed in a debate. Share your conviction to connect with the audience. Develop a practice regimen to ensure your nerves are quelled and your voice is calm and direct.

If you've gotten this far, then it's clear you are up to the challenge, and you are asking yourself, "Well, what's next?"

INSPIRATION ABOUNDS

"She is the greatest living teen of our generation."
"I am speechless."
"I need to stop complaining about going to school."

That's how American teenagers reacted to learning about the bravery of Nobel Prize recipient Malala Yousafzai.[2] The teens came away with a deeper appreciation of what is possible after hearing how Malala survived a Taliban gunman attack and continues her mission to reach the 66 million girls worldwide who are denied an education.

Along with the women you already admire, more inspiration can be found at women's conferences where leaders like Malala are featured: the National Coalition of 100 Black Women, Women in the World Summit, *Forbes* Women's Summit, TEDWomen, MAKERS Conference, Lesbians Who Tech, Grace Hopper, S.H.E. Summit, and the list goes on. These gatherings showcase a variety of women speakers from the private, public, and nonprofit sectors tackling issues from sex trafficking to work/life balance.

Some high-profile events can come with expensive ticket prices. Scholarships may be available, but, if not, many events are livestreamed and/or videos are available online afterward. In your community, look for regional meetings on women's leadership sponsored by universities and community colleges. TEDx programs are independent TED-like events held in many cities.

If you're running for office and want to get a feel for candidate debates and stump speeches, tune into C-SPAN. During an election cycle, the cable channel follows candidates on the campaign trail. In addition to daily coverage of congressional hearings and floor speeches, C-SPAN cameras record public-policy forums, panel discussions, and talks by authors. The website's video library logs party convention speeches and congressional and presidential debates. Additionally, attend local candidate forums, go to a fundraiser, join a political party, and take part in organizing events to get a feel for campaigning.

BALANCED MIC TIME

Check out the speaker lineups at professional conferences and industry conventions for gender balance. How many speakers are women, and are they showcased in prime speaking slots? If women aren't on the program, find out why not. Event organizers need to prioritize diversity at the mic and take corrective action when needed. When CES 2018, the largest consumer electronics trade show announced its headliners speakers, the six keynote slots were given to men, five of whom were white.

The advocacy group Gender Avenger generated headlines about CES 2018's all-pale, male lineup, which prompted a discussion with the organizers about the lack of women in high-profile roles. The initial response was that senior women and women of color were not available; "the pool" of speakers was too small.[3] The "Yeah, but" excuse has been used for too long to exclude women from technical, scientific, medical, and academic conferences.

The notion that there aren't enough women available might hold water if it were true. Researchers at Rice University built a database to look at academic conferences held at the top fifty universities. After adjusting for the relative number of men and women in six disciplines, they found that male speakers outnumbered women nearly two to one.

With a pool of qualified women to draw from, men are still 20 percent more likely to be invited to speak.[4]

The cry for change about pale, male lineups also needs to come from within professional fields and industries. Gender Avenger mobilized leading voices in the tech industry to push back on the claims that there are too few women. Individual men can refuse to speak on panels without people of color and women, and they can make their objections public. Public shaming on social media can shine a much-needed spotlight on the problem.

SECURITY MATTERS

Increasing the numbers of women speakers can do much to change the climate at large conferences, and some organizers have pledged to include more women in the future. Another necessary change is the establishment and enforcement of anti-harassment policies so all conference attendees are safe and speakers don't suffer harassment or abuse. Well-publicized codes of conduct are a sign that concerns or accusations will be taken seriously and appropriate action will be taken. Inquire beforehand to see what, if any, policies are in place. By asking about codes of conduct, you can raise the visibility of the issue and signal its importance.

The logistics of an event matter. Don't allow neglectful event planners to jeopardize your personal safety. They may not have safety concerns in mind when they plan and relay logistical information. Ask for complete directions and contact information so you don't find yourself in a cab leaving an airport late at night with a dead cell phone, wondering where the hotel is.

The cheapest hotel may not be the best option, especially if you are traveling alone. Consider the following: How far is it from the venue? Are other conference attendees staying there? Will transportation be provided? It's one thing to navigate familiar surroundings by yourself;

it's another to be in a new city or a new country where you don't know the lay of the land and may be jet-lagged from a long flight.

VISIBILITY COUNTS

An invitation to speak is more than a break from work or a nice thing to do if you have the time. National and regional conferences are a chance to raise your personal visibility and advance your career as well as elevate the cause. Presenting research and/or sharing expertise and ideas at a prestigious gathering brings recognition to your work, enhances your standing with your peers, and can lead to funding.

A speaking slot means you are in a position not just to be a part of an agenda but to shape the conversation. Technical conferences, public-policy forums, and conventions are the places where thought leaders emerge. Your presence provides the chance to elevate an issue that might otherwise languish. Share a unique perspective to solve a problem. Initiate debate on the best approach to bring change.

Along with recognition and high-level networking, speaking events provide opportunities for personal growth. Declining an invitation means you are missing out on a chance to stretch your abilities by trying something new. Accepting gives you a forum to speak to a different audience that may not be familiar with your work. It gives you a reason to brush off a previous talk and update it with a fresh perspective. As a featured speaker, your work may be brought to the attention of a media organization covering the event. Media exposure brings your ideas to an even-larger audience.

GIVE YOURSELF PERMISSION

This can be a tough one—stop saying no. Be honest and ask yourself, are you taking the steps needed to boost your visibility?

Is a lack of confidence holding you back? Are family obligations used as an excuse? Does the speech topic seem like a stretch beyond your expertise? Are you waiting for the perfect fit?

If you're saying no because the event is outside your comfort zone, you may want to try the Shonda Rhimes approach to turn nos into yeses. The award-winning television producer wrote a book about how she faced down speaking fears and conquered the panic attacks she had suffered her entire life.[5] It wasn't easy, and it was often painful, but she found that she could take her armor off. Let her hair down. Even be herself. Not only did disaster not ensue, she discovered she could enjoy speaking in public.

Even women like Shonda Rhimes with strong evidence of high achievement can feel like frauds before an audience. The imposter syndrome is an equal-opportunity affliction suffered by both men and women. However, women tend to blame themselves for any perceived shortcomings. Men tend to place the blame on external factors beyond their control, such as bad luck. While a sense of feeling like a phony afflicts many, research shows that some minority students may be particularly susceptible. A study published in the *Journal of Counseling Psychology* found that the imposter phenomenon can negatively impact the mental health of minority students who already perceive prejudices against them.[6] African American college students reported that feelings of imposterism exacerbated the impact of discrimination.

One way to combat imposter syndrome is to seek out colleagues with similar backgrounds and experiences. Many organizations offer affinity groups or shared-interest groups for people who would like the support of peers. Recruit a mentor who will encourage you to value your unique perspective and hone your skills. A mentor can serve as a sounding board and share approaches for how to manage feelings of inadequacy.

Another way to combat the syndrome is to remind yourself of the importance of adding your voice to the discussion. If you don't agree to speak, what will be the outcome? Will only one perspective be heard?

Will the topic be shelved? This may be just the impetus you need to move forward. If you are an inexperienced presenter, have you thought about how this might actually be a benefit? You bring a fresh pair of eyes to the discussion. You are not steeped in conventional wisdom and held back by it. You can think creatively about a problem without being burdened by all the reasons it won't work. You can help the group break out of groupthink. If you make a mistake, it is a way to learn—not evidence of a personal shortcoming.

It is time to throw off what holds you back. It's time to recognize that some of those restraints have been imposed by society. Actress Laura Dern, who is a leader in the Times Up movement, encouraged us to rethink the lessons we learned as children that are no longer applicable.

> Many of us were taught not to tattle. It was a culture of silencing, and that was normalized. I urge all of us to not only support survivors and bystanders who are brave enough to tell their truth, but to support restorative justice. May we also please protect and employ them. May we also teach our children that speaking out without fear of retribution is our culture's new North Star.[7]

EQUAL PAY FOR EQUAL SAY

There are costs involved to saying yes—time spent preparing, time away from family, and sometimes travel expenses. First off, you deserve to be fairly compensated for time, effort, and expenses. Pay equity should apply to public speaking fees like any other job. Negotiating speaker fees is a tricky business because there are no hard-and-fast rules. Ask around to learn whether you're receiving the same fee as men who have similar speaking slots. Find out whether and how much colleagues have been compensated for speaking at similar conferences. Backstage at an event, you can ask other speakers. It may feel uncomfortable or seem rude, but unless you have an agent, there isn't any other way to find out the going rates.

In some cases, it is enough to be invited—the gig may be good for your personal branding, or a to-die-for networking opportunity. But don't allow your first impulse to be settling for having your Lyft receipt reimbursed. There is nothing wrong with asking for an honorarium, and the worst that can happen is you will be told the organization doesn't have a budget for speaker fees. Then you can make a more-educated decision about whether or not it is worth it for you to give your time.

LET GO OF THE DEATH GRIP

> *"A woman with a voice is, by definition, a strong woman. But the search to find that voice can be remarkably difficult."*[8]
>
> —Melinda Gates

Start your search where you need to. Recognize that may mean starting small. If you are battling anxiety, asking a question is a good place to begin. Raising a question at a conference or a meeting is a low-risk way to raise your visibility as well as learn something. Not surprisingly, just as men are more likely to interrupt other speakers, they are also more likely than women to ask questions, especially at scientific meetings. Researchers found that men asked 80 percent more questions than women scientists at a conservation biology conference, even though the audiences were between 40 and 75 percent female.[9]

Asking a question in a large room or speaking up in a meeting can be nerve-racking for fear of becoming tongue-tied or having your comment judged harshly. Write out what you want to say and run through it in your head. It doesn't have to be perfect, but it should not be long. Taking a quick second to jot it down will help you phrase it the way you want and avoid rambling. Joining in versus remaining a spectator in the back row can help you feel more connected to the community. There is no way to figure out what type of forum you are best at other than by giving them a try. You may discover that you are adept at asking questions and would like to participate in more events in the role of moderator. Toastmasters International is a great option for practicing your speaking skills and experimenting with different formats.

Every speaking engagement with a live audience is an opportunity to learn how you can improve your interaction with them. The only way to learn how to read an audience is to be up in front of audiences. What lines did they react to? Did you lose them in the middle? Could the visual aids be improved? Feedback helps you develop a repertoire of high-quality material.

DON'T TRY THIS AT HOME

Sometimes knowing what not to do is more important than knowing what to do.

Liquid Courage

The head of a national organization confessed that before her first live appearance on the *Today* show she needed Jack Daniels to boost her courage. A shot of whiskey might take the edge off pre-show jitters, but you also run the risk of slurring your words. Follow the guidance in chapter 9 about preparing for television interviews.

Palm Pilot

Sarah Palin used notes when she spoke at a large Tea Party conference; unfortunately, they were written on her hand, just like a grocery list. But, rather than *bread, milk, eggs*, she had written "energy, budget cuts, lift American spirits."[10] The media roundly criticized her for having to remind herself to lift the American spirits. Use notecards.

Starting with a Joke

Getting a laugh can be a wonderful way to open, but therein lies the rub. Humor at the top can be an icebreaker that signals to the audience that this isn't going to be nearly as bad as they thought. It can also signal that the speaker doesn't take herself too seriously.

However, what Leslie Jones and Amy Schumer do for a living is not easy. Avoid setting yourself up for a kill-me-now moment with a joke. Even Kathy Griffin says she doesn't tell jokes and can't write one-liners. But she does tell stories. Humor drawn from everyday life that is used to illustrate an essential point can be an icebreaker that connects you with the audience.

Multitasking

A gubernatorial candidate once did a live radio interview with the state's most senior political reporter while in the car, driving along mountain roads.

That is both foolish and dangerous. The interview was worth her undivided attention because it was a chance to make a favorable impression with the voters and a knowledgeable reporter who was closely following the campaign.

LIFT UP YOUR SISTERS

Women in the worlds of politics and entertainment are leading the way for other women by providing a helping hand up. Reese Witherspoon started her own production company to put "different, dynamic women on film."[11] Late-night comedienne Samantha Bee fills the *Full Frontal* writer's room with "people who've been underestimated"[12] by creating a blind application process. The results were a writing staff that is half women and one-third people of color.

For Ava DuVernay, "diversity is a must." The award-winning, visionary movie director has prioritized providing space for people with different backgrounds. The director of *Selma* hired an all-female directing crew for the TV series *Queen Sugar* and has long called for inclusion in a profession she never thought would be a "viable alternative" for her. And for diverse voices in an industry that wasn't interested in "telling the inner stories of black women."[13]

> We should be remembered for the work we put in the world. Even more important is the way that we work. The people that we actually choose to see, that we choose to amplify in the moments when no one is looking and the moments when everyone is looking.[14]

When thousands of first-time candidates expressed a desire to get off the sidelines and run, the women's political community responded with open arms. And strategic support and resources. The experts at the Center for American Women and Politics, Emerge America, EMILY's List, Higher Heights, Ready to Run, Running Start, Run for Something, She Should Run, and others raised their game so women across the country wouldn't have to take the plunge alone.

Supporting women candidates pays off in multiples. Most women seek office not to further a career track but to make a difference, and, once elected, they govern differently than their male counterparts do. Women are more likely to introduce and work on legislation for providing access to healthcare, pushing for pay equity, ending sexual harassment, stopping violence against women, and offering paid family leave.[15] Importantly in this age of extreme partisanship, the women in Congress have been more willing to work across party lines to save the Affordable Care Act and to pass breast cancer and childcare bills.

Women in corporate America and Wall Street might see practices they could emulate to bolster women in business. The Times Up movement has established a sexual-harassment legal defense fund to assist people who are farm laborers, factory employees, restaurant workers, and caregivers. Many companies provide in-house diversity training and leadership conferences, which are a start, but more could be done.

Leadership from the C-Suite is needed to elevate the concerns of women in the workplace. The annual World Economic Forum held in Davos, Switzerland, which attracts the world's most powerful people to discuss society's most pressing issues, took up the issue of sexual harassment for the first time in 2018. Corporate boards remain the ultimate manels, with representation of women remaining at less than 15 percent globally.[16] More than a decade ago, countries in Europe began to increase the representation of women by instituting quotas. Research from all over the world shows that gender-balanced boards create benefits with companies enjoying higher returns on investment and suffering fewer governance-related controversies.[17]

On a personal level, look for opportunities to raise up the women around you. If you've got a colleague or a friend who has speaking talent, be sure to let her know. She may not see it in herself, and your positive reinforcement can be just the boost she needs. Perhaps there is a colleague who lacks skills or confidence. Create a safe space where she can get the feedback and guidance she needs to grow. We need to encourage one another to take risks, and be there to celebrate the successes and offer support for the learning experiences.

FINAL THOUGHT

In conclusion, let me say that ending this book brings mixed emotions. I'm excited to get it to you. But the writing has been a welcome distraction from the daily news cycle. It has provided an outlet for my fear and unease about the current political environment. And it has been a place to celebrate the women who have come forward with stories of change.

It has been an honor to be a part of the women's political community and the broader progressive advocacy community. I continue to have adventures, experience moments of great inspiration, and meet truly dedicated public servants.

It's also a tough business. For every election won, there have been more defeats. For every policy victory, there are setbacks, so it often feels as if you are running in place. But I couldn't turn away if I tried. I've learned you must persevere. If you keep your eyes and ears open, you take away as much, if not more, from failure as you do from victory. If there's something I've tried to impart to the amazing people I've worked with, it is this one thing:

Be yourself on purpose.

It's all you can do. And it's everything.

When someone has done everything there is to do to be ready, then there is no stopping her. There will be uncooperative audiences and difficult people. But, if you've taken the time to be well-prepared and if you believe in what you are doing, there is nothing more. The rest is luck and good timing.

Be yourself on purpose.

Let's march on together.

Well-spoken women drive change!

ACKNOWLEDGMENTS

Many thanks to my husband, Paul Hagen, for his steadfast support; my sister, Lisa Hanson, for being the best sounding board; and my parents and marketing team, Wayne and Sharon Jahnke. My agent, Paul Fedorko, for his humor and sage advice; and Steve Lysohir for making the introduction. Artist Kersti Frigell, for her talent, professionalism, and good spirits. The wise and wonderful Becky Fleischauer. The entire team at Prometheus Books for supporting two books on public-speaking skills for women.

Many thanks for all I've learned from the brilliant and tenacious women leaders and strategists who mostly toil behind the scenes to drive progressive change. Jill Alper, Elizabeth Arledge, Libby Benedict, Jen Bluestein, Donna Brazile, Julie Burton, Jessica Byrd, Venessa Cardenas, Cristal Williams Chancellor, Amy Conroy, Jane Danowitz, Kelly Dittmar, Judith Hope, Mary Hughes, Adrienne Kimmell, Muthoni Wambu Kraal, Karin Johanson, Dawn Laguens, Celinda Lake, Barbara Lee, Ann Lewis, Haven Ley, Jean Lloyd-Jones, Ruth Mandel, Capricia Marshall, Shanelle Matthews, Kate McCarthy, Martha McKenna, Mary Ellen Miller, Sacha Millstone, Lissa Muscatine, Ramona Oliver, Carol Pensky, Andrea Dew Steele, Stephanie Schriock, Catherine St. Laurent, Marion Sullivan, Debbie Walsh, Amy Walter.

ACKNOWLEDGMENTS

WELL-SPOKEN WOMEN
GREAT MOMENTS

Oprah Winfrey's speech at the 2018 Golden Globes immediately shot to the top of my all-time fave list. Her commanding presence was a masterful display of poise, precise language, and poignant urgency. What are the moments that stay with you?

Here are well-spoken women working their magic. They are exemplars of skill, talent, experience, and expertise in a variety of venues. There are many, many women who could be showcased, so the list below is a sampling of remarks for which a transcript or a video is available. Watch, enjoy, and learn!

AWARD ACCEPTANCE SPEECHES

Viola Davis, Emmy acceptance, 2015, https://www.youtube.com/watch?v
=QCCQxsGN-n4.
Viola Davis, Hunger Is Initiative, *Variety* Power of Women, 2014, https://www
.youtube.com/watch?v=AMtKz54UcxQ.
Mia Hamm, National Soccer Hall of Fame Induction, August 27, 2007, https://
www.youtube.com/watch?v=7qdwmhidOL0.
Karen Panetta, professor, Anita Borg Institute Women of Vision, 2011, https://
www.youtube.com/watch?v=G5JhwuFCHlk.
Issa Rae, *Essence* Black Women in Hollywood, March 5, 2017, https://www
.youtube.com/watch?v=cIkWRup2MjM.

Meryl Streep, 2017 Golden Globe Cecil B. DeMille Lifetime Achievement Award acceptance, https://www.youtube.com/watch?v=WVUHntJ7FCY.

Pat Summitt, Naismith Memorial Basketball Hall of Fame Induction, 2002, https://www.youtube.com/watch?v=ac6oBOcjBro.

Serena Williams, *Sports Illustrated* Sportsperson of the Year, December 15, 2015, https://www.youtube.com/watch?v=I9eoPS1Rzug.

Oprah Winfrey, 2018 Golden Globes Cecil B. DeMille Lifetime Achievement Award acceptance, https://www.youtube.com/watch?v=fN5HV79_8B8.

COMMENCEMENT ADDRESSES

Jill Abramson, Wake Forest University, 2014, https://www.youtube.com/watch?v=wC0idAdoxbI.

Nora Ephron, Wellesley College, 2012, https://www.youtube.com/watch?v=DVCfFBlKpN8.

Melissa Harris-Perry, Wellesley College, May 25, 2012, https://www.youtube.com/watch?v=JO4mepx-7vU.

Mindy Kaling, Harvard Law School, 2017, https://www.youtube.com/watch?v=a7_49EXuLoQ.

Barbara Kingsolver, Duke University, 2008, https://today.duke.edu/2008/05/kingsolver.html.

Wangari Maathai, Connecticut College, May 21, 2006, https://www.c-span.org/video/?192688-1/connecticut-college-commencement-address.

Toni Morrison, Wellesley College, May 28, 2004, https://www.youtube.com/watch?v=SAJH03U7aHM.

Michelle Obama, Tuskegee University, 2014, https://www.youtube.com/watch?v=JACTrIRjGos.

Dolly Parton, University of Tennessee, 2009, https://www.youtube.com/watch?v=EuOm2lLIOoU.

Susan Rice, Stanford University, June 15, 2010, https://www.youtube.com/watch?v=o38B5mPbGCI.

J. K. Rowling, Harvard University, 2011, https://www.youtube.com/watch?v=wHGqp8lz36c.

Sheryl Sandberg, Barnard College, May 2011, https://www.youtube.com/watch?v=AdvXCKFNqTY.

CONGRESSIONAL/LEGISLATIVE SPEECHES

US Senator Margaret Chase-Smith, Declaration of Conscience, June 1, 1950, https://www.senate.gov/artandhistory/history/resources/pdf/Smith Declaration.pdf.

Texas State Senator Wendy Davis, opening remarks of eleven-hour filibuster, June 25, 2013, https://www.youtube.com/watch?v=1lOijHOdx8c.

US Representative Barbara Jordan, Watergate Impeachment Hearing, July 25, 1974, https://www.youtube.com/watch?v=UG6xMglSMdk.

US Representative Jackie Speier, abortion story, February 18, 2011, https://www .youtube.com/watch?v=Nz5DZJgclKQ.

DEBATES

Chimamanda Ngozi Adichie, debate interview with R. Emmitt Terrell, BBC *Newsnight*, November 16, 2016, https://www.youtube.com/watch?v =_LAUgq8KX4U.

Hillary Clinton, First Democratic Primary Debate, October 13, 2015, https:// www.youtube.com/watch?v=l0M8P24AGcY.

Hillary Clinton vs. Donald Trump, Presidential Debate, September 26, 2016, https://www.youtube.com/watch?v=855Am6ovK7s.

Hillary Clinton vs. Donald Trump, Presidential Debate, October 9, 2016, https:// www.youtube.com/watch?v=FRlI2SQ0Ueg.

Hillary Clinton vs. Donald Trump, Presidential Debate, October 19, 2016, https:// www.youtube.com/watch?v=ye0Xblp_Nb0.

Geraldine Ferraro vs. George H. W. Bush, 1984 Vice Presidential Debate, Philadelphia, PA, October 11, 1984, https://www.youtube.com/watch?v =42scedX5MT8.

Jennifer Granholm vs. Dick DeVos, Gubernatorial Debate, Michigan State University, October 2, 2006, https://www.c-span.org/video/?194580-1/ michigan-gubernatorial-debate.

Jennifer Granholm vs. Dick DeVos, Gubernatorial Debate, Michigan State University, October 10, 2006, https://www.youtube.com/watch?v =8pd09PSBr9Y.

Maggie Hassan vs. Kelly Ayotte, US Senate Debate, October 29, 2016, https:// www.c-span.org/video/?417411-1/hampshire-senate-debate.

Gina Raimondo, Gubernatorial Debate, October 24, 2014, https://www.c-span
.org/video/?322235-1/rhode-island-governors-debate.
Symone Sanders, debate interview with Jeffrey Lord, CNN New Day, April 13,
2017, https://www.youtube.com/watch?v=Hk9ajgkAOLA.
Elizabeth Warren vs. Scott Brown, US Senate Debate, October 1, 2012, https://
www.c-span.org/video/?308386-1/massachusetts-senate-debate.
Elizabeth Warren vs. Scott Brown, US Senate Debate, October 10, 2012, https://
www.c-span.org/video/?308580-1/massachusetts-senate-debate.

GOVERNMENT/LEGAL TESTIMONY

Hillary Clinton, former secretary of state, Select Committee on Benghazi, October
22, 2015, https://www.c-span.org/video/?328699-1/hillary-clinton
-testimony-house-select-committee-benghazi-part-1.
Ruth Bader Ginsburg, Senate confirmation hearing for Supreme Court, July 1993,
https://www.youtube.com/watch?v=-VfUB7PgW4o.
Anita Hill, law professor, US Senate Judiciary Committee Hearing, October 11,
1991, https://www.c-span.org/video/?22097-1/clarence-thomas
-confirmation-hearing.
Aly Raisman, Olympic gymnast at sentencing hearing for Lawrence Nassar, County
Court Ingham County, Michigan, January 19, 2018, https://www.youtube
.com/watch?v=yW4Cm5vRutM.
Cecile Richards, president, Planned Parenthood, US Committee on Oversight
and Government Reform, September 29, 2015, https://www.youtube.com/
watch?v=gPDszR4195k.
Sally Yates, former deputy attorney general, US Senate subcommittee investigating
Russian ties to 2016 presidential election, May 8, 2017, https://www.youtube
.com/watch?v=YtIQdneqlq4.

KEYNOTES

Chimamanda Ngozi Adichie, "We Should All Be Feminists," TED Talk, April
2013, https://www.youtube.com/watch?v=hg3umXU_qWc.
Maya Angelo, "On the Pulse of the Morning," presidential inauguration poem,
January 20, 1993, https://www.youtube.com/watch?v=Fg0mu32h5IY.

Charlene Carruthers, "Killing the Black Imagination," Illinois Wesleyan University, May 12, 2016, https://www.youtube.com/watch?v=m_UlTTUvJDw.

Laverne Cox, "Creating Change," National LGBTQ Task Force, February 2014, https://www.youtube.com/watch?v=6cytc0p4Jwg.

Anna Marie Chavez, CEO Girls Scouts of USA, National Press Club, June 13, 2016, https://www.c-span.org/video/?410958-1/ceo-anna-maria-chvez-speaks-future-girl-scouts.

Kelly Dittmar, "Navigating Gendered Terrain," New Brunswick, New Jersey, March 2015, https://www.youtube.com/watch?v=44-_aCMii4Y.

Alicia Garza, "From Protest to Power," Iowa Citizens for Community Improvement, July 2017, https://www.youtube.com/watch?v=08hM1ewXTqM.

Melinda Gates, "Let's Put Birth Control Back on the Agenda," TED Talk, 2012, https://www.youtube.com/watch?v=2BOTS9GAjc4.

Ruth Bader Ginsburg, Stanford Rathbun Lecture, Stanford University, February 2017, https://www.youtube.com/watch?v=83XnwyWg_q8.

Jane Goodall, primatologist, "Sowing the Seeds of Change," Concordia University, March 28, 2014, https://www.youtube.com/watch?v=vibssrQKm60.

Carla Harris, "How to Own Your Power," Take the Lead Conference, February 19, 2014, https://www.youtube.com/watch?v=0rWmtyZXkFg.

Dolores Huerta, Netroots Nation 2017, August 12, 2017, https://www.facebook.com/NetrootsNation/videos/10155491655864827/.

Winona LaDuke, Seeds of Our Ancestors, TEDx, Minneapolis, MN, March 4, 2012, https://www.youtube.com/watch?v=pHNlel72eQc.

Christine Lagarde, managing director International Monetary Fund, "Three Ls of Leadership," June 8, 2016, https://www.youtube.com/watch?v=EK2s1gq2uIM.

Fei Fei Li, computer scientist, "Google Gets Aggressive in A.I." Google Cloud Next, March 2017, https://www.youtube.com/watch?v=Rgqgdddl018.

Ellen Sirleaf Johnson, President of Liberia, United Nations General Assembly, September 19, 2017, https://www.youtube.com/watch?v=gHNMCINFCDY.

Wilma Mankiller, "Challenges Facing 21st Century Indigenous People," Arizona State University, October 2008, https://www.youtube.com/watch?v=9K_rVUmV7Y8.

Ai-jen Poo, labor leader, "Building a Caring America," TEDx Middlebury, VT, August 18, 2013, https://www.youtube.com/watch?v=ColFFPNgtK4.

Anita Sarkeesian, "Feminist Frequency," XOXO Festival, Portland, OR, 2014, https://www.youtube.com/watch?v=ah8mhDW6Shs.

Amy Webb, futurist, "The Signals Are Talking," John Adams Institute, March 2017, https://www.youtube.com/watch?v=JICXBu8Y4ak.

MODERATOR/PANELIST/EMCEE

Madeleine Albright, "America's Place in the World," conversation CSIS conference, Washington, DC, January 30, 2017, https://www.youtube.com/watch?v=SWdQQbayiYk.

Grace Hopper, Rear Admiral, *The Late Show with David Letterman*, 1986, https://www.youtube.com/watch?v=1-vcErOPofQ.

Tina Fey and Amy Poehler, Golden Globes Opening Monologue, January13, 2013, https://www.youtube.com/watch?v=F4rSKCXqEw0.

Tina Fey and Amy Poehler, Golden Globes Opening Monologue, January12, 2014, https://www.youtube.com/watch?v=b5ZnnE1nPrQ.

Tina Fey and Amy Poehler, Golden Globes Opening Monologue, January 11, 2015, https://www.youtube.com/watch?v=8cyrltnOQm8.

Sallie Krawcheck, "Investing Gender Gap," Tech Crunch, May 2016, https://www.youtube.com/watch?v=dBpTwLHgL_s.

Sonia Sotomayor, "My Beloved World," conversation, University of Washington, 2014, https://www.youtube.com/watch?v=cnHwRTovPv4.

Elaine Welteroth, editor, *Teen Vogue*, conversation with Rowan Blanchard, Inbound 2017, https://www.youtube.com/watch?v=u2iyuBIYjkA.

POLITICAL CONVENTIONS/RALLIES

Sister Simone Campbell, 2012 Democratic National Convention, Charlotte, NC, https://www.youtube.com/watch?v=Yw-m8Hfj4rw.

Shirley Chisholm, Presidential Campaign Announcement, January 25, 1972, https://www.youtube.com/watch?v=7s_0cYIs2gs.

Hillary Clinton, 2016 Democratic National Convention, presidential nomination acceptance, Philadelphia, PA, July 28, 2016, https://www.youtube.com/watch?v=pnXiy4D_I8g.

Geraldine Ferraro, 1984 Democratic National Convention, vice presidential nomination acceptance, San Francisco, CA, https://www.youtube.com/watch?v=Lw0MF-I85XE.

Barbara Jordan, 1976 Democratic National Convention, New York City, https://www.youtube.com/watch?v=Bg7gLIx__-k.

Michelle Obama, 2016 Democratic National Convention, Philadelphia, PA, July 25, 2016, https://www.youtube.com/watch?v=4ZNWYqDU948.

Michelle Obama, 2016 Presidential Campaign, Manchester, NH, October 13, 2016, https://www.youtube.com/watch?v=SJ45VLgbe_E.

Ann Richards, 1988 Democratic National Convention, Atlanta, GA, https://www.youtube.com/watch?v=wtIFhiqS_TY.

PROTESTS/RALLIES

Angela Davis, Women's March 2017, Washington, DC, https://www.youtube.com/watch?v=TTB-m2NxWzA.

America Ferrera, Women's March 2017, Washington, DC, https://www.youtube.com/watch?v=c5bOsXj4wYo.

Ashley Judd, Women's March 2017, Washington, DC, https://www.youtube.com/watch?v=ffb 5X59 DA.

Coretta Scott King, Ten Commandants on Vietnam, New York City, April 27, 1968, https://www.youtube.com/watch?v=2B-7RhNgYNA.

Linda Sarsour, Women's March 2017, Washington, DC, https://www.youtube.com/watch?v=DnaT8JxUTY0.

Gloria Steinem, Women's March 2017, Washington, DC, https://www.youtube.com/watch?v=4ukHjJzRCas.

Phyllis Young, Sioux elder at Standing Rock, North Dakota, December 4, 2016, https://www.youtube.com/watch?v=xLwErEqVtb4.

NOTES

INTRODUCTION

1. Theodore Roosevelt, "Citizenship in a Republic," speech at Sorbonne, Paris, France, April 23, 1910.

2. Eleanor Roosevelt, *You Learn by Living: Eleven Keys for a More Fulfilling Life* (New York: Harper, 1960), p. 30.

CHAPTER 1: THE FUTURE IS FEMALE

1. Ashley Bennett, interview by Lawrence O'Donnell, MSNBC, November 8, 2017, "Meet the NJ Woman Who Beat Republican That Mocked Women's March | The Last Word | MSNBC," YouTube video, 6:29, https://www.youtube.com/watch?v=kZEDaKUauHI.

2. Emma González, speech, March for Our Lives, Washington, DC, March 24, 2018.

3. Marcus Christenson, "Swedish Women's Team Replace Shirt Names with Messages of Empowerment," *Guardian*, March 2, 2017, https://www.theguardian.com/football/2017/mar/02/sweden -women-team-shirt-names-empowerment.

4. Ibid.

5. Amy S. Rosenberg, "Jersey GOP Official: Will Women's March End in Time for Them to Cook Dinner?" *Inquirer Daily News*, January 24, 2017, http://www.philly.com/philly/blogs/downashore/Shore-official -interviewed-on-Fox-criticized-for-misogynist-post-on-womensmarch-john -carman-atlantic-county-freeholder-facebook.html.

6. Isaac Saul, "Ashley Bennett Ran Because of a Meme and Joined a

Movement," *APlus*, December 27, 2017, https://aplus.com/a-plus-game
-changer-of-the-year/ashley-bennett-atlantic-county-freeholder-john
-carman-sexist-meme?no_monetization=true.

7. Amy S. Rosenberg, "Woman Who Ran After Atlantic County
Freeholder Mocked the Women's March Knocked Him off the Board,"
Inquirer Daily News, November 8, 2017, http://www.philly.com/philly/
news/new_jersey/shore/run-for-something-ashley-bennett-womens-march
-dinner-john-carmam-atlantic-county-freeholder-20171108.html.

8. Carmen Perez, panel discussion, Women's Convention, Detroit,
MI, October 28, 2017.

9. Carmen Yulín Cruz, press conference, San Juan, Puerto Rico,
September 29, 2017.

10. Richard Fausset and Frances Robles, "Who Is Carmen Yulín Cruz,
the Puerto Rican Mayor Criticized by Trump," *New York Times*, September 30,
2017, https://www.nytimes.com/2017/09/30/us/san-juan-mayor-cruz.html.

11. Mary Wang, "Trump Attack on San Juan Mayor As a 'Nasty'
Woman Only Emphasizes His Failures in Puerto Rico," *Vogue*,
September 30, 2017, https://www.vogue.com/article/trump-nasty
-woman-san-juan-mayor-puerto-rico.

12. Vann R. Newkirk II, "Puerto Rico's Power Scandal Expands,"
Atlantic, November 3, 2017, https://www.theatlantic.com/politics/
archive/2017/11/puerto-rico-whitefish-cobra-fema-contracts/544892/.

13. Brené Brown, "The Power of Vulnerability," speech, TEDx Talk,
Houston, TX, June 2010, video, 20:13, https://www.ted.com/talks/
brene_brown_on_vulnerability.

14. Chris L. Jenkins, "Marshall Admits No Doubts about Marriage,"
Washington Post, November 4, 2006, http://www.washingtonpost.com/
wp-dyn/content/article/2006/11/03/AR2006110301580.html
?tid=a_mcntx.

15. Ashley Dejean, "One of the Most Anti-LGBTQ Lawmakers in
the Country May Lose His Seat to a Transgender Journalist," *Mother Jones*,
November 6, 2017, https://www.motherjones.com/politics/2017/11/one-
of-the-most-anti-lgbt-lawmakers-in-the-country-might-lose-his-seat-to-a-
transgender-journalist/.

16. Danica Roem, Prince William County Democratic Committee
Election Night Celebration, speech, Manassas, VA, November 8, 2017.

17. Frank Bruni, "Danica Roem Is Really, Really Boring," *New York Times*, November 14, 2017, https://www.nytimes.com/2017/11/14/opinion/danica-roem-virginia-transgender.html.

18. Danica Roem, "Danica Roem: Why I Got into Politics," interview by Kiran Moodley, UK Channel 4 News, November 23, 2017, https://www.channel4.com/news/transgender-state-legislators-thanksgiving-message.

19. Katty Kay and Claire Shipman, "The Confidence Gap," *Atlantic*, May 2014, https://www.theatlantic.com/magazine/archive/2014/05/the-confidence-gap/359815/.

20. Pauline Rose Clance and Suzanne Imes, "The Imposter Phenomenon in High Achieving Women: Dynamics and Therapeutic Intervention," *Psychology Theory, Research and Practice* 5 no. 3 (Fall 1978), http://www.paulineroseclance.com/pdf/ip_high_achieving_women.pdf.

21. Brook Baldwin, interview, CNN Newsroom, September 15, 2017, "Clay Travis Stuns CNN Host When He Says He Believes in Two Things: The First Amendment and Boobs," Washington Free Beacon, YouTube video, 2:41, https://www.youtube.com/watch?v=XSCneVakGGk.

22. Callum Borchers, "Clay Travis Used His 'First Amendment and Boobs' Line Long before He Shocked CNN," *Washington Post*, September 15, 2017, https://www.washingtonpost.com/news/the-fix/wp/2017/09/15/clay-travis-used-his-first-amendment-and-boobs-line-long-before-he-shocked-cnn/?utm_term=.bdd8be1926cf.

23. Maxine Waters, US House Financial Services Committee hearing, C-SPAN, July 27, 2017, video, 3:00:09, https://www.c-span.org/video/?431675-1/treasury-secretary-testifies-state-international-finance-system.

24. Rose McGowan, opening speech, Women's Convention, Detroit, MI, October 27, 2017.

25. Jodi Kantor and Megan Twohey, "Harvey Weinstein Paid Off Sexual Harassment Accusers for Decades," *New York Times*, October 5, 2017, https://www.nytimes.com/2017/10/05/us/harvey-weinstein-harassment-allegations.html.

26. Justin Jones, "When It Comes to Politics, Friendship Has Its Limits," *New York Times*, July 23, 2007, http://www.nytimes.com/2007/07/23/us/politics/23oprah.html.

27. Emma González, anti-gun rally speech, Fort Lauderdale, FL, February 17, 2018, "Florida Student to NRA and Trump: 'We Call BS,'"

CNN, YouTube video, 11:40, https://www.youtube.com/watch?v =ZxD3o-9H1lY.

28. Audrey Carlson and Jugal Patel, "March for Our Lives Maps of the More Than 800 Protests around the World," *New York Times*, March 22, 2018, https://www.nytimes.com/interactive/2018/03/22/us/politics/march-for-lives-demonstrations.html.

29. Steve Collins, "Maine Candidate Calls Teen Who Survived Florida School Shooting a 'Lesbian Skinhead,'" *Sun Journal*, March 12, 2018, https://www.pressherald.com/2018/03/12/maine-house-candidate-from -sabattus-calls-activist-teens-from-florida-a-skinhead-lesbian-and-another-a -bald-faced-liar/.

30. May Rhodon, "This Post about Emma Gonzalez on Rep. Steve King's Facebook Is Making People Mad," *Time*, March 26, 2018, http://time.com/5215844/steve-king-facebook-post-emma-gonzalez/.

CHAPTER 2: THE SELF-AWARENESS QUOTIENT

1. Nikolas Westerhoff, "The 'Big Five' Personality Traits," *Scientific American*, December 17, 2008, https://www.scientificamerican.com/article/the-big-five/.

2. *Norma Rae*, directed by Martin Ritt (1979, Twentieth Century Fox).

3. Jelani Cobb, "The Matter of Black Lives," *New Yorker*, March 14, 2016, https://www.newyorker.com/magazine/2016/03/14/where -is-black-lives-matter-headed.

4. Yolanda Renee King, speech at March for Our Lives, Washington, DC, March 24, 2018.

5. Ioana Latu, Marianne Schmid Mast, Joris Lammers, and Dario Bammari, "Successful Female Leaders Empower Women's Behavior in Leadership Tasks," *Journal of Experimental Social Psychology* 49 (January 16, 2013): 444–48, https://www.ed.ac.uk/files/atoms/files/latu2013.pdf.

6. Moria Forbes, "Laverne Cox on Why She Still Has Something to Prove," *Forbes*, June 30, 2016, https://www.forbes.com/sites/moira forbes/2016/06/30/laverne-cox-on-why-she-still-has-something -to-prove/#5ab20d265638.

7. Rebecca Solnit, "Silence and Powerlessness Go Hand in Hand—Women's Voices Must Be Heard," *Guardian*, March 8, 2017, https://www.theguardian.com/commentisfree/2017/mar/08/silence-powerlessness-womens-voices-rebecca-solnit.

8. Aalayah Eastmond, speech at March for Our Lives, Washington, DC, March 24, 2018.

9. Edna Lizbeth Chavez, speech at March for Our Lives, Washington, DC, March 24, 2018.

10. Tyra Hemans, speech at March for Our Lives, Washington, DC, March 24, 2018.

11. Naomi Wadler, speech at March for Our Lives, Washington, DC, March 24, 2018.

CHAPTER 3: READING THE ROOM

1. Personal communication with the author.

2. Stacy Schiff, *Cleopatra: A Life* (New York: Little, Brown, 2010), p. 31.

3. Carroll Brooks Ellis, "A Good Man Speaking Well," *Southern Speech Journal* 11, no. 4 (1946): 85, http://www.tandfonline.com/doi/abs/10.1080/10417944609370967?journalCode=rsjc18.

4. Thomas Jefferson, letter to Samuel Kercheval, September 6, 1816, in John P. Foley, ed., *The Jeffersonian Cyclopedia* (New York and London: Funk & Wagnalls, 1900), entry 7282.

5. Institute for Women's Policy Research, "Political Participation, Status of Women in the States," 2015, https://statusofwomendata.org/explore-the-data/political-participation/#section-a.

6. United States Census Bureau, "Age and Sex Composition: 2010," https://www.census.gov/prod/cen2010/briefs/c2010br-03.pdf.

7. Ibid.

8. Olga Kahzan, "Why Pence's Dudely Dinners Hurt Women," *Atlantic*, March 30, 2017, https://www.theatlantic.com/science/archive/2017/03/pences-gender-segregated-dinners/521286/.

9. Tamara Cofman Wittes and Marc Lynch, "The Mysterious

Absence of Women from Middle East Policy Debates," *Washington Post*, January 20, 2015, https://www.washingtonpost.com/news/monkey-cage/wp/2015/01/20/the-mysterious-absence-of-women-from-middle-east-policy-debates/?utm_term=.970ad5f976ad.

10. Michelle Cottle, "Why Sexual-Harassment Legislation Stalled in the Senate," *Atlantic*, April 17, 2018, https://www.theatlantic.com/politics/archive/2018/04/sexual-harassment-bill-senate/558176/.

11. Julia Bullez, "Once Again 13 Men Wrote a Bill That's Bad for Women's Health," *Vox*, June 23, 2017, https://www.vox.com/2017/6/22/15845832/republican-senate-healthcare-bill-planned-parenthood-better-care-reconciliation-act.

12. Halle Tecco, "Women's Voices Largely Missing from Health Care Conferences (and How We Can Fix It in 2014)," (study) Rock Health, December 13, 2013, https://rockhealth.com/xx-health-can-better-2014/.

13. Vidhi Doshi, "Why Doctors Still Misunderstand Heart Disease in Women," *Atlantic*, October 26, 2015, https://www.theatlantic.com/health/archive/2015/10/heart-disease-women/412495/.

14. Susan Danziger, "Speaking Up for More Women Speakers at Conferences," *Forbes*, August 30, 2016, https://www.forbes.com/sites/susandanziger/2016/08/30/speaking-up-for-more-female-speakers-at-tech-conferences/#12d4466a0d12.

15. Arielle Dohaime-Ross, "Apple Promised an Expansive Health App, So Why Can't I Track Menstruation," *Verge*, September 25, 2014, https://www.theverge.com/2014/9/25/6844021/apple-promised-an-expansive-health-app-so-why-cant-i-track.

16. Rebecca Robins and Meghana Keshavan, "Men Named Michael Outnumber Female CEOs," Stat, January 7, 2018, https://www.statnews.com/2018/01/07/jpm-gender-diversity/.

17. Nadia Khoja, "Women Still Not Welcome: The Ongoing Problem with MarTech Conferences," Venngage, June 18, 2017, https://venngage.com/blog/women-speaker-marketing-tech-diversity/.

18. Elizabeth Cady Stanton, Susan B. Anthony, and Matilda Jocelyn Gage, eds., *History of Women's Suffrage*, vol. 1 (New York: Fowler & Wells, 1881), pp. 53–54.

19. Ibid.

20. Lorraine Boisseneault, "The Original Women's March on Washing-

ton and the Suffragists Who Paved the Way," Smithsonian.com, January 21, 2017, https://www.smithsonianmag.com/history/original-womens-march-washington-and-suffragists-who-paved-way-180961869/.

21. Elizabeth Dwoskin and Danielle Paquette, "The TED Talks Empire Has Been Grappling with Sexual Harassment, Interviews and Internal Emails Show," *Washington Post*, November 17, 2017, https://www.washington post.com/business/economy/the-ted-talks-empire-has-been-grappling-with-sexual-harassment-interviews-and-internal-emails-show/2017/11/17/39f9 374a-cae7-11e7-b0cf-7689a9f2d84e_story.html?utm_term=.faeb0db4604c.

22. Andrea Moore Kerr, *Lucy Stone: Speaking Out for Equality* (New Brunswick, NJ: Rutgers University Press, 1992), p. 44.

23. Ibid., p. 24.

24. Collier Meyerson, "The Founders of Black Lives Matter: We Gave Tongue to Something We All Knew was Happening," *Glamour*, November 1, 2016, https://www.glamour.com/story/women-of-the-year-black-lives-matter-founders.

25. "Violence against the Transgender Community in 2017," Human Rights Campaign, report, 2018, https://www.hrc.org/resources/violence-against-the-transgender-community-in-2017.

26. Anita Samuels, *Rants and Retorts* (North Charleston, SC: CreateSpace, 2016), pp. 1–6.

27. Soraya Nadia McDonald, "Gamergate," *Washington Post*, October 15, 2014, https://www.washingtonpost.com/news/morning-mix/wp/2014/10/15/gamergate-feminist-video-game-critic-anita-sarkeesian-cancels-utah-lecture-after-threat-citing-police-inability-to-prevent-concealed-weapons-at-event/?utm_term=.d0450e74f167.

28. Adi Robertson, "The FBI Has Released Its Gamergate Investigation Records," Verge, January 27, 2017, https://www.theverge.com/2017/1/27/14412594/fbi-gamergate-harassment-threat-investigation-records-release.

29. Doug Glanville, Who Gets to Call the Game? *New York Times*, July 29, 2017, https://www.nytimes.com/2017/07/29/opinion/sunday/jessica-mendoza-baseball-espn.html.

30. Tim Hill, "Jessica Mendoza Receives Sexist Backlash after Calling MLB Playoff Game," *Guardian*, October 7, 2015, https://www.theguardian.com/sport/2015/oct/07/jessica-mendoza-espn-mlb-yankees-astros.

31. Domenico Montanaro, "ESPN Flap Shows People Can't Even Agree What They Are Arguing Over in the Trump Era," NPR, September 17, 2017, https://www.npr.org/2017/09/17/551636211/espn-flap-shows -people-cant-even-agree-on-what-theyre-arguing-over-in-trump-era.

32. Deborah Tannen, *You Just Don't Understand* (New York: HarperCollins, 1990), p. 90.

33. Leah Sinclair, "The Angry Black Girl Stereotype Shows How Little We Are Respected," *Guardian*, October 8, 2015, https://www .theguardian.com/commentisfree/2015/oct/08/stereotype -angry-black-girls-racial.

34. Catalyst, *The Double-Bind Dilemma for Women in Leadership: Damned If You Do, Damned If You Don't* (New York, 2007), p. 1, https:// books.google.com/books?id=okXTiuDlAGAC&pg=PA1&lpg=PA1 &dq=gender+double-bind+feeling+of+being+trapped&source= bl&ots=TnuJHmPu5n&sig=3o9lP3fdOYF7BKfP1MfoTGp6bwc&hl= en&sa=X&ved=0ahUKEwjHpevlytXbAhUwvlkKHZUNBrEQ6 AEIVDAI#v=onepage&q=gender%20double-bind%20feeling%20of %20being%20trapped&f=false.

35. Sheryl Sandberg, "Speaking While Female," *New York Times*, January 12, 2015, https://www.nytimes.com/2015/01/11/opinion/ sunday/speaking-while-female.html.

36. Victoria Brescoll, "Who Takes the Floor and Why," *Administrative Science Quarterly* 56, no. 4 (February 29, 2012), http://journals.sagepub .com/doi/abs/10.1177/0001839212439994.

37. Cristal Williams Chancellor, ed., '"*The Status of Women in the US Media 2017*" (New York and Washington, DC: Women's Media Center, March 21, 2017), p.1, http://www.womensmediacenter.com/assets/site/ reports/10c550d19ef9f3688f_mlbres2jd.pdf.

38. Personal communication with the author.

39. Sharon Kann, "How Cable News Keeps Getting It Wrong on Abortion and Reproductive Rights," (study) Media Matters for America, April 18, 2017, https://www.mediamatters.org/research/2017/04/18/ study-how-cable-news-keeps-getting-it-wrong-about-abortion-and -reproductive-rights/216069.

40. Ella Nilson, "Mark Halperin Once Downplayed Sexual Harassment Claims against Trump. Now He Is Facing His Own," *Vox*,

October 27, 2017, https://www.vox.com/2017/10/27/16559880/
mark-halperin-trump-sexual-harassment.

41. Michelle Mark, "A Former NBC Employee Has Accused Matt
Lauer of Locking Her in His Office and Sexually Assaulting Her During the
Day," *Business Insider*, November 30, 2017, http://www.businessinsider
.com/matt-lauer-accused-sexual-assaulting-nbc-employee-office-2017-11.

42. Anna North, "Matt Lauer Was Fired for Reported Sexual
Harassment. Watch Him Question Hillary Clinton's 'Judgment,'"
Vox, November 29, 2017, https://www.vox.com/identities/
2017/11/29/16714964/matt-lauer-sexual-harassment-nbc-hillary-clinton.

43. Claire Cain Miller, "From Sex Object to Gritty Woman: The
Evolution of Women in Stock Photos," *New York Times*, September 7, 2017,
https://www.nytimes.com/2017/09/07/upshot/from-sex-object-to-gritty
-woman-the-evolution-of-women-in-stock-photos.html.

44. Martha Lauzen, *It's a Man's Celluloid World: Portrayals of
Female Characters in the Top 100 Films in 2016* (report; San Diego,
CA: Center for the Study of Women in Television and Film, San Diego
State University, 2017), http://womenintvfilm.sdsu.edu/wp-content/
uploads/2017/02/2016-Its-a-Mans-Celluloid-World-Report.pdf.

45. Tonja Jacobi and Dylan Schweers, "Justice Interrupted: The Effect
of Gender, Ideology, and Seniority at Supreme Court Oral Arguments,"
Virginia Law Review 102, no. 1379 (2017), Northwestern Law & Econ
Research Paper No. 17–03, October 24, 2017, https://papers.ssrn.com/
sol3/papers.cfm?abstract_id=2933016.

46. Lauzen, *It's a Man's Celluloid World*.

47. Kelly Lawler, "Ava DuVernay: I Hate the Word Diversity," *USA
Today*, January 26, 2016, https://www.usatoday.com/story/life/movies/
2016/01/26/ava-duvernay-oscars-academy-awards-diversity/79338066/

48. Donald Trump, press conference remarks, Trump Tower, New
York, August 15, 2017, https://www.politico.com/story/2017/08/15/
full-text-trump-comments-white-supremacists-alt-left-transcript-241662.

49. Josh Dawsey, "Trump Derides Protections for Immigrants from
'Shithole' Countries," *Washington Post*, January 12, 2018, https://www
.washingtonpost.com/politics/trump-attacks-protections-for-immigrants
-from-shithole-countries-in-oval-office-meeting/2018/01/11/bfc0725c
-f711-11e7-91af-31ac729add94_story.html?utm_term=.22368d2f61ec.

50.   Phyllis Schlafly, "What's Wrong with Equal Rights' for Women?" *Phyllis Schlafly Report*, no. 7, February 1972, p. 4.

51.   Ella Alexander, "Karl Lagerfeld: How My Fat Comments Helped Adele," *Vogue*, June 4, 2013, http://www.vogue.co.uk/article/karl-lagerfeld-adele-fat-comments-helped-her-to-lose-weight.

52.   Charli Carpenter, "Five Don'ts for Introducing a Female Speaker," *Duck of Minerva*, May 10, 2016, http://duckofminerva.com/2016/05/five-donts-for-introducing-a-female-speaker-and-why-this-matters.html.

53.   Scott Wilson, "Obama Apologizes to California Attorney General over Comment about Looks," *Washington Post*, April 5, 2013, https://www.washingtonpost.com/politics/obama-apologizes-to-california-attorney-general-kamala-harris-over-comment-on-looks/2013/04/05/0d080766-9e28-11e2-9a79-eb5280c81c63_story.html?utm_term=.f02828e888d8.

54.   Ari Fleischer, tweet, July 25, 2012, https://twitter.com/AriFleischer.

55.   Daisuke Wakabayashi, "Google Fires Engineer Who Wrote Memo Questioning Women in Tech," *New York Times*, August 7, 2017, https://www.nytimes.com/2017/08/07/business/google-women-engineer-fired-memo.html.

56.   Rebecca Solnit, "Men Explain Things to Me," chap. 1 in *Men Explain Things to Me* (Chicago, IL: Haymarket Books, 2014). Essay originally published 2008.

57.   Gail Collins, "Bernie Sanders Yells His Mind," *New York Times*, May 1, 2015, https://www.nytimes.com/2015/05/02/opinion/gail-collins-bernie-sanders-yells-his-mind.html.

CHAPTER 4: RESISTING BOORS AND BULLIES

1.   Jessicah Lahitou, "Who Is Don Young? The GOP Lawmaker Berated His Female Colleague on the House Floor," *Bustle*, September 8, 2017, https://www.bustle.com/p/who-is-don-young-the-gop-lawmaker-berated-his-female-colleague-on-the-house-floor-2303061.

2.   Rob Hotakainen and Lindsay Wise, "Dear Women: You Can't Read. Your Hair Looks Bad. And Stop Shaking Your Head," *McClatchy*,

March 21, 2017, http://www.mcclatchydc.com/news/politics-government/
article141996689.html.

3. Andrea Gonzalez-Ramirez, "This Immigrant Is the First Indian
American Elected to the US House," *Refinery 29*, November 9, 2016,
http://www.refinery29.com/2016/10/125469/pramila-jayapal
-washington-woman-running-congress.

4. Patricia Sullivan, "Marshall Ad Accuses Roem of 'Lewd Behavior'
in Old Video of Her Band," *Washington Post*, October 25, 2017, https://
www.washingtonpost.com/local/virginia-politics/marshall-ad-accuses
-roem-of-lewd-behavior-based-on-old-video-of-her-band/2017/
10/25/ca12f208-b9a8-11e7-9e58-e6288544af98_story.html?utm
_term=.5b14819666d7.

5. Danica Roem, "Virginia Elections a Sweep for Democrats,"
WAMU's the Kojo Nnamdi Show, November 8, 2017, https://
thekojonnamdishow.org/shows/2017-11-08/virginia-election-wrap-up.

6. Juliet Eilperin, "White House Women Want to Be in the Room
Where It Happens," *Washington Post*, September 13, 2016, https://www
.washingtonpost.com/news/powerpost/wp/2016/09/13/white-house
-women-are-now-in-the-room-where-it-happens/?utm_term=.a415347
aeee4.

7. Dylan Kickham, "Amy Schumer Heckler Shut Down by Comedian
During Show," *Entertainment Weekly*, September 1, 2016, http://ew.com/
article/2016/09/01/amy-schumer-heckler/.

CHAPTER 5: POWER WORDS—
INTENTIONAL STORYTELLING

1. Patrick Marley, "Dem Governor Candidate Kelda Roys Talks
about Banning BPA while Breastfeeding Daughter in Campaign Video,"
Milwaukee Journal Sentinel, March 6, 2018, https://www.jsonline.com/
story/news/politics/2018/03/06/dem-governor-candidate-kelda-roys
-talks-banning-bpa-while-breastfeeding-her-daughter-campaign-video/
400198002/.

2. Pamela Meyer, "How to Spot a Liar," TED Global speech,

July 2011, video, 18:49, https://www.ted.com/talks/pamela_meyer _how_to_spot_a_liar.

3. The American Association of University Women, https://www .aauw.org/. At the time of writing, this line appeared on the organization's website, but it has since been removed.

4. Diane Horvath-Cosper, "How Does an Abortion Provide Work," interview by Jacob Brogan, *Slate's Working*, November 22, 2016, http:// www.slate.com/articles/podcasts/working/2016/11/how_does_obgyn _diane_horvath_cosper_work.html.

5. Ayanna Pressley, interview by Chris Lovett, *BNN News*, February 9, 2018, "Pressley Mounts Challenge for Congress," Chris Lovett, YouTube video, 9:44, https://www.youtube.com/watch?v=x9OFk0yGUDs.

6. Sophie Cruz, speech at Women's March, Washington, DC, January 21, 2017.

7. Winona LaDuke, "Seeds of Our Ancestors Seeds of Life," TEDxTC speech, March 4, 2012, "TEDxTC – Winona LaDuke – Seeds of Our Ancestors, Seeds of Life," TEDx TALKS, YouTube video, 16:36, https://www.youtube.com/watch?v=pHNlel72eQc&vl=en.

8. Aaron Gottlieb, "The Effects of Message Frames on Public Attitudes toward Criminal Justice Reform for Nonviolent Offenses," *Crime and Delinquency* 63, no. 5 (2017), http://journals.sagepub.com/ doi/10.1177/0011128716687758.

9. Emma Watson, "He for She Campaign," United Nations speech, New York, September 22, 2014, "Emma Watson at the HeForShe Campaign 2014 – Official UN Video," United Nations, YouTube video, 13:15, https://www.youtube.com/watch?v=gkjW9PZBRfk.

10. Elizabeth Warren, "America Needs You," University of Massachusetts Amherst Commencement Address, May 12, 2017, "Senator Elizabeth Warren Commencement Speech at UMass Amherst," WWLP-22News, YouTube video, 15:43, https://www.youtube.com/ watch?v=9zbcPxi4X14.

11. Aly Raisman, sentencing hearing for Lawrence Nassar, County Court Ingham County, Michigan, January 19, 2018, "Aly Raisman Addresses Larry Nassar, Calls Out U.S.A. Gymnastics in Victim Impact Statement," ESPN, YouTube video, 12:48, https://www.youtube.com/ watch?v=e6McY8yMdd0.

12. Ibid.

13. Clara Moskowitz, "Mind's Limit Found: 4 Things at Once," *Live Science*, April 27, 2008, https://www.livescience.com/2493-mind-limit-4.html.

14. Jedidah Isler, "How I Fell in Love with Quasars, Blazers, and Our Incredible Universe," TED Talk, March 2015, video, 4:20, https://www.ted.com/talks/jedidah_isler_how_i_fell_in_love_with_quasars_blazars_and_our_incredible_universe.

15. Ibid.

16. Tom McCarthy and Ben Jacob, "Melania Trump convention speech seemed to plagiarize Michelle Obama," *The Guardian*, July 19, 2016, https://www.theguardian.com/us-news/2016/jul/19/melania-trump-republican-convention-plagiarism-michelle-obama.

17. Jillian Kearney, "The When, Where, & How of Using GIFs in Content Marketing," *Scribble Live*, December 21, 2016, https://www.scribblelive.com/blog/2016/12/21/the-when-where-how-of-using-gifs-in-content-marketing/.

18. Shonda Rhimes, *Year of Yes* (New York: Simon & Schuster, 2015), pp. 167–73.

19. Patrick McCarthy, TED Talk speech, Washington, DC, June 24, 2015, http://www.aecf.org/blog/annie-e-casey-foundation-ceo-calls-for-states-to-close-youth-prisons/.

20. Cameron Knight, "New Councilwoman Tamaya Dennard's Folding Chair Goes Viral," Cincinnati.com, January 3, 2018, https://www.cincinnati.com/story/news/politics/2018/01/03/new-councilwoman-tamaya-dennards-folding-chair-goes-viral/999485001/.

21. Chimamanda Ngozi Adichie, "Dangers of a Single Story," TED Global 2009, https://www.ted.com/talks/chimamanda_adichie_the_danger_of_a_single_story/transcript?language=en.

22. Ibid.

CHAPTER 6: POWER WORDS—
PERSUASIVE MEDIA MESSAGES

1. Erik Wemple, "Sarah Huckabee Sanders: 'We Give the Very Best Information Possible at the Time.' That's the Problem," *Washington Post*, May 3, 2018, https://www.washingtonpost.com/blogs/erik-wemple/ wp/2018/05/03/sarah-huckabee-sanders-we-give-the-very-best -information-possible-at-the-time-thats-the-problem/?utm_term= .e0d19e249192.

2. Glenn Kessler, "Trump Made 2,140 False or Misleading Claims during His First Year as President," *Washington Post*, January 21, 2018, https://www.washingtonpost.com/news/fact-checker/wp/2018/01/20/ president-trump-made-2140-false-or-misleading-claims-in-his-first -year/?utm_term=.7f177112cb6d.

3. David Leonhardt, "Trump's Lies v. Obama's," *New York Times*, December 14, 2017, https://www.nytimes.com/interactive/2017/12/14/ opinion/sunday/trump-lies-obama-who-is-worse.html.

4. Claire Phipps, "Kellyanne Conway Blames Refugees for 'Bowling Green Massacre' That Never Happened," *Guardian*, February 3, 2017, https://www.theguardian.com/us-news/2017/feb/03/ kellyanne-conway-refugees-bowling-green-massacre-never-happened.

5. Richard Perez Pena, "Anti-Abortion Activists Charged in Planned Parenthood Video Case," *New York Times*, March 29, 2017, https://www .nytimes.com/2017/03/29/us/planned-parenthood-video-charges.html.

6. David Ingram, "Facebook Says 126 Million Americans May Have Seen Russia Linked Political Posts," *Reuters*, October 30, 2017, https:// www.reuters.com/article/us-usa-trump-russia-socialmedia/facebook -says-126-million-americans-may-have-seen-russia-linked-political-posts -idUSKBN1CZ2OI.

7. Art Swift, "Americans' Trust in Mass Media Sinks to New Low," *Gallup News Politics*, September 14, 2016, http://news.gallup.com/ poll/195542/americans-trust-mass-media-sinks-new-low.aspx.

8. "Americans Attitudes about the News Media Deeply Divided along Partisan Lines," Pew Research Center, Washington, DC, May 9, 2017, http://www.journalism.org/2017/05/10/americans

-attitudes-about-the-news-media-deeply-divided-along-partisan-lines/
pj_2017-05-10_media-attitudes_a-05/.

   9. Barbara Lee Family Foundation, "Politics Is Personal," April 2016,
Cambridge, MA, https://www.barbaraleefoundation.org/wp-content/
uploads/BLFF-Likeability-Memo-FINAL.pdf.

   10. Jugal Patel and Alicia Parlapiano, "The Senate's Official
Scorekeeper Says the Republican Tax Plan Will Add $1 Trillion to the
Deficit," *New York Times*, December 1, 2017, https://www.nytimes.com/
interactive/2017/11/28/us/politics/tax-bill-deficits.html.

   11. Robin Morgan, *Fighting Words: A Toolkit for Combating the
Religious Right* (New York: Nation Books, 2006.)

   12. Fred Barbash, "Disneyland Measles Outbreak Strikes in Anti
Vaccination Hotbed of California," *Washington Post*, January 22, 2015,
https://www.washingtonpost.com/news/morning-mix/wp/2015/01/22/
disney-measles-outbreak-strikes-in-anti-vaccination-hotbed-of-california/
?utm_term=.c4abcc396f2e.

   13. Matthew Harrington, "Survey: People's Trust Has Declined in
Business, Media, Government, and NGOs," *Harvard Business Review*,
January 16, 2017, https://hbr.org/2017/01/survey-peoples-trust-has
-declined-in-business-media-government-and-ngos.

CHAPTER 7: THE NEW LOOK AND SOUND
OF LEADERSHIP

   1. University of Alberta, "Hand Gestures Linked to Better
Speaking," *Science Daily*, May 11, 2005, https://www.sciencedaily.com/
releases/2005/05/050511105253.htm.

   2. Caitlin Gibson, "Scientists Have Discovered What Causes Resting
Bitch Face," *Washington Post*, February 2, 2016, https://www.washington
post.com/news/arts-and-entertainment/wp/2016/02/02/scientists-have
-discovered-the-source-of-your-resting-bitch-face/?utm_term=
.d38fbb46faf6.

   3. Terry Gross, "From Upspeak to Vocal Fry: Are We Policing
Young Women's Voices?" NPR's *Fresh Air*, July 23, 2015, https://

www.npr.org/2015/07/23/425608745/from-upspeak-to-vocal
-fry-are-we-policing-young-womens-voices.

4. Nik DeCosta Kipla, "Read the Massive Speech Elizabeth Warren
Gave Ripping Moderate Democrats at Netroots Nation," Boston.com,
August 13, 2017, https://www.boston.com/news/politics/2017/08/13/
read-the-massive-speech-elizabeth-warren-gave-ripping-moderate
-democrats-at-netroots-nation.

5. Helene Cooper, "Fashion Police Have Reporter Up in Arms," *New
York Times*, October 19, 2017, https://www.nytimes.com/2017/10/19/
reader-center/dear-helene-could-you-not-wear-beachwear-on-sunday-am
-talk-shows.html.

6. She Should Run and Women's Media Center, "*Name It. Change It*,"
March 2013, http://www.nameitchangeit.org/page/-/Name-It-Change-It
-Appearance-Research.pdf.

7. Katherine Fritz, "Meet the Inspiring Bride Obliterating Wedding
Dress Stereotypes," MTV News, August 6, 2015, http://www.mtv.com/
news/2233654/lindy-west-wedding-dress/.

CHAPTER 8: PREPARATION IS QUEEN

1. Mindy Kaling, Harvard Law School Class Day speech, May 29,
2015, Cambridge, MA, "Mindy Kaling's Speech at Harvard Law School
Class Day 2014," Harvard Law School, YouTube video, 16:56, https://www
.youtube.com/watch?v=a7_49EXuLoQ.

2. Jill Bolte Taylor, "My Stroke of Insight," TED Talk, February
2008, https://www.ted.com/talks/jill_bolte_taylor_s_powerful
_stroke_of_insight.

3. Amy Tan, "Where Does Creativity Hide?" TED Talk, February
2008, https://www.ted.com/talks/amy_tan_on_creativity.

4. John Hashner, "'I Prepared to be President,' Clinton Tells Trump
in Debate Zinger," *USA Today*, September 27, 2016, https://www.usa
today.com/story/news/politics/onpolitics/2016/09/27/prepared
-president-clinton-tells-trump-debate-zinger/91151506/.

5. Nick Skillicorn, "The 10,000-Hour Rule Was Wrong, According to

the People Who Wrote the Study," *Inc.*, June 9, 2016, https://www.inc
.com/nick-skillicorn/the-10000-hour-rule-was-wrong-according-to-the
-people-who-wrote-the-original-stu.html.

6. Abby Jones, "Beyoncé Reportedly Booking 11-Hour Rehearsal
Days for Coachella," *Billboard*, April 3, 2018, https://www.billboard.com/
articles/columns/pop/8283636/beyonce-rehearsal-coachella.

7. Antoniette Bueno, "Lady Gaga Reveals Intense Preparation for
Super Bowl Halftime Show," *ET*, February 3, 2017, https://www.etonline
.com/news/209378_lady_gaga_reveals_intense_preparation_for_the
_super_bowl_halftime_show.

8. Jesse Holland, "Mock Exercises Prepare Sotomayor for Hearings,"
San Diego Union Tribune, July 10, 2009, http://www.sandiegounion
tribune.com/sdut-us-sotomayor-preparation-071009-2009jul10-story.html.

9. Viola Davis, interview by Steve Heisler, *AV Club*, February 18,
2009, https://film.avclub.com/viola-davis-1798215762.

10. Kathryn Shattuck, "Jane Krakowski Tap, Tap, Taps, into a
Christmas Story Live," *New York Times*, December 8, 2017, https://www
.nytimes.com/2017/12/08/arts/television/jane-krakowski-a-christmas
-story-30-rock.html.

11. Oprah Winfrey, "What Oprah Knows about the Power of
Gratitude," *Oprah Master Class*, video, October 28, 2011, http://www
.oprah.com/oprahs-lifeclass/what-oprah-knows-about-the
-power-of-gratitude-video.

12. Francesca Rise, "20 of Beyoncé's Best and Most Brilliant Quotes,"
Marie Claire, September 7, 2015, http://www.marieclaire.co.uk/
entertainment/people/bow-down-bitches-15-beyonce-quotes-that
-cemented-her-place-as-one-of-the-most-inspiring-women-ever-101061.

13. Zach Seemayor, "Céline Dion shares career advice from late
husband," *ET*, March 15, 2017, https://www.etonline.com/tv/213057
_celine_dion_shares_career_advice_from_late_husband_rene_angelil_the
_voice_battle_rounds_preview.

14. Martin Belam and Sam Levin, "Woman Behind 'Inclusion Rider'
Explains Frances McDormand's Oscar Speech," *Guardian*, March 5, 2018,
https://www.theguardian.com/film/2018/mar/05/what-is-an
-inclusion-rider-frances-mcdormand-oscars-2018.

CHAPTER 9: MEDIA INTERVIEWS AND DEBATES

1. Matthew Shaer, "How Far Will Sean Hannity Go?" *New York Times*, November 28, 2017, https://www.nytimes.com/2017/11/28/magazine/how-far-will-sean-hannity-go.html.

2. Ana Marie Cox, "At the Heart of a Celebrity Interview," *New York Times*, October 21, 2017, https://www.nytimes.com/2017/10/19/reader-center/for-ana-marie-cox-goodbyes-can-be-awkward.html.

3. Louis Nelson and Daniel Strauss, "Libertarian Candidate Gary Johnson: 'What Is Aleppo?'" *Politico*, September 8, 2016, https://www.politico.com/story/2016/09/gary-johnson-aleppo-227873.

4. Anna Menta, "Debra Messing Calls Out E! for Equal Pay on Golden Globes Red Carpet," *Newsweek*, January 7, 2018, http://www.newsweek.com/golden-globes-2018-debra-messing-equal-pay-773466.

5. Symone Sanders, interview, CNN *New Day*, April 13, 2017, "Symone Sanders Sic Burn of Jeffrey Lord, 'You CAN'T Compare MLK to Your V*GINA Grabbin' President,'" Act Now 2017, YouTube video, 1:21, https://www.youtube.com/watch?v=C6BO4Bi2ch4.

6. Kelly Dittmar, "Navigating Gendered Terrain," speech, New Brunswick, New Jersey, February 2, 2015, YouTube video, 1:27:08, "'Navigating Gendered Terrain' Author Kelly Dittmar Discusses Gender and Political Campaigns," Eagleton Institute of Politics, https://www.youtube.com/watch?v=44-_aCMii4Y.

7. Ali Vitali, "Trump Calls Warren 'Pocahontas' at Event Honoring Native Americans," *NBC News*, November 27, 2017, https://www.nbcnews.com/politics/white-house/trump-calls-warren-pocahontas-event-honoring-native-americans-n824266.

8. Tobin Harshaw, "CNN and the Questionable Question," *New York Times*, November 16, 2007, https://opinionator.blogs.nytimes.com/2007/11/16/cnn-and-the-questionable-question/.

9. Sarah Wheaton, "Cruz Unloads on CNBC Moderators," *Politico*, October 28, 2015, https://www.politico.com/blogs/live-from-boulder/2015/10/debate-ted-cruz-cnbc-moderators-215306.

10. Hillary Rodham Clinton, *What Happened?* (New York: Simon & Schuster, 2017), pp. 135–37.

11. Ibid., p. 136.

CHAPTER 10: KEYNOTES, PANELS, INTRODUCTIONS, AND AWARDS

1. Oprah Winfrey, Golden Globes Cecil B. DeMille Lifetime Achievement Acceptance speech, January 7, 2018, "Oprah Winfrey's Golden Globes Speech, Annotated," Washington Post, YouTube video, 3:08, https://www.youtube.com/watch?v=CKuKc7KTt9g.

2. Lynn Sherr, *Failure Is Impossible: Susan B. Anthony in Her Own Words* (New York: Times Books, 1995), p. 103.

3. Ann Richards, keynote speech, 1988 Democratic National Convention, July 18, 1988, Atlanta, GA.

4. Hillary Clinton, United Nations Fourth World Conference on Women, speech, September 5, 1995, Beijing, China, http://www.un.org/esa/gopher-data/conf/fwcw/conf/gov/950905175653.txt.

5. Maria Perez, "Harriet Tubman Quotes: Six Sayings to Celebrate Abolitionist on the 105th Anniversary of Her Death," *Newsweek*, March 10, 2018, http://www.newsweek.com/harriet-tubman-quotes-105th-anniversary-slavery-history-839450.

6. Nikki Waller, "Melinda Gates Talks Philanthropy and Her Push to Empower Women," *Wall Street Journal*, December 14, 2014, https://www.wsj.com/articles/melinda-gates-talks-philanthropy-and-her-push-to-empower-women-1418597178.

7. Louisa Loveluck, "Egypt Threatens to Arrest Human Rights Lawyer Amal Clooney," *Business Insider*, January 2, 2015, http://www.businessinsider.com/human-rights-lawyer-married-to-george-clooney-threatened-with-arrest-2015-1.

8. Kim K. Azzarelli and Melanne Verveer, *Fast Forward: How Women Can Achieve Power and Purpose* (New York: Houghton Mifflin Harcourt, 2015), p. 65.

9. Maria Godoy, "Dolores Huerta: The Civil Rights Icon Who Showed Farmworkers Si Se Puede," *NPR*, September 17, 2017, https://www.npr.org/sections/thesalt/2017/09/17/551490281/dolores-huerta-the-civil-rights-icon-who-showed-farmworkers-si-se-puede.

10. Michelle Obama, Democratic National Convention, speech, July 25, 2016, Philadelphia, PA, "Watch First Lady Michelle Obama's Full

Speech at the 2016 Democratic National Convention," PBS NewsHour, YouTube video, 14:45, https://www.youtube.com/watch?v=4ZNWYqDU948.

11.   Oprah Winfrey, Golden Globes Cecil B. DeMille Lifetime Achievement Acceptance speech, January 7, 2018.

12.   Obama, Democratic National Convention.

13.   Ashley Judd, "Nasty Woman," Women's March, speech, January 21, 2017, Washington, DC, "Ashley Judd's EPIC 'Nasty Woman' Speech at the Women's March on Washington," Reflect, YouTube video, 6:59, https://www.youtube.com/watch?v=ffb_5X59_DA.

14.   America Ferrera, Women's March speech, January 21, 2017, Washington, DC, "America Ferrera Speaks at Women's March on Washington," CBS News, YouTube, 6:08, https://www.youtube.com/watch?v=SpdgPTUGFQw.

15.   "Chants," Ferguson Response Network, http://fergusonresponse.org/action-resources/chants/.

16.   Christie D'Zurilla, "Madonna Clarifies 'Blowing Up the White House' Comment: 'Taken Wildly Out of Context,'" *LA Times*, January 23, 2017, http://www.latimes.com/entertainment/gossip/la-et-mg-madonna-womens-march-secret-service-20170123-htmlstory.html.

17.   Tania Lombrozo, "Think Your Credentials Are Ignored Because You Are a Woman? Could Be," NPR, May 22, 2017, https://www.npr.org/sections/13.7/2017/05/22/529391023/think-your-credentials-are-ignored-because-youre-a-woman-it-could-be.

18.   *Pitch Perfect: Winning Strategies for Women Candidates* (report; Cambridge, MA: Barbara Lee Family Foundation, 2012), http://www.barbaraleefoundation.org/research/pitch-perfect-winning-strategies-for-women-candidates/.

19.   Viola Davis, Golden Globes Award ceremony, introduction of Meryl Streep, January 8, 2017, "Viola Davis Introduces Meryl Streep Lifetime Achievement Award – Golden Globe Awards 2017," YouTube video, 12:23, https://www.youtube.com/watch?v=fjSiCkz_bEo.

20.   Michelle Kort, "Gloria Steinem Receives Top National Honor," *Ms.* blog, November 20, 2013, http://msmagazine.com/blog/2013/11/20/gloria-steinem-receives-top-national-honor/.

21.   Malala Yousafzai, Nobel Lecture transcript, December 20,

2014, Oslo, Sweden, https://www.nobelprize.org/nobel_prizes/peace/laureates/2014/yousafzai-lecture_en.html.

22. Laverne Cox, Logo Trailblazer Award Ceremony, acceptance speech, June 26, 2014, "Laverne Cox & Orange Is the New Black Cast | 2014 Logo Trailblazers," YouTube video, 4:30, https://www.youtube.com/watch?v=FjnwX4d7MXY.

23. Mia Hamm, National Soccer Hall of Fame Induction, speech, August 26, 2007, "Mia Hamm Hall of Fame Induction Speech – 1 of 2," CenturyCouncil, YouTube video, 7:50, https://www.youtube.com/watch?v=7qdwmhidOL0.

24. Karen Panetta, Anita Borg Institute Women of Vision Award, acceptance speech, May 23, 2011, "Karen Panetta Acceptance Speech: 2011 Anita Borg Institute Women of Vision Award for Social Impact," AnitaB_org, YouTube video, 7:12, https://www.youtube.com/watch?v=G5JhwuFCHlk.

EPILOGUE

1. Max Londberg, "Teacher Arrested for Asking about Salary, Called a Poor Little Woman by Board President," *Kansas City Star*, January 12, 2018, http://www.kansascity.com/news/article194414944.html.

2. Teens React to Public Figures, FBE Video, November 17, 2014, "Extended – Teens React to Malala Yousafzai," FBE, YouTube video, 19:46, https://www.youtube.com/watch?v=o_p3wTJR8SA.

3. Gender Avenger, "CTA Senior VP Karen Chupka Defends Gender Imbalance at CES. We Are Not Buying It," Gender Avenger, December 8, 2017, https://www.genderavenger.com/blog/cta-senior-vp-karen-chupka-gender-imbalance-ces.

4. Ed Wong, "Women Are Invited to Give Fewer Talks than Men at Top Universities," *Atlantic*, December 18, 2017, https://www.theatlantic.com/science/archive/2017/12/women-are-invited-to-give-fewer-talks-than-men-at-top-us-universities/548657/.

5. Shonda Rhimes, *Year of Yes* (New York: Simon & Schuster, 2015), p. 294.

6. K. Cokley, L. Smith, D. Bernard, A. Hurst, S. Jackson, S. Stone, D. Roberts, et al. "Impostor Feelings as a Moderator and Mediator of the Relationship between Perceived Discrimination and Mental Health among Racial/Ethnic Minority College Students," *Journal of Counseling Psychology*, 64, no. 2 (2017): 141–54, http://dx.doi.org/10.1037/cou0000198.

7. Laura Dern, Golden Globes Ceremony, Best Supporting Actress Acceptance Speech, January 7, 2018, "Laura Dern Wins Best Supporting TV Actress at the 2018 Golden Globes," NBC, YouTube video, 1:42, https://www.youtube.com/watch?v=geCIXy7nvFY.

8. Melinda Gates, speech at Powerful Voice Annual Luncheon, October 16, 2003, https://www.gatesfoundation.org/media-center/speeches/2003/10/melinda-french-gates-2003-powerful-voices-luncheon.

9. Maggie Kuo, "Women Ask Fewer Questions than Men at Conference Talks, Study Shows," *Science*, October 23, 2017, http://www.sciencemag.org/careers/2017/10/women-ask-fewer-questions-men-conference-talks-new-studies-suggest.

10. Richard Adams, "Hand It to Sarah Palin," *Guardian*, February 9, 2010, https://www.theguardian.com/world/richard-adams-blog/2010/feb/09/sarah-palin-obama-hand-teleprompter.

11. Ali Montag, "Here's What Makes Reese Witherspoon Angry about Hollywood—And How She Is Solving the Problem," CNBC, September 7, 2017, https://www.cnbc.com/2017/09/07/how-reese-witherspoon-is-helping-fix-the-entertainment-industry.html.

12. Megan Lasher, "How Samantha Bee Built a Diverse Writer's Room," *Time*, January 10, 2017, http://time.com/4630075/samantha-bee-full-frontal-diverse/.

13. "Ava DuVernay, Filmmaker," Makers, video, 5:09, https://www.makers.com/ava-duvernay.

14. Dino Ray-Ramos, "Ava DuVernay Says Diversity Is an Absolute Must in Industry," Deadline Hollywood, January 20, 2018, http://deadline.com/2018/01/ava-duvernay-pga-awards-visionary-award-wrinkle-in-time-queen-sugar-diversity-inclusion-1202264680/.

15. Laura Ratliff, "What Actually Happens When Women Run & Win Elections," Bustle, November 7, 2017, https://www.bustle.com/p/what-actually-happens-when-women-run-win-elections-3231157.

16. "*Quick Take: Women on Corporate Boards Globally*" (report; New

York: Catalyst, March 16, 2017), http://www.catalyst.org/knowledge/
women-corporate-boards-globally.

  17. *"The Bottom Line: Corporate Performance and Women's
Representation on Boards (2004–2008)"* (report; New York: Catalyst,
March 1, 2011), http://www.catalyst.org/knowledge/bottom-line
-corporate-performance-and-womens-representation-boards-20042008.

INDEX

AATM technique, 229–30, 235
AAUW. *See* American Association of University Women
abortion, 79, 117–18, 140
academies, ancient Greek, 68
Academy of Motion Picture Arts and Sciences, 81
acceptance speeches, 221, 249, 273–76, 295–96
acronyms, 127
active voice, writing with, 126
Adichie, Chimamanda Ngozi, 58, 113, 136
affirmations, positive, 217
Affordable Care Act, 290
African American women
    assertive speaking style by, 77
    excluded from first women's march (1913), 72
    impostor syndrome and, 285
    pay equity and, 116–17
agreeableness, 41–42
Ailes, Roger, 113
alcohol use, 288
alliteration, 132
alt-right groups, 74, 225

Amazing Interrupting Technique, 98–99
American Association of University Women (AAUW), 116
amplification technique, 100–101, 221
analogies, 132–33
ancient Greece, 68–69
Anderson, Marian, 255
Angelou, Maya, 31, 58
angry questioners, 108–109
Anita Borg Institute, 275
ankle turns, 216
Annie E. Casey Foundation, 131
Anthony, Susan B., 250
anti-slavery convention (1840), 72
anxiety
    causes of, 47
    dealing with triggers for, 217–19
    linked to other SAQ factors, 47
    obligatory speaking situations and, 44
    preparation and, 214–15

relaxation techniques, 215–17
Self-Awareness Quotient
  (SAQ) and, 37, 38, 46–47,
  215
appeal, making an, 274
apple boxes, 178
apps, 207
Aristotle, 68–69
Arrington, Courtlin, 61
Atlantic County freeholder
  meeting, 22
atmospheric (audience) bias,
  67–69
attire, 190–94, 245, 263
audience
  answering questions from,
    106–109
  appealing to self-interest of,
    119–21
  appeals/requests of, 121–23
  compassion from, 114
  dialogue between speaker
    and, 105
  eye contact with (*see* eye
    contact)
  flat, 219
  gathering information about,
    201, 203
  getting the attention of, 116
  good and bad news about, 65
  heckling by, 103–105
  misreading your, 127–28
  poker faces from, 101–102

quieting down an, 102
recognition of bias in, 66
relationship to the topic,
  120–21
toxic people, 82–83, 85–89
understanding your motivation to speak, 117–19
use of climate indicators, 67
awards, accepting. *See* acceptance
  speeches

Baldwin, Brooke, 27–28
banners, 105
Bannon, Steve, 83
Barbara Lee Family Foundation,
  10, 143, 271
bar stools, 180
"bathroom bills," 74
Bee, Samantha, 59, 171–72, 289
being yourself on purpose, 292
belief in yourself, 20, 21–23
benefits, in Issue Message Box
  (IMB), 151–52
Bennett, Ashley, 19, 21–22
Beyoncé, 211, 219
bias
  atmospheric, 67–69
  by Donald Trump, 82
  exclusion of women from
    speaking, 67–72
  explicit, 66, 67, 70
  flipping the script and,
    93–95

implicit, 66, 67
treatment of female Supreme Court justices, 81
by white men, 82–83
women speaking up in the workplace and, 77–78
Biba, Erin, 110
biblical passages, on women keeping silent, 67–68
Biden, Jill, 59
"Big Five" personality traits, 38–42
Bill & Melinda Gates Foundation, 12
Billy Graham Rule, 69
#BlackLivesMatter, 12, 17, 43, 74
Black Panther (film), 80
body language. *See* power moves
body movement, for relaxation, 216
body shaming, 85, 96
"Bowling Green massacre," 140
boxes. *See* power boxes and triangles
brain-driven approach to public speaking, 38–39
breath/breathing, 215, 218
Breitbart News Network, 225
Brescoll, Victoria L., 77–78
briefings, informal, 46
Brookings Institution, 70
bropropriation, 85, 100

broviators (bros), 85, 86, 99
Brown, Brené, 25
Brown, Michael, 262
Brown, Scott, 241
Burke, Tarana, 30–31

C3PO media message principles, 141–46
connecting with target audience, 143–44
connection, 143–44
contrast, 144
credibility, 142–43
prioritize, 144–45
cable news programs, 79
call-and-response, 262
call to action, 121–22, 123, 136, 150, 156, 189, 262
camera appearances
debates, 243–44
eye contact, 170–71
hand gestures, 173
makeup and, 193
stance on, 166
wardrobe for, 193–94
Candidate Message Triangle (CMT), 146, 154–57, 226, 240
Carlson, Gretchen, 113
Carlson, Tucker, 83, 87–88
Carman, John, 22
Carruthers, Charlene, 255
cell phone, used while delivering a speech, 207

Center for American Women and Politics, 69, 290

CES trade show, 70, 282

Chaffetz, Jason, 106

chants, 262, 263

character, argument by (ethos), 68–69

Chavez, Edna Lizbeth, 61

chest voice, vs. head voice, 183

Chisholm, Shirley, 135

Chu, Judy, 92

Cleopatra, 68

Clinton, Hillary, 48, 53, 210
    debate question asked of, 242
    as first woman to accept a
        presidential nomination,
        250
    keynote address by, 252
    Matt Lauer's interview with,
        79–80
    "may the force be with you"
        used by, 135
    Opposition Message Box
        used by, 158–59
    propaganda against, 140
    town hall debate with
        Donald Trump, 244

clipped sentences, 189

Clooney, Amal, 253

closing lines, 127

clothing. *See* wardrobe

CNN, 79, 234, 242

coaches, speech, 220–21

colleague, interruptions from, 98

collective voice, power of, 28–33

college campuses, speaking out
    against misogyny and racism
    on, 74–75

Collins, Gail, 88

comedians, 103–104

commencement addresses, 122,
    199, 205, 296

Community Coalition, 61

compelled, being, 43–44

conclusions, 124, 127, 137

conferences/professional forums
    asking questions at, 287–88
    confidence monitors used at,
        258
    exclusionary practices against
        women at, 69–70
    gender imbalance of speakers
        at, 282–83
    manels at, 70
    raising your visibility at, 284
    security issues at, 283–84
    women's, 281
    women speaking at health-
        care, 71

confidence, 20, 27–29, 165–66

confidence monitors, 258

Congress. *See* US Congress

congressional/legislative
    speeches, 297

congresswomen, 91–93

connection, 143–44

conscientiousness, 42

conservative media groups, 225

conservatives
  communicating their bias
    and hatred, 82–83
  female commentators, 84
  framing techniques used by,
    150
  receiving speaking requests
    from, 225
  straightsplaining by, 89

Consumer Electronics Show, 70,
  282

contrast, 144, 255

contrast message, in Issue
  Message Box (IMB), 151

conversational rate for speaking
  pace, 182–83

conviction, showing your, 24–25

Conway, Kellyanne, 84, 140

Cooper, Helene, 190–91

corporate boards, 291

cotton mouth, 218

Coulter, Ann, 84

Cox, Ana Marie, 226

Cox, Laverne, 49, 51, 274–75

credibility
  eye contact and, 166
  in media messages, 142–43
  owning your, 25–26

Crime and Delinquency
  (journal), 120–21

criminal-justice system, 120–21

Cruz, Carmen Yulín, 24–25

Cruz, Sophie, 119

C-SPAN, 281

Cullors, Patrisse, 74

cultural references, used in
  keynote addresses, 254

"Danger of a Single Story, The"
  (Adichie), 136

data, 128, 142

Davis, Angela, 57

Davis, Bette, 65

Davis, Viola, 51, 211, 271–72

Davis, Wendy, 135

Davos, Switzerland, 291

death threats, 75

debates
  agreeableness and, 41–42
  best practices for, 246–47
  formats for, 238
  links to examples of great,
    297–98
  messaging in, 240–41
  questions on format of,
    238–40
  rehearsing for, 243–44
  tricky questions asked
    during, 242
  worst practices for, 245

deep breathing, 103, 166–67,
  215, 218

delivery of your message. *See*
  presentation/delivery

Democratic National Conventions, 10, 254, 256
Dennard, Tamaya, 135
Dern, Laura, 286
dialogue, between audience and speaker, 105
Dion, Céline, 220
director's chairs, 180
direct quotes, use of, 130
Dittmar, Kelly, 240–41
documents, use of, 253
double bind, the, 77
down-ballot races, 243–44
Dreamers (under the DREAM Act), 60
DuVernay, Ava, 81, 110, 290
dynamic visuals, 41

Eastmond, Aalayah, 61
edited interviews, 230–31
editing a speech, 125–26
Election (film), 245
elections (2018), 194. *See also* presidential election (2016)
emcees, 300
Emerge America, 10, 290
EMILY's List, 10, 290
emotion, argument by (pathos), 68
E! News (entertainment news show), 228
enunciation, 184
Ephron, Nora, 35, 205
equal pay, 228, 286–87

Equal Rights Amendment (ERA), 84, 88
erasable boards, 209–10
ethos, 68–69
exaggerated pronunciation, 188
examples, using vivid, 131–32
explicit bias, 66, 67, 70
extroverts/extroversion, 39, 47
eye contact
    with angry questioner, 108
    with broviators, 99
    don'ts of, 169
    establishing, 166–68
    importance of steady, 170
    maintaining, 168–69
    on-camera, 170–71
    quadrant system, 168, 177
    speaking with conviction and, 170
    turning the body for, 177

facial expressions
    neutral, 99
    poker faces, 101–102
    reflecting your words, 174
    "Resting Bitch Face," 175
    smiling during interruptions, 99
female candidates. *See* political candidates
feminism
    conservative female commentators on, 84

pink pussy hats as symbol of, 263

plastic feminists, 88

Ferguson Response Network, 262

Ferraro, Geraldine, 250

Ferrera, America, 261

Fey, Tina, 51, 87

Field, Sally, 42

Fighting Words (Morgan), 150

Filipovic, Jill, 133

filler words, 190

films

    making references to popular, 135

    stereotypes of women in, 80–81

First Amendment rights, 18

first impressions, 175–76, 232

flat audience, 219

Fleischer, Ari, 86

flip charts, 209–10

flipping the script, 93–110

Flores, Sol, 115

font, on full-text script, 204

Fontana, Anthony, 280

foot stance, 165

Forbes Women's Summit, 281

forearms, positioning your, 180

founding fathers of America, 69

4 *W* questions, 115–23, 148, 259

Fox News, 79, 113, 226

framing the issue, 149–50

Francis, Pope, 119, 132

Franks, Trent, 83

Fuentes, Samantha, 163

Full Frontal with Samantha Bee (television show), 171–72, 289

full-text script, 204–205

Garner, Eric, 262

Garza, Alicia, 43, 55, 74

Gates, Melinda, 53, 253, 287

gay people. *See* LGBTQ community

Gay, Roxane, 133

Gender Avenger, 282, 283

gender balance

    corporate boards, 291

    speaker lineups at conferences and conventions, 282

gender balance, in speaker lineups, 282–83

gender differences

    displays of emotion, 212

    how people see themselves on videos, 35–36

    socialization on speaking and, 77

gender equity, 121, 228. *See also* pay equity

gender gap, on representation in the media, 78–80

genetically modified plants, 119–20

Gifford, Kathie Lee, 231

Ginsburg, Ruth Bader, 53, 81, 91
Gladwell, Malcolm, 211
Glass, Ira, 185
Golden Globe Awards (2018), 12, 228, 249, 256, 271
González, Emma, 19, 31–33, 61
government/legal testimonies, 298
grabbers, 131–36, 152–53
Grace Hopper, 281
Grammarly, 130
Grassley, Charles, 82
Gray, Freddie, 262
Griffin, Kathy, 168, 289
Gross, Terry, 185
groups of threes, as an audience grabber, 131
groupthink, 18
guided meditation apps, 207
gun violence/gun control, 31–33, 60

Halperin, Mark, 79–80
Hamilton (musical), 254
Hamm, Mia, 275
hand gestures, 171–74
Handler, Chelsea, 182, 186
hand placement, 180
Hannity, Sean, 87–88, 225
Hargrave, Deyshia, 280
Harris, Carla, 56
Harvard Law School commencement speech (2014), 199

headline points, in power boxes and triangle, 148–52, 154–55, 156, 159, 160
head voice, vs. chest voice, 183
healthcare conferences, 71
heart-driven approach to public speaking, 39
hecklers, 103–105, 219
HeForShe campaign, 121
Hemans, Tyra, 61
Higher Heights, 290
high-road comments, 95–96
Hill, Anita, 11, 17
Hill, Jemele, 76
holding the floor, 97–99
Hollaback!, 104
Hollywood Reporter, The (digital and print magazine), 130
Horvath-Cosper, Diane, 117–18
Houlahan, Chrissy, 9
House Financial Services Committee hearing, 28–29
Huckabee, Mike, 83
Huerta, Dolores, 254
Hughes, Cheryl, 117
Human Rights Campaign, 74
humblebragging, 86
humor, 133, 275, 289
Hurricane Maria, 24–25

"I," use of the word, 143
IFB (interruptible foldback), 235
immigration reform, 60

impetus for speaking, 37, 42–44, 47, 117–19

implicit bias, 66, 67

imposter syndrome, 27, 222, 285

inflection, 186, 187–88

information overload, 144–45

Ingraham, Laura, 84

Inquirer Daily News (New Jersey), 22

insults
name-calling, 87–88
toward US congresswoman, 91–93

intentional storytelling. *See* storytelling

internet-based slides, 209

interrupting/interruptions
how to handle, 97–99
by men, 87
on panel discussions, 267–68
of Supreme Court justices, 81

intersectionality, 23, 72

interviews
building public-speaking skills with, 220
declining request for, 225
edited, 230–31
live, 46, 231–32
maximum message points for, 145
with multiple guests, 232–34
multitasking during, 289

pivot technique for, 229–30

power boxes and triangles used for, 147, 148, 160, 161

questions asked during, 226–28, 227

satellite and online video, 235–37

staying on message during, 228–30

understanding media format for, 224

introducing yourself, 272

introductions, 124, 126, 137, 269–73

introverts/introversion, 39–40, 44, 47

Isler, Jedidah, 126, 127

Issue Message Box (IMB), 146, 147–54, 241, 261

jargon, 127, 231

jaw opener, 217

Jayapal, Pramila, 91–93, 104

Jefferson, Thomas, 69

Johnson, Gary, 227

Joint Committee on Taxation, 144

jokes, 289

Jones, Leslie, 165, 289

Jones, Monica, 274

Jordan, Barbara C., 139, 251

Journal of Counseling Psychology, 285

Journal of Experimental Social Psychology, 48
J. P. Morgan Health Care, 70
Judd, Ashley, 57, 261

Kagan, Elena, 81
Kaling, Mindy, 199
Kelly, Megyn, 231
keynote addresses, 46, 251, 252–59, 298–99
key target, eye contact and, 166–67, 168, 170
King, Steve, 32, 83
Krakowski, Jane, 214
Krawcheck, Sallie, 56

LaDuke, Winona, 119–20
Lady Gaga, 211
Lagerfeld, Karl, 85
Lake, Celinda, 194
Lauer, Matt, 79–80
laughter punctuation, 190
leadership, redefining the look and sound of, 194–95
Lean In (Sandberg), 77
Lean In Collection (Getty Images), 80
lecterns, 177–78
Lee, Barbara, 92
Lesbians Who Tech, 281
LGBTQ community
    name-calling, 88
    straightsplaining and, 89
    violence against, 74

liars/lying, 116, 117, 140
list making, 127
literary references, use of, 134–35
live interviews, 46, 158, 227, 228, 230, 231–33, 289
"locker room talk," 83
logos (pillar of persuasion), 68
Logo Trailblazer Award, 274
Lord, Jeffrey, 234
lying. *See* liars/lying
Lyon, Cookie, 199

MAKERS Conference, 281
makeup, 193
Malala Fund, 50
male chauvinists, 86
manelists, 86
manels, 67, 70, 71, 291
mansplainers, 86–87
manterrupters, 87, 97
March for Our Lives (2018), 32, 48, 60–61, 260
March for Science on Earth Day (2017), 263
Marjory Stoneman Douglas High School, 31–32, 61
Marshall, Bob, 26, 97
MarTech, 70
Martin, Trayvon, 43
Mary Tyler Moore Show, The (television show), 11
mass media, American trust in, 142

maternity care, insurance coverage for, 71
Mayo Clinic, 269
McDormand, Frances, 221
McKinnon, Kate, 174
Mead, Margaret, 133
mean girls, 87
Mean Girls (film), 87
measles outbreak, Disney theme park (2015), 149, 150–54
media and media messages
    assessing opportunities to speak in, 223–24
    connecting with your target audience for, 143–44
    contrast messaging, 144
    declining interviews on, 225
    edited interviews, 230–31
    editing content for, 144–45
    gender imbalance in, 78–80
    handling questions on, 226–28
    Issue Message Box (IMB) tool for, 147–61
    lies/lying in, 140
    live interviews, 231–32
    live television/cable programs with multiple guests, 232–34
    Oh, Wow! factor for, 145–46
    preparing for interviews, 224, 226
    satellite/online video interviews, 235–37
Media Matters, 79
meetings, 46
    amplification at, 100–101
    bropropriating at, 85
    broviators at, 99
    getting the nerve to speak up at, 100
    handling interruptions at, 97–99
    poker faces from audience members at, 101 102
    resisting boors and bullies at, 97–101
memorization, debates and, 245
memorizing speeches, 204
men
    bias and hatred by white, 82–83
    gender imbalance in speakers, 282–83
    inflating their credentials, 110
    lecterns designed and built for, 178
    as space consumers, 164
    See also gender differences
Mendoza, Jessica, 75
"Men Explain Things to Me" (Solnit), 86–87
mental release, 217
Merkel, Angela, 48

message boxes, 226, 227, 228, 231. *See also* Issue Message Box (IMB); Opposition Message Box; power boxes and triangles

Messing, Debra, 228

metaphors, 133

#MeToo movement, 12, 17, 30, 79, 114, 228

Meyer, Pamela, 116, 117

Michigan State University, 122–23

Mikulski, Barbara, 11

Miranda, Lin-Manuel, 254

mirroring, 174

misogyny, 74–75

Mnuchin, Steve, 28–29

mock-debate practice, 243

moderators, 105, 106, 238, 264–66, 300

Moore, Michael, 261

Moore, Roy, 82–83

Morgan, Robin, 150

Morning Joe (television show), 227

Mott, Lucretia, 72

MSNBC, 79

MTV Video Music Awards (2009), 87

multitasking during interviews, 289

mumbling, 184

name-callers, 87–88

names of audience members, Q&A sessions and, 107

narrative, use of data vs., 128

Nassar, Larry, 122

National Coalition of 100 Black Women, 281

National Domestic Workers Alliance, 50

natural facial expression, 174

Navarro, Ana, 52

neck turns, 216

Nerd Girls, 275

Netroots Nation speech (2015), 186–89

neuroticism/neurotics, 40–41, 47

#NeverAgain, 17

New York Times (newspaper), 80, 190

New York Times Sunday Magazine, 226

Nineteenth Amendment, 250

Nnamdi, Kojo, 97

Nobel Peace Prize, 274

nonstop conjunctions, 190

Norma Rae (film), 42–43

note cards, 106, 206

notepad apps, 207

notes
    added to visual aids, 207
    eye contact and looking down at, 166, 170
    full-text script approach to, 204–205

outline approach to, 206
using prepared, 203
written on your hand, 288
NPR (National Public Radio), 185
numbers, use of, 133–34

Obama, Barack, 100–101, 140, 255
Obama, Michelle, 59
    amount and level of speaking experience, 45
    Democratic Convention (2016) speech, 257
    Melania Trump plagiarizing, 129
    speaking from personal observation, 254–55
    "What Would Michelle Do" statements, 95–96
Oberlin College, 73
obligation, impetus and, 44
O'Connor, Sandra Day, 254
offensive comments/statements
    in Congress, against Pramila Jayapal, 91–93
    flipping the switch, 93–95
    taking the high road, 95–97
    "What Would Michelle Do" responses to, 95–96
Oh, Wow! factor, 145–46
Old Executive Office building, 69
Olympic gymnasts, 60, 122–23

on-camera. See camera appearances
one-liners, 133
one-syllable words, extending, 188
online trolls, 74
online video interviews, 235–37
opening lines, 126
openness, 40, 47
Opposition Message Box, 146, 157–59, 234, 240
Orange Is the New Black (television show), 274
orators, principles of early, 68–69
O'Reilly, Bill, 87–88
outline approach to notes, 206

pace of speaking. See speaking pace
Palin, Sarah, 288
panel discussions, 46, 67, 70, 86, 179, 264–68, 300
Panetta, Karen, 275–76
party conventions, 250. See also Democratic National Conventions
passive voice, 126
passive writing style, 126
pathos, 68
pauses, 129, 183–84
pay equity, 116–17, 286–87
PBS NewsHour (television show), 231–32

Pence, Mike, 69
Perez, Carmen, 23
personal brands, 157
personality types, 37, 38–42, 47
personalizing your story, 110
persuasion, Aristotle's three
    pillars of, 68–69
Pew Research Center, 142
phone apps, 207
photographs
    of hecklers, 104
    of role models, 48–49
    stereotypes in images of
        women, 80
physical appearance, described
    during introductions, 269
physical movement, while
    speaking, 41
physical relaxation techniques,
    215–16
Physicians for Reproductive
    Health, 12
pink hats, 135, 263
"pinkwashing," 86
pitch, voice, 98, 183, 187
pivot technique, 219, 228–30,
    235
plagiarism, 129–30
Planned Parenthood, 12, 140
plastic feminists, 88
pockets, putting your hands in,
    172
podcasts, 46, 145

point-counterpoint discussions,
    41
poker faces, 101–102
police violence, 43, 74
political candidates, 10
    Candidate Message Triangle
        (CMT) for, 154–56
    changing how leadership is
        defined, 115
    C-SPAN and, 281
    debates, 237–47
    media coverage on wardrobe
        of, 191
    questions asked of, 226
    storytelling by, 115
    stump speeches by, 45–46
political conventions, 300–301.
    See also Democratic National
    Conventions
Poo, Ai-jen, 50
popular culture references, use of,
    134–35
Populist Party, 250
positive affirmations, 217
positive visualization, 217
power boxes and triangles, 146–61
    Candidate Message Triangle
        (CMT), 154–57
    how to use, 159–61
    Issue Message Box (IMB),
        146–61
    Opposition Message Box,
        157–59

power moves, 163, 164–82
    animated hands, 171–74
    behind a lectern, 177–78
    eye contact, 166–71
    facial expression, 174–75
    first impressions, 175–76
    for a purposeful perfor-
      mance, 181–82
    reviewing, on videotape of
      yourself, 212–13
    "three-star" technique,
      178–79
    waist turns, 176–77, 258
power outfit, 190–94
PowerPoint, 207
power sounds, 163, 182–90
    clipped sentences, 189
    enunciation, 184
    exaggerated pronunciation,
      189
    inflection, 185–86, 187–88
    one-syllable words,
      extending, 188
    pace of speaking, 182–83
    pauses, 183–84
    pitch, 183
    pronunciation, 184
    repetition, 189
    reviewing, on videotape of
      yourself, 213
    vocal faux pas, 190
    vocal power controls,
      182–84

voice projection, 184
    volume drops, 188–89
#PowerToThePolls, 17
power-word techniques
    active voice, use of, 126
    avoiding stream of conscious-
      ness, 128
    C3PO principles, 141–42
    citing sources/avoiding pla-
      giarism, 129–30
    connecting with target audi-
      ence, 143–44
    content flow, 124–25
    contrast messaging, 143–44
    credibility, 142–43
    developing just a few ideas,
      125–26
    editing content, 144–45
    grabbers, 131–36
    knowing your audience and,
      127–28
    reviewing, on videotape of
      yourself, 213
    strong openings and closings,
      126–27, 137
    use of story vs. data, 128
    verbal/vocal signposts,
      128–29
    visual imagery, 130–31
    See also power boxes and tri-
      angles; storytelling
preparation, 199–222
    apps used for, 207

calming nerves and, 214–17

dealing with anxiety, 217–19

for debates, 237–38

effort involved in, 199–200

equation for time spent on, 200

formatting full-text script, 204–205

keynote speeches, 259

learning about the audience, 203

for media scenarios, 224

of note cards, 206

power boxes and triangles used for, 160

by practicing, 210–12

reconnaissance and logical questions, 202

researching the speaking event, 201

reviewing tapes/feedback from others, 214

scheduling preliminaries, 201

videotaping yourself, 212–13

See also preparation time; rehearsing

preparation time, 47

presentation/delivery

dealing with anxiety triggers during, 217–19

full-text script approach to notes for, 204–205

interjecting in a friendly way, 268

keynote addresses, 256–57

outline approach to notes for, 206

power boxes and triangles useful for, 161

preparation for (*see* preparation)

at protests and rallies, 264

Q&A session following, 106–109

relaxation methods for, 215–17

tips for, 264

well-laid-out notes for, 203–204

presentations at conferences, 46. *See also* speeches/talks/presentations

presentation software, 209

presidential election (2016), 10

Candidate Message Triangles used by candidates in, 156–57

media coverage of, 79

Opposition Message Box from, 158–59

Russian-government-backed trolls during, 140

Presidential Medal of Freedom, 274

press conferences, 166, 177

Pressley, Ayanna, 118

Pride and Prejudice (Austen), 134

principles of the well-spoken woman, 20–33
  belief and certainty about yourself, 21–23
  claiming confidence, 27–29
  collective voice, power of, 29–33
  owning your credibility, 25–26
  showing your conviction, 24–25
prioritizing messages, 144–45
Proceedings of the National Academy of Sciences (journal), 125
pro-choice women candidates, 11
procrastination, 44, 47
professional forums. *See* conferences/professional forums
professional title, used for women, 269
projection, voice, 184
pronunciation, 184, 188
proportional numbers, 134
props, 135, 210
protests, 260–64, 301
publications, referencing your, 110
public speaking
  amount and level of experience in, 38, 45–46
  brain-driven approach to, 38–39
  early definition of what constitutes effective, 69
  efforts at improving in, 219–22
  neuroticism and, 40–41
  vitamin Cs of, 20
  women's exclusion from, 67–72
  See also conferences/professional forums; debates; interviews; speeches/talks/presentations; women, public and private speaking by
Puerto Rico, 24–25
purposeful performance, 181–82

quadrant system, for eye contact, 168–69, 177, 219
qualified/qualifications
  introductions stating you as, 110, 270–71
  making known, in debates, 246
Queen Sugar (television series), 290
questions
  asked during conferences, 287–88
  asked off the beaten path, 228–29
  debate format, 238–40
  gotcha debate, 242

handling interview, 226–28
interjecting on a panel using, 268
at panel discussions, 265
types of interview, 227
used in a speech/talk, 135–36
Quintilian, 69
quivering voice, 218
quotas, 291
quotes, use of, 130, 132

racial disparities, in criminal-justice system, 120–21
racist comments/language, 17, 28, 83, 91–93, 225
radio talk shows, 46, 145
Raimondo, Gina, 246
Raisman, Aly, 122–23
rallies, 105–106, 260–64, 300, 301
Rants and Retorts (Samuels), 74
rational approach to public speaking, 41
Ready to Run, 290
"reclaiming my time," 28–29
rehearsing
    for debates, 243–44
    teleprompters and, 258
    for using visual aids, 208
    watching yourself on video and, 35
relative numbers, 134

relaxation methods, 215–17
repetition, in speeches, 124, 125, 132, 189
research
    messages based on, 142
    on speaking event, 201
Resting Bitch Face (RBF), 175
rhetoric, Aristotle's three pillars of, 68–69
rhetorical questions, 268
Rhimes, Shonda, 35, 130–31, 285
Rice University, 282–83
Richards, Ann, 54, 250–51
Richards, Cecile, 50, 223
Rivera, Sylvia, 274–75
Roem, Danica, 25–26, 97
Roe v. Wade, 144
role models, 48–62
    Alicia Garza, 55
    Ana Navarro, 52
    Chimamanda Ngozi Adichie, 58
    Hillary Clinton, 53
    Laverne Cox, 51
    Linda Sarsour, 57
    Malala Yousafzai, 50
    Oprah Winfrey, 54
    Sallie Krawcheck, 56
    young women and girls as, 60–61
Roosevelt, Eleanor, 10, 211
routine speaking situations, 44

Rowling, J. K., 58
Roys, Kelda, 115
RT (Russian Television), 191
Run for Something, 290
Running Start, 290

Samuels, Anita, 74
Sandberg, Sheryl, 56, 77
Sanders, Bernie, 88
Sanders, Sarah Huckabee, 140
Sanders, Symone, 52, 234
San Diego State University,
    Center for the Study of
    Women in Television and Film,
    80
San Juan, Puerto Rico, 24–25
SAQ. See Self-Awareness
    Quotient
Sarkeesian, Anita, 75
Sarsour, Linda, 57
satellite interviews, 171, 235
Scandal (television show), 135
Schlafly, Phyllis, 84, 88
school safety, 31–33
Schumer, Amy, 103–104, 164,
    289
security issues, 283–84
self-awareness, 35–36. See also
    Self-Awareness Quotient
    (SAQ)
Self-Awareness Quotient (SAQ),
    36–48
        anxiety and, 38, 46–48

experience and, 38, 45–46
personality type and, 37,
    38–42
role of impetus and, 37,
    42–44
self-doubt, 26–27
Selma (film), 81, 290
Seneca Falls convention, 72
sexist remarks/language, 17,
    27–28, 191, 280
sexual harassment
    legal defense fund, 290–91
    power of the collective voice
        and, 30–31
    security issues and, 283
    talk to professional women
        about, 113–14
    at TED events, 73
    World Economic Forum
        (2018) and, 291
    See also #MeToo movement
sexual misconduct, by USA
    Gymnastics doctor, 122–23
shaming the ignorant, 93. See also
    body shaming
#ShePersisted, 17
She Should Run, 17, 191, 290
S.H.E. Summit, 281
short-term memory, 125
shoulder drop, 165
shoulder turns, 216
shouters, 88
Sierra Club, 12

Silverman, Sarah, 94, 184

Sinclair Broadcasting, 225

"6 Minute and 20 Second Speech" (Emma González), 32

slide decks, 209

smartphone apps, 207

smiling, 98, 99, 103, 174, 175

Soccer Hall of Fame induction, 275

software apps, 207

Solnit, Rebecca, 60, 86–87

solutions, in Issue Message Box (IMB), 150–51

Sotomayor, Sonia, 81, 211, 279

sound-bite form, 147, 152

speaker fees, 286

speaking pace, 41, 98, 129, 182–83, 256

speech coaches, 220–21

speeches/talks/presentations
    getting the crowd to quiet down at, 102
    grabbers for, 131–36
    hecklers at, 103–105
    keynote, 251, 252–59, 298–99
    mistakes in speech writing, 125–31
    organization of content, 124–25, 129
    at protests and rallies, 260–64
    Q&A session following, 106–109

special occasions, 249–50

town hall events, 105–106

writing for the ear, 124

See also storytelling

Spicer, Sean, 140

sports, women commentators in, 75–76

staff/board meetings, 46

stance, having a sure, 165–66

standing posture, 179–80

Stanton, Elizabeth Cady, 72

startling numbers, 134

state legislators, women in, 69

Steinem, Gloria, 55, 261, 274

stereotypes, 80–81

Stone, Lucy, 73–74

storytelling
    appealing to self-interest of audience, 119–21
    call to action in, 121–23
    choosing a topic and, 115–16
    4 *W*s of, 115
    Issue Message Box (IMB) and, 147
    motives for talking about your topic and, 117–19
    on sexual harassment, 113–14
    by women candidates, 115

straightsplainer, 89

stream of consciousness, 128

Streep, Meryl, 51, 271–72

stump speech, 45–46, 156

supporting material, for Issue Message Box (IMB), 152–53
sure-stance position, 165–66
sweating, dealing with, 218
Swift, Taylor, 87
Sykes, Wanda, 178

taking the high road, 95–96, 97
Tan, Amy, 210
Tannen, Deborah, 77
targeted eye contact, 166–71
tax bill (2017), 144
Taylor, Jill Bolte, 210
technical glitches, 219
TED Talks, 73, 116, 126, 127, 131–32, 258
TEDWomen, 281
TEDx programs, 281
teleprompter apps, 207
teleprompters, 257–58. *See also* teleprompter apps
terminology, choice of, 127
theme, Issue Message Box (IMB), 153–54, 160
Thomas, Clarence, 11
"three-star" technique, 178–79
Times Up movement, 17, 249, 286, 290–91
titles, using your, 110
Toastmasters, 220
Today show, 79, 288
Tometi, Opal, 74
topic sentence, 116

town hall debates, 238, 244
town halls, 105–106
toxic people, 82–83, 85–89
training workshops, 46, 209
Traister, Rebecca, 55
transgender people/rights, 12, 18, 25–26, 74, 97. *See also* Cox, Laverne
Travis, Clay, 28
triangles. *See* power boxes and triangles
Trump, Donald
  on Carmen Yulín Cruz, 25
  false or misleading claims by, 140
  Jemele Hill and, 76
  Mark Halperin's interviews with, 79–80
  mean-spirited commentary by, 82
  Opposition Message Box used by (2016 presidential election), 158–59
  "Pocahontas" name-calling by, 241
  request to voice opposition to, 121–22
  town hall debate with Hillary Clinton (2016), 244
Trump, Ivanka, 88
Trump, Melania, 129–30
trustworthiness, establishing, 142

Tubman, Harriet, 49, 252
Tully, Paul, 158
Tully Message Box, 158
TV interviews, 46
Twitter, 91–92, 94, 110
Tzu, Sun, 157, 158

undocumented people, speaking about, 119
Union of Concerned Scientists, 12
University of Alberta, 171
University of Massachusetts Amherst, 122
upper-body movement, 179–80
USA Gymnastics, 122–23
US Congress
    congressional/legislative speeches, 297
    congresswomen pushing back in, 91–93, 104
    C-SPAN coverage on hearings/speeches, 282
    giving nonanswers to women in, 28–29
    insults from males, 91–93
    women in, 69, 71
    women working together in, 290
US Olympic Committee, 122–23
Utah State University, 75

Valenti, Jessica, 52
verbal signposts, 129
Vermilion Parish School District, New Orleans, 280
video
    notepad apps and, 207
    reviewing, from actual speaking events, 214
    as visual aid, 208, 209
    watching yourself practice a speech on, 35–36, 181, 212–13
video chat, 235–37
video conferences, 171
video games/gaming, 75
video interviews (online), 235
violence, 73–75. See also gun violence/gun control
virtual-reality app, 207
visual aids, 135, 207, 208–10
visual imagery, 130–31
visualization technique, 217
vitamin Cs of public speaking, 20
vocal signposts, 129
voice
    quivering, 218
    volume, 184, 188–89
    See also power sounds
voting rights, 69
vulnerability, power of, 25

Wadler, Naomi, 61
waist turns, 176–77, 258

wardrobe, 190–94, 245, 263

Warren, Elizabeth, 54, 92, 110, 122, 186–89, 241

Washington Post (newspaper), 73, 100, 140

Waters, Maxine, 28–29

Watson, Emma, 121

webcasts, 171

Weinstein, Harvey, 30

Wells-Barnett, Ida, 72

West, Kanye, 87

West, Lindy, 191

"wetbacks," use of term, 91

White Earth reservation, 119

whitesplainers, 89

Williams, Serena, 210

Williams, Venus, 210

Winfrey, Oprah, 12, 54, 249, 256

Witherspoon, Reese, 245, 289

Wittes, Tamara Cofman, 70

"woman," use of word, 10

women

    barriers and biases against, 17–18

    congresswomen pushing back, 91–93, 104

    conservative commentators, 84

    credentialing themselves, 110

    executives, speaking out by, 77–78

    importance of speaking out, 280–81

    inspiration for, 281

    lifting each other up, 221, 289–91

    political candidates (*see* political candidates)

    political participation of, 69

    in politics, progress in, 10

    progress made by, 279–80

    "Resting Bitch Face," 175

    role models for the well-spoken (*see* role models)

    as space savers, 164

    speaking out against misogyny and racism on college campuses, 74–75

    stereotypes of, 80–81

    ways of telling "shut up" to, 185

    See also gender differences

women, public and private speaking by

    ancient Greece, 68–69

    Bill Graham Rule, 69

    Cleopatra and, 68

    exclusionary practices, 67–72

    manels and, 67, 70, 71

    in the media, 78–80

    professional forums and conferences, 69–70

    risks involved with, 73–75

    sports commentators, 75–76

    suffragist and abolition movement, 72

Women in Entertainment Power 100 breakfast, 130
Women in the World Summit, 281
women of color
    excluded from first women's march (1913), 72
    insult by congressman to congresswoman, 91–93
    speaking roles in film, 80
    underrepresented in speaker lineups, 70, 282
    See also African American women
Women's Campaign Fund, 11
women's conferences, 281
Women's Convention, 23, 30
Women's March (2017), 22, 121–22, 135, 260
Women's Media Center, 78, 79, 191

Wonder Woman (film), 80, 279
Woodruff, Judy, 231–32
working memory, 125
workplace, bias against women talking in, 77–78
World Conference on Women (1995, China), 252
World Economic Forum, 291
Wrinkle in Time, A (film), 81
writing, techniques for elevating the scope and depth of, 253–56
Wu, Brianna, 75

"yes, and" technique, 268
Young, Don, 91
Yousafzai, Malala, 50, 274, 281

Zimmerman, George, 43